LIVING A PREDICAMENT: Young people surviving unemployment

For Rose and Maria

Living a Predicament: Young People Surviving Unemployment

STEPHEN HUTCHENS
Anglia Polytechnic University
Norwich City College

Avebury
Aldershot · Brookfield USA · Hong Kong · Singapore · Sydney

Published by
Avebury
Ashgate Publishing Company
Gower House
Croft Road
Aldershot
Hants GU11 3HR
England

Ashgate Publishing Company
Old Post Road
Brookfield
Vermont 05036
USA

British Library Cataloguing in Publication Data
Hutchens, Stephen
Living a Predicament: Young People
Surviving Unemployment
I. Title
170
ISBN 1 85628 641 X

Library of Congress Cataloging-in-Publication Data
Hutchens, Stephen, 1950–
Living a predicament : young people surviving unemployment / Stephen Hutchens.
p. cm.
Includes bibliographical references. (p.)
ISBN 1-85628-641-X
1. Youth--Employment--Great Britain. 2. Youth--Great Britain--Psychology. 3. Unemployed--Great Britain--Psychology. I. Title
HD6276.G7H877 1994 94-24781
331.3'4137941--dc20 CIP

Typeset by Simon Marshall, Print Unit,
Norwich City College of Further and Higher Education
Ipswich Road, Norwich, NR2 2LJ

Printed and bound by Athenæum Press Ltd.,
Gateshead, Tyne & Wear.

Contents

Figures and tables

Acknowledgements

I would like to thank the following people; Jon Gubbay for his excellent academic advice; Denise for her help with proof reading; Simon Marshall for his invaluable assistance with preparing the manuscript; Hilary for her essential practical and moral support without which I could not have finished. Finally to the young women and men whose problems and attempts to deal with them are the subject of this book and generously gave me their time.

Foreword

'Unemployment', as Kumar (1984) has pointed out, is a term of quite recent origin. Its arrival in Britain in the late nineteenth century signalled the extent to which employment had eclipsed other opportunities for making a living in a highly industrialised economy. It has become difficult subsequently to think of 'work' as anything but employment, whether work takes place inside or outside the market. Moreover, as social policy came to address the fate of the unemployed, especially in the 1930s, it tightened the bonds between paid work and making a living, because entitlements to benefit were based on regular previous employment and contributions and taxes extracted from employer and employee at source.

The post war settlement associated with the Beveridge report recognised that only an active labour market policy aimed at 'full employment' could produce the tax revenue need to insure people against the vicissitudes of employment under capitalism - sickness and retirement and the demand for educational qualifications, as well as unemployment. Thus did history set the context for social reaction to the second great depression of the twentieth century beginning in the 1970s.

As unemployment reached levels that few thought could return (the registered unemployed exceeded three million for much of the 1980s in Britain), it began to be suggested that employment might not regain the central importance it had in the society of the post war boom. An inexorable trend towards relatively casual employment and informal economies was discerned (or imagined) as if the clock were turning back to pre-industrial forms as it moved forward to 'post-modernity'. On the other hand, much research (eg Pahl 1984) demonstrated that formal employment continued to be the mainstay of making a living in Britain, as elsewhere in the world, including newly industrialising countries (Redclift and Mingione 1985). Even the increasing trend for women without dependent children to enter employment was concentrated among those whose partners had permanent full time jobs, not in households where the man was out of work. Alternative lifestyles that were not dependent on formal employment were negligible statistically in developed countries and probably transitional in the less developed.

Among the features that marked out this great depression from its precursor of the 1930s was youth unemployment on an unprecedented scale. While the typical unemployed of the 1930s were men with families in the heavy industry regions of Britain, epitomised by the Jarrow hunger marchers, the typical unemployed of the 1970s to 1990s included many young people who were seeking but had yet to find employment, especially secure employment, and - during the 1990s, these were to be found in almost all regions of the country, including the Midlands and South East which had prospered during the 1930s. A frequently changed kaleidoscope of youth educational and training programmes and benefit rules concealed the true extent of youth unemployment by reducing the numbers on the register.

Stephen Hutchens' book addresses this group. He is concerned not with its statistical extent, nor its economic causes, but the experience of young people confronting unemployment. He seeks first to present the world from their point of view. His second concern is with the social and cultural factors, many of them just beyond the awareness of the young unemployed themselves, which nevertheless demonstrably shape their worlds. These factors are teased out from the data. There is no predetermined theory, far less an ideological agenda, to which the data have been made to conform.

The results complement those of previously published research, including the major study of Social Change and Economic Life commissioned by the Economic and Social Research Council, the findings of which on the experience of unemployment in the 1980s are published in Gallie et al (1994). Here there is statistical support from various parts of Britain and for all ages for the evidence Hutchens presents on a small scale for Norfolk young people about the implications of unemployment for psychological health, for income, for participation in social life and for short-term prospects in the labour market.

However, it is the way that the factors involved in being unemployed that emerge from surveys of large numbers fit together in the individual case that Hutchens is able to demonstrate with particular effect. He tries literally to give voice to the young unemployed. Accordingly he eschews the use of questionnaire-based scales, such as the General Health Questionnaire, in favour of qualitative accounts elicited in semi-structured interviews. He has tape recorded each of these, and maintains, with justification, that the way the young unemployed speak about themselves is as indicative of their situation as what they say. The tapes have to be heard of course for the full effect, and I can confirm Hutchens' claim that they document spoilt identity and lack of self-esteem.

For similar reasons, he finds the psychological stage theory of adjustment to unemployment, developed initially by Jahoda in the 1930s, to be both over-deterministic and lacking in explanatory power. The process of adjustment to unemployment, if and when it happens, must be set in the social and cultural context of those experiencing it, and that context is crucial to explaining why it happens. Among the changes that have occurred among the unemployed since the 1930s is the number of young women who find themselves in this position. Usefully, there are sufficient young women in the sample data to indicate that, at least among single young people, the experience of unemployment does not vary systematically with gender.

This book emerges at a time when there are definite signs that politicians are taking 'full employment' to be a serious issue once again. The misery of youth unemployment and the waste of productive potential it represents needs to be at the head of that agenda.

Paul Bellaby - University of East Anglia
July 4 1994

References

Kumar K (1984) 'Work, Employment and Unemployment in the Development of Industrial Society' *Sociological Review* 22(2): 185-233

Pahl R E (1984) *Divisions of Labour* Oxford: Basil Blackwell

Redclift N and Mingione E (edited) (1985) *Beyond Employment* Oxford: Basil Blackwell

Gallie D et al (1994) *Social Changes and the Experience of Unemployment* Oxford: Oxford University Press

1 Introduction

This book arose from concern over the return of a problem that a fuller understanding of economic management was supposed to have banished forever - that of mass unemployment. What was surprising to me, however, was not so much the return of this phenomenon, but the low level of reaction to it. Active concern seemed the province of a tiny minority. The Government that presided over the bulk of this huge rise continued to receive votes, and campaigns around the subject grew for a while but did not really take off. As for the unemployed themselves, they remained largely passive. Riots did break out in 1981, and these did involve unemployed youths, but by historical and international standards, they were brief, small-scale affairs.

Concern with why reactions should be so muted, broadened into a general interest in how unemployment affects people, how they react to these effects and how they try to cope with them. Young people are a relatively unresearched group and are disproportionally affected by unemployment so it was interesting and relevant to concentrate on their experience rather than the more thoroughly investigated group; older men made redundant after years of work.

The research was qualitative, involving questionnaires, but relied more heavily on 40 tape-recorded, in-depth, semi-structured interviews with 22 unemployed young women and 18 unemployed young men. All the respondents came from Norwich or villages in Norfolk, an area of low unemployment in comparison to many large industrial cities, but high compared with the norm since the war. This means considerable numbers of people were unemployed, so describing the area as one of 'low' unemployment should not lead one to ignore its attendant misery; fifteen years ago such figures would have seemed intolerable.

It is in this and similar areas that the recession/depression of the early 1990's has taken root. Regions that previously escaped relatively untouched by unemployment are those that have been most effected recently. The plight of the young unemployed living in formerly affluent areas is examined here and so this book is particularly relevant to recent preoccupations

This was, in fact, an 'inbetween' situation - unemployment considerably exceeding the special groups, with disadvantageous positions in the labour market, such as people with a handicap or mental illness. My sample consisted of 'ordinary' 'employable' intelligent people, most of whom wanted desperately to work. On the other hand, the situation was not one where unemployment affected so many that a community of unemployed was created, where it was self-evidently not the fault of the individual and where individuals would have the support of a community of people in the same position. Most had friends who were working and were aware of the fact that not everyone was in the same position as themselves. This is part of the distinctiveness of this research. Most other research has either been done in times of very low unemployment concentrating on why certain socially disadvantaged groups find themselves unable to take advantage of the situation, or has concentrated on areas of large-scale unemployment, where the unemployed may feel less visible, less singled out and may benefit from more community understanding and support.

My sample are the unlucky ones in a situation that may not be good but is no economic disaster area either. Each of these young person's situations gets worse as their unemployment lengthens, as employers are then likely to perceive their history as one of a bad working record. It has often been noticed that 'in practice therefore, a recently unemployed person is much more likely to be offered a job than someone who has been unemployed for many months' (Kelvin and Jarrett, 1985, p.33).

I shall argue that their situation is different, and in some ways worse, than that of an unemployed young person in, say, Liverpool or Newcastle. The effects of unemployment do not occur in a vacuum and will be strongly influenced by the social environment, be it a large industrial city, town or small village. These comparisons are part of the theme of this research. The aim is to identify direct and indirect factors in the generation of negative psychological states, the conditions that affect these factors and the strategies adopted to cope with their predicaments.

At the start of the research I had a number of general hypotheses and questions that arose both from reading and from my own thinking about the subject, in particular that money worries would be the most important problem and also that lack of a wage would have further repercussions. Shortage of money would inhibit social life, prevent the acquisition of desired clothes, consumer goods, and act as barrier to establishing a separate home, and thus achieving a transition to adulthood based on independence. I also expected to encounter a number of non-monetary factors, as categorised by Jahoda as 'latent functions of work':

> First among them is the fact that employment imposes a time structure on the working day. Secondly, employment implies regularly shared experiences, contacts with people outside the nuclear family. Thirdly, employment links an individual to goals and purposes which transcend his own. Fourthly, employment defines aspects of personal status and identity. Finally, employment enforces activity (Jahoda, 1979, p.313)

I expected problems with time to loom particularly large as young people are used to having their time structured by school, and will expect work to do the same. Of course, they are also used to filling in time in summer holidays so time may not be such as problem as it would be for someone who has worked twenty years, but I did not expect many to relish a permanent summer holiday situation. I also expected to encounter particular problems with Jahoda's second and fourth latent functions.

Another working hypothesis was that the feeling and behaviour of the young unemployed would be strongly influenced (but not completely determined) by the culture of the general employed working class and, in particular, the taste and standards of employed working class youth. This could be expected to be especially true of young people living in an area where the majority are not unemployed. I expected that my sample of young unemployed people would want and desire conventional things from clothes and consumer goods, a commercial social life, - courtship, marriage, a separate home and so on, and that they would be dissatisfied and in some way hurt if these desires were frustrated. These young people would feel deprived relative to employed friends and the working culture that surrounds them. They would also tend to refer to the general working culture when judging their own status and worth.

Experience of working with young people over some years had led me to believe that in spite of a visible but small minority appearing to belong to seemingly exotic subcultures, most had values and aspirations not so very different from their elders; that other factors, principally class and gender are more important than age, with most young people heavily influenced by mainstream social values. Indeed, when questioned on this issue, most described themselves by using such phrases as 'ordinary, everyday person'.

The research generally supported the above expectations but some other the working hypotheses did not stand up so well.

I expected to find men suffering more than women because of a general cultural belief that work is more important to men, more crucial to their identity and that therefore they would feel the lack of it more heavily. Other research seemed to back this up. For example, Kelvin and Jarrett in their review of the literature say: 'Unemployment does not seem to induce in women, a sense of failure as a woman, in a way it so frequently seems to produce a sense of failure as a man, amongst men' (p.66) and later: 'To hold a job still does not seem to be as central to the social psychological situation of a woman as to a man ... who is much less likely to see the situation as personally deeply demeaning' (p.67)

I expected to find this correct, and for this to manifest itself in noticeably less distress. I found the opposite to be true: the women in my sample seemed to suffer more, I shall try to explain this in the thesis, it is but worth pointing out straight away that women's reaction to unemployment has been assumed rather than researched, as there has been very little research on the situation of unemployed women of any age. To quote Kelvin and Jarrett again: 'We found scarcely any research on the unemployed woman ... For all practical purposes, though women do feature in the literature, they do so first and foremost as the wives of unemployed men'

Similarly, Marshall (May 1984) reports that unemployed women are almost totally neglected. Most research concerns 'The Unemployed Man and his Family' and women appear only as 'fleeting shadows', or 'housewives under stress', and almost never in their own right.

The present thesis is therefore unusual in that it has not neglected the position and views of unemployed young women.

I also came to doubt my implicit belief in the 'work ethic' - the secular offspring of the 'Protestant Work Ethic'. The research indicated that the undoubted problems of life on the dole can be explained without referring to a supposedly deep seated work ethic. The work ethic is partly a myth, yet only partly because many people *do* believe that to work is a good thing in itself. However, it is not the most important factor. Most people work to earn money in order to make other things possible and, being unable to do the things they want, explains the pain of unemployment better than involving the work ethic. For example, it is frustrating and shaming not being able to buy desired consumer goods, go to nightclubs, being unable to return hospitality by buying rounds of drinks at pubs for working friends and having future plans blocked by an inability to afford an independent house. The effects of non-monetary factors can also be explained without citing a supposed work ethic; for example, worklessness itself involves long hours of boring, unfilled time during the day.

Questions I wanted answered range from the specific, such as 'How does the experience of being unemployed in a small village compare with that of a city?' to the more general, such as 'How do they see their situation?', 'What mechanisms and factors exist that ameliorate or exacerbate their situation?' 'How do these factors interrelate?' and 'How do they attempt to cope with a difficult situation or do they just flounder on?'

In short, I was interested in the experiences and definitions these young people gave of their situations, but my own selection of questions and interpretation of their responses is unavoidable. In effect, I am in the same position as Coffield et al (1986) when they say that 'it would be disingenuous of us not to admit that the selection from the wealth of data we collected, the organisation of the material, and the final conclusions are all our own work, although heavily influenced by discussions with the young adults.' (p.62)

A look at the idea that unemployed people go through several 'stages' or 'phases' might help to clarify the purpose of the present thesis. In a classic review of the literature on the psychology of unemployment, Eisenberg and Lazerfield (1938) argue that unemployment has been found to be a miserable and damaging experience and that people pass through a number of set phases:

> We find that all writers who have described the course of unemployment seem to agree on the following points: first there is shock, which is followed by an active hunt for a job, during which the individual is still optimistic and unresigned, he still maintains an unbroken attitude. Second, when all efforts fail, the individual become pessimistic, anxious and suffers active distress, this is the most crucial stage of all. And third, the individual becomes fatalistic and adapts himself to his new state but with a narrower scope. He now has a broken attitude. (p.378)

Many modern writers and researchers have come to similar conclusions (for example, Hayes and Nutman, 1981; Fagin and Little, 1984). They report that the unemployed go through similar stages - shock, optimism ('a holiday feeling'), despair and lastly adaption, but at a low psychological level. Other writers such as Sinfield (1981, p.38-39) suggest that this idea has become so influential that it has conditioned later research to look for it and prevented other patterns from being discovered.

Sinfield may well be right. Certainly, the above quotation appears again and again in the literature and may rank as the most commonly reproduced passage on the effects of unemployment. Kelvin and Jarrett (1985) claim that the concept of stages has been so often uncritically used that: 'However unwittingly, this literature has thereby created a general stereotype of the behaviour of the unemployed, with all the potentially misleading oversimplification which this implies.' (p.25)

The objection to the stages concept is not that it is wrong, for there is a great deal of evidence to suggest that many people do indeed pass through these stages and, in particular, there is strong evidence to support the existence of the last stage. Prolonged unemployment does very often result in apathy, resignation and low psychological health. (See Chapter 3)

What is wrong with the stages concept is that it is deterministic and descriptive. It is deterministic in that unemployment is seen as a leveller, forcing all people along the same route regardless of other factors. Any individual differences according to Eisenberg and Lazerfield may affect the timing - that is, how long it takes to pass through each stage, but not the eventual outcome.

> Of course there are large individual differences, but one would suspect

> that the various types of attitudes monitored are more a function of the other predisposing factors that have been discussed above. It would seem instructive to map the course of events of those beginning unemployment with differing attitudes. It may be that all have the same courses, except that the unbroken take a longer time before becoming broken, than those who began as distressed or broken individuals. (Eisenberg and Lazerfield, 1938, p.378)

There may be factors that lead to different patterns; these stages may be less valid for groups other than that most researched of groups, that is older males made redundant after years of work. (Indeed not even all of these pass through the same stages).

My research seems to indicate that the phase model has less application to young people. Firstly, leaving school or a YTS scheme without a job may be disappointing but is hardly likely to match the shock felt by someone made redundant after say 10 - 20 years work. Secondly, the redundant adult will have had much longer to internalize the view of himself as a worker with a certain status, an independent self reliant provider and of course will have greater commitments. None of this applies to youth and initially unemployment will not be dissimilar to starting another school summer holiday. My sample shows that response will vary with the majority suffering to varying degrees and a minority coping fairly well. One common pattern seems to be a slow decline in both activity (job search and hobbies etc) and morale from the level found on leaving school or schemes to a fairly low level.The unemployed person then drifts along, usually in the company of a small group of others but not really accepting unemployment, in fact blaming all their troubles on unemployment so that worklessness becomes in their minds the central blight on their lives. Being thinking human beings the young people recognize the corrosive effect this has ("vegetate" seems to be a common expression they use to describe this situation) and make periodic efforts to `do something' - a conscious act of will. This may be to increase job searching or develop hobbies or interests. The consequent increase in activity causes morale to rise. After a short while the failure of attempts to find work erodes confidence, or hobbies come to be perceived as pointless time fillers so they lapse back into the pattern of low activity and morale. Next, after a further period of time, comes another attempt to `do something' and so on. Of course this pattern will not apply to all - not for example those who are coping well.

One problem which attempts to set out phases of responses to unemployment is that it either assumes the individual is totally unemployed, or eventually finds a job which ends the problem, or at least those problems associated with worklessness. Most of my sample have had periods of temporary work - and schemes followed by periods of unemployment complicated by a bit of illegal work on the side will be even less likely to fit Eisenberg and Lazerfield's phase model.

Linked to the point that different patterns may be more common for different groups, is the fact that the stages model is descriptive rather than explanatory. It does not explain what factors cause transition from one stage or another, or block this transition or perhaps result in alternative outcomes. It does not adequately explain differential vulnerability to being unemployed, or the specific mechanisms generating more or less distress and apathy.

The stages model is a reality for many but I argue that it is a contingent reality rather than a predetermined, inevitable process. It is contingent on a number of interrelated factors, some of which may be the product of the individual's conscious activity, some of which are out of his or her control, and consequently they can lead towards differing outcomes. The aim is to illuminate in detail: '.. the chain or set of casualties which indicate particular outcomes from many possible ones.' (Willis, 1977)

There are many possible outcomes - some adapt but with a broken attitude, as Eisenberg and Lazerfield suggest. Others may go further into despair, depression or even to the point of suicide. Many, my research suggests, are dissatisfied and unhappy about their situation, but without having a 'broken attitude' or being depressed. A very few form satisfactory and happy lives in spite of their worklessness.

All research indicates that for most, unemployment hurts. This thesis hopes to offer some evidence as to what causes that hurt, and what factors exacerbate or ameliorate that hurt.

A model of interrelated factors

From the research emerged a web of interrelated factors that tend to push unemployed young people in the direction of depression. However, these do not affect every individual uniformly and there are other factors, some of which help them avoid such an outcome and some which exacerbate the situation, making such an outcome more likely. A brief explanation of the 'core' model and these exacerbating factors will be helpful in setting the scene for the substantive chapters.

The 'Core' model of causally related factors

In order to facilitate the exposition, the core model (fig 1:1) is built up by combining three simpler partial models (Figs 1:1, 1:2 and 1:4). It should be noted that even figure 1:1 is simplified by leaving out some factors, for example inability to replace worn out clothes, buy desired consumer goods, and so on. These have been omitted to avoid over-complication. Fig. 1:1 should therefore be seen as an aid to understanding rather than as a complete coverage of all the negative effects of youth unemployment. [Numbers in brackets refer to numbers on the diagrams. (see Figs 1:1, 1:2, 1:3 and 1:4 overleaf)

The factors illustrated in Fig.I produce a low self-image and a tendency to blame oneself for a situation not of one's own making [13]. These factors are stigma [1]; the belief that other people are judging you and finding you wanting. If a person perceives others view him or her negatively, then one's self-image tends to become negative. (The concept of the 'work ethic' could enter here. The belief that other people possess a work ethic may cause the suspicion in the minds of the unemployed that others are judging them harshly.)

Certainly, many in my sample believe that others consider them 'wasters' or 'scroungers' and feel 'degraded'.

Feelings of rejection [2] and lack of status [3] also reinforce the unemployed's sense of blame and low self-image. Being unable to get a job when it is desperately wanted is to feel rejected generally, and applying for jobs and failing reinforces this. Jobs are still the prime sense of a person's status in our society

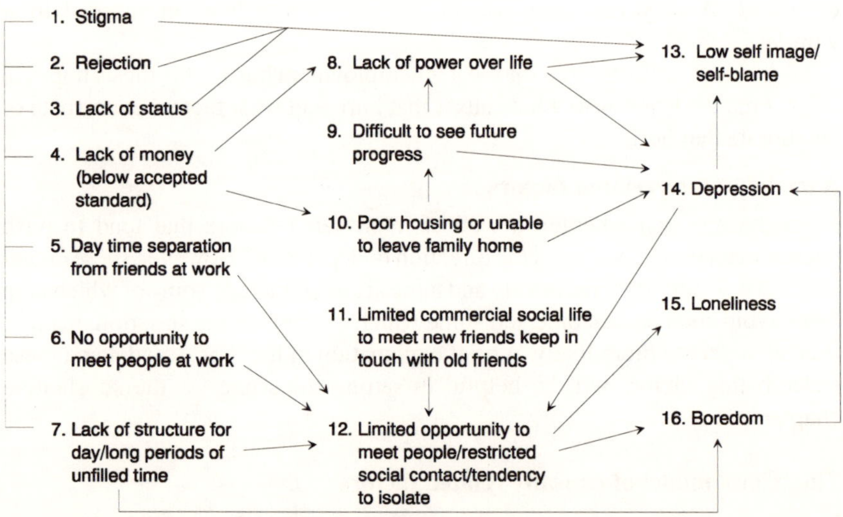

Fig.1.1 Core model of causally related factors

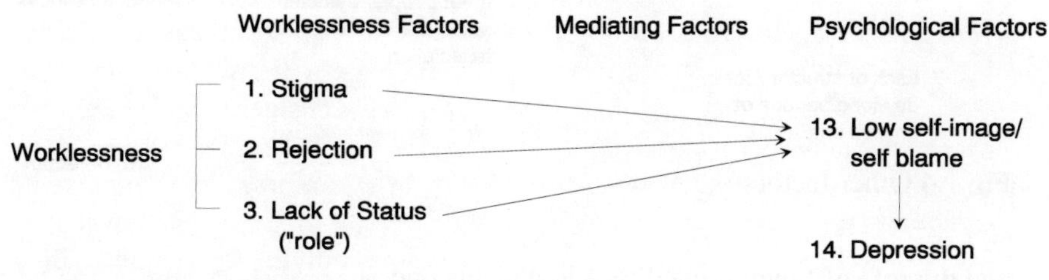

Fig 1.2 Worklessness factors

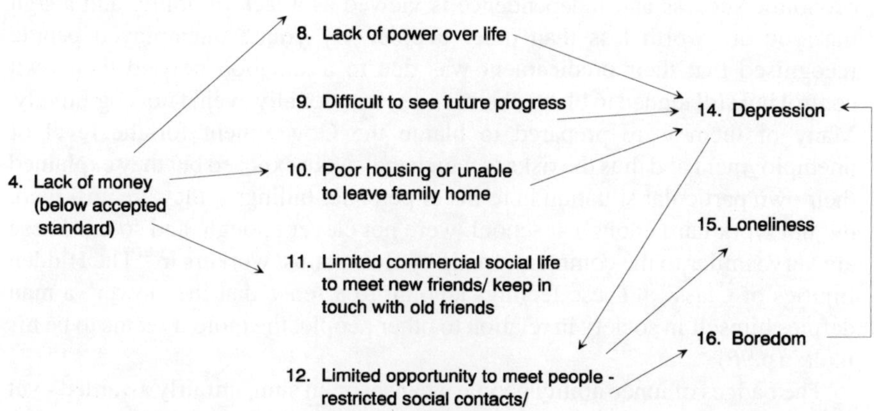

Fig 1.3 Money factors

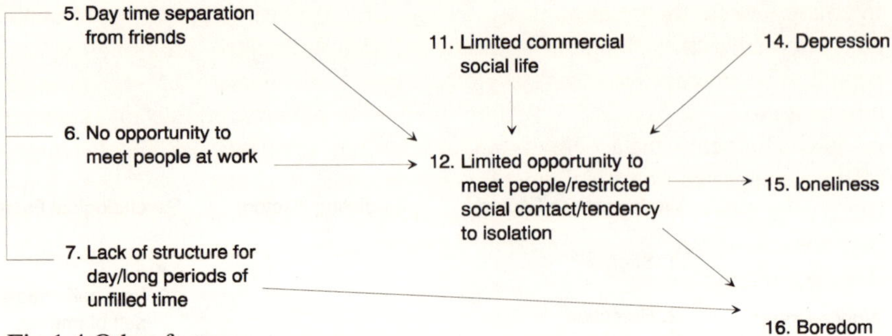

Fig 1.4 Other factors

and the role of 'unemployed' is a low status one.

The tendency to blame themselves for the situation not of their own making was marked. The situation is similar to that experienced by American workers as described by Sennett and Cobb in their explanation of the 'Hidden Injuries of Class' (1972). Success is seen as a 'Badge of Ability', failure as a sign of lack of ability, as one's own fault and a sign of lack of worth. So Sennet and Cobb's industrial workers and my unemployed young people are injured by the cultural assumption that people do well in life if they have ability. Not to achieve economic success and independence is viewed as a lack of ability and a sign that you are worth less than other people. My young unemployed people recognised that their predicament was due to a situation beyond their own control but still tended to blame themselves, emotionally even if not cognitively. Many of them were prepared to blame the Government for the level of unemployment and thus the risks to which they were exposed but they explained their own particular situation in terms of personal failings - they are unskilled, did not work hard enough at school, were not clever enough, and so on. These are very similar to the comments made by 'low status' workers in "The Hidden Injuries of Class": 'These feelings amount to a sense that the "lower" a man defines himself in society in relation to other people, the more it seems to be his fault.' (p.96)

'The badges of inner-ability people wear seem, in sum, unfairly awarded - yet hard to repudiate.' (p.118)

These feelings of self-blame and self-accusation help explain the missing ingredient from almost all of my interviews - the lack of a sense of anger (except that directed against themselves) about their situation. Intellectually, many may blame the Government or 'Mrs Thatcher' but emotionally they tend to blame themselves.

The next factor and probably most important factor is money [see Fig.1.3]. Worklessness equals wagelessness which for most unemployed young people means financial deprivation relative to those with whom they compare themselves.

In an area where the great majority are working, the tendency will be to make comparisons with the general working culture, particularly employed young people. The unemployed, whatever their age, will, unless there are unusual circumstances, be existing in a state of relative poverty, coping on financial resources far below the accepted standard. It might seem obvious that this might affect feelings, coping mechanisms, and psychological states, but there have been very few attempts to relate the poverty of the unemployed to their psychological state. An exception is Jahoda's linking of increasing poverty to stages of unemployment:

> We have distinguished four basic attitudes; the predominant one is "resignation"; a more active one we named "unbroken"; and two deteriorated forms we called "in despair" and "apathetic". As we look back on these two forms, it now appears that they are probably but two different stages of a process of psychological deterioration that runs parallel to the narrowing of economic resources and the wear and tear of personal belongings. (Jahoda, 1933/72, p.87)

What then are the effects of wagelessness?

Lack of money leads to feelings of being unable to have control over life, of lack of power, of dependency, perhaps upon parents for example. Poverty results in living in poor housing conditions which is directly depressing, or an inability to leave their parents' home. [10]This makes it difficult to see future progress in life [9], the desired path of which is the general cultural pattern of courtship, leading to a separate home and family. Progress in this direction appears blocked, so underpinning the feeling of being unable to control one's life. [8]

Emerging strongly from the data is that a commercial social life is strongly desired and money limits access to this [11]. Limited access to pubs, discos and night clubs, means limited ability to keep in touch with old friends (usually school friends) who are employed and so not suffering from this disadvantage. It also becomes harder to meet new friends including new boy/girlfriends. This limited opportunity to meet people is one cause of the restricted social contacts that many of my sample suffer from [12]. This in turn contributes to feelings of loneliness [15] and boredom [16], which can lead to depression [14].

So an important result of lack of money is limited access to a commercial social life leading to restricted social contacts. [12] A sense of isolation or at least restricted social contacts was felt to be very important by the young people in the sample and was keenly regretted. It was reinforced by the daytime separation from working friends [5] (see Fig.1:1V) and by lack of opportunity to meet new people at work [6] - work being valued as a meeting place in its own right. Both these factors lead to loneliness [15] and boredom [16], which in turn increases the possibility of depression [14]. Work also provides a time structure for the working day[7] and lack of this means periods of unfilled time, causing boredom and increasing the likelihood of depression.

Finally, depression tends to paralyse the will, causing people to become apathetic, to sleep in late, and to make less effort to meet people (perhaps to feeling that others will consider them worthless and not worth meeting). So there is a tendency for depressed people to cut themselves off and thus increase their tendency towards isolation. So depression [14] feeds back limiting social contact [12] and therefore worsening the situation.

Ameliorating and exacerbating factors

There are a number of ameliorating factors - those that help prevent individuals from moving towards depression, and exacerbating factors that tend to make the situation worse. Some of the ameliorating factors in particular are very important and go a long way to explain why so many are 'low' about their situation and are dissatisfied but do not have a 'broken attitude', and do not appear to be depressed. Some of the exacerbating factors are also important and explain to a large degree why it may well be worse to be unemployed in an area of low rather than high unemployment.

i) Support from parents and other relatives. This is the most important survival aid. A majority have supportive parents and this is one factor that sets them aside from older unemployed people who are expected to be more independent. This help can be both emotional, helping to boost self-image [13] and combat loneliness (15); or it can be financial: free or subsidised board, housing, giving or lending money, buying clothes, and so on. It means that a higher proportion (or in some cases, all) of the benefit money is spending money helping to maintain at least some social life. So it directly influences factor [4] in the Core Model (Figs.1.2 and 1.4) and through that helps the linked factors particularly [11] and [13]. It is not likely however to completely make up for lack of a wage.

The reverse of this - lack of support from parents and other relatives is an important exacerbating factor. Individuals who have parents who are unable or unwilling to subsidise them are the poorest group with less spending power even than other unemployed people. In the worst position are the minority who have parents who are hostile and blame them for their unemployment. This will increase their feelings of stigma [1], rejection [2] and self-blame [13], particularly if because of financial circumstance they are still living in the parental home.

ii) Financial support from partner. A minority have working partners which directly influences money aspects [4]. Although some feel guilty, having a partner pay is one avenue to a desired commercial social life [11], helping to prevent the tendency towards isolation.

iii) Company and emotional support from a partner. This has direct effects on psychological states, influencing self image [13], loneliness [15] and boredom [16].

iv) Friends in the same position. Unemployment tends towards restricted social contacts but usually falls short of complete isolation. A common pattern is to spend a great deal of time with a few unemployed friends - directly influences. self image (13) and tends to combat loneliness (15). Continued availability of school friends is an asset, especially if some are unemployed.

v) Being isolated from other unemployed people. This is a major exacerbating factor. For example, being the only unemployed person in a small village. However, this may apply even to Norwich city dwellers with only a few unemployed friends when compared to the situation in larger industrial cities with a higher rate of youth unemployment. This makes the individual more visible to others as unemployed and makes him or her more likely to compare themselves with others such as working friends and to judge themselves as wanting. Support from a community of others 'in the same boat' is lacking and having only or mainly employed friends means being unable to keep up with their social life. As well as being unable to afford night clubs and such like, it can also mean being unable to return hospitality by buying drinks in pubs for example (Gouldener's 'Norm of Reciprocity') and feeling ashamed of this. The net result is a tendency to lose contact with friends gained at school or on schemes.

vi) Living with parents. This influences housing situations [10], in that it avoids poor housing and as previously stated, often involves emotional and financial support. However, it may involve a trade-off because it can mean loss of independence and postponing future progress. [9]

(vii) Possessing a life interest. Sports and hobbies help but are not seen as a satisfactory substitute by most people. Exceptions are those with an overriding interest that they hope to develop into a career. This factor directly influences structuring of time [7] and boredom [16].

viii) Work. Temporary work schemes, part-time work and illegal work 'on the side', are another very important ameliorating factor. Other things being equal, the more work the better. Getting work on the side depends largely on contacts and it shall be demonstrated that this is a valuable asset. Women do much less illegal work than men and this puts them at a considerable disadvantage and partly explains why they often seem more distressed. This influences a number of factors such as by providing money (4) the opportunity to meet people at work (6) structuring the day (7) and combatting boredom (16)

ix) Belonging to a subculture. This is protective if the subculture downgrades the importance of material means and consumer goods - smart clothes, discos, nightclubs or a conventional life career - job, marriage, family, home and other conventional trappings. For it is the lack of these things that account for much of the pain of unemployment. What is less valued is less missed and, practically, less money is needed if budgets are not strained by attempts to have a commercial social life and meet conventional dress standards. This factor directly influences [4], [13] and [8].

x) Having a baby. This can be an ameliorating factor, providing a role and status [3], reducing feeling of stigma [1], filling time with meaningful activity [7], boosting self-image [13] and perhaps by making council housing more available [10]. However, the difficult circumstances of unemployment, lack of money and isolation could make it an extra burden.

xi) Difficult or expensive travel. This can be a large added burden to those with already overstretched budgets and is very significant in rural areas for the possibility of social contacts and job search depend on travel, [11] and [12]. Apart from city dwellers, those with the highest level of financial subsidies from parents or partners are the least affected, which is an example of how these factors interrelate.

xii) Living in a rural area with poor provisions. Having 'nothing to do', as the young unemployed tend to put it, will exacerbate matters, by providing less alternative ways of structuring the day (7)

xiii) Living in poor housing that is not considered temporary. 'Poor' is a relative term. Students for example may not object to poor housing as they consider it a temporary phase of their lives. At first the young unemployed may be pleased with any housing that offers the novelty of independence. In time, however, squalid conditions may become wearing, as might the expense of independent living whilst unemployed. For these reasons, there are examples of people in the sample who retreated from independence back to the family home and examples of others who, lacking this choice, were very dissatisfied with their living conditions. [10]

xiiii) Long duration of unemployment. This could be an exacerbating factor in combination with the other factors listed above and also, with the exhaustion of any savings, and the worsening of poverty [4].

xv) Personal factors. The above are social factors and they are the concern of this thesis, but it is not claimed that this is the end of the matter. Some may be more vulnerable to adverse circumstances than others. The possession of a strong 'will' helps, that is, the ability to make deliberate efforts to 'do things' and to keep in touch with friends. Being a conventionally minded individual, that is a person who wants smart clothes, a commercial social life and a conventional life career, is also relevant and personality factors influence which individual adopt such attitudes. However, although these sorts of factors are noted, the main focus of this thesis is sociological rather than psychological.

2 Description of Youth Employment Study

This research is essentially a qualitative study relying on in depth interviews with forty unemployed young people living in Norwich and small villages in rural Norfolk. Over one hundred detailed questionaires were collected but after an initial attempt to use the data they provided I found myself concentrating increasingly on the evidence gained by interview and consequently almost abandoning the questionnaire data. Both the reasons for choosing in depth intensive but focused interviews and for down grading the information gleaned by my questionnaire will be discussed below. Firstly, however, the procedure for gaining respondants will be described.

The first problem was obtaining a reasonably random sample of young unemployed people and this presented a problem because this is a geographically scattered group and there was no way of obtaining lists of names and addresses. Certainly, understandable concerns about confidentiality meant that organisations such as the DSS would not allow access to their files and, even if this had been allowed, this option would have been declined for fear of raising suspicions in the minds of the respondents as to the purpose and independance of the study by associating it with the world of officialdom. The problem was solved by using young women students, who generously agreed to act as voluntary research assistants, who administered the questionnaire to people, as they emerged from 'signing on' at the DSS. In order to achieve randomness these student helpers approached every third person who appeared to be in the correct age group (16-22) and asked if they would mind filling in a questionnaire on unemployment. If they agreed, they were taken to a convenient grassed area with benches, and low wall to sit on, that is only minutes away from the DSS offices, and which is regularly used by young unemployed and others. The students then went through the questionnaire with the respondant, a process which took ten to fifteen minutes. Respondants were assured of an anonymity and that this was an independant study unrelated to social security investigations and so on. They were then asked if they would mind being contacted later for a larger, more in depth, interview. This was at first in Norwich, but because of concern to reach a population of rural unemployed this was switched in the later stages to Wymondham, an office which caters not only for the town itself but also for a wide area of very small villages.

The refusal rates when the students were involved was low, and calculations indicate it was probably less than 10%. There is a margin of uncertainty because, although they were asked to record every refusals, they sometimes failed to do so. The most consistent helper explained that she found the whole thing so interesting and absorbing she simply forgot. Going by memory and the occassion when they did remember to record refusals there were very few. Typically they would do five or six questionnaires in a morning and often they would get no refusals at all, sometimes one, never more than two.

This is in contrast to the day when no students could make it and I tried to administer questionnaires. After eight straight refusals, some of them obviously suspicious, I gave up. Clearly 17-19 year old young women were regarded as less threatening than a male in his thirties. It is possible to speculate as to why this should be so. Firstly, I am of the age whereby I could have been a social security 'snooper', whereas the students were not. Secondly, young women approached by an older man and asked if they would mind coming to one side for an interview could be forgiven for considering an obvious alternative explanation of the encounter. Also, contrary to my experience the students reported virtually no signs of suspicion. People refusing seemed friendly and the usual explanations that they had arranged to meet people after 'signing on' seemed genuine. This may have introduced a slight bias in the sample in that their 'busyness' may indicate people who have their time well filled. This sample may therefore have been somewhat slanted in the directions of respondents who were experiencing problems with time.

When it came to contacting people for the second stage, the interviews, there seemed to be very little suspicion and there can be little doubt that this was due to the ground being prepared by the student helpers.

A sub sample was then chosen by the following method. First the forms were separated into male and female files. This was because the positions of unemployed women had been very neglected and the aim was to have at least as many young women as men. Then the forms were randomly mixed ('shuffled') and an attempt was made to contact every other person. This was of course started before the students had finished collecting questionnaires, as time was always short and there seemed no reason in principle to wait until that stage was finished before starting the next. There was also the danger of losing contact with people if there was too long a gap between them filling in the questionnaire and being interviewed. Those people contacted outside the Wymondham office were treated somewhat differently in that only people living in small villages were interviewed, as by this time I was interested in a rural sample.

Every effort was made to contact those picked for interview, with as many as six attempts made if people were not immediately available.

This failed in exactly six cases. One young woman had changed her mind and sounded (on the phone) suspicious, and a young man's neighbours informed me he had been removed to prison so I excused myself from further attempts at contact. Another was homeless and living in a night shelter in Norwich; he had moved on by the time contact was attempted and was said to be living in a derelict car 'somewhere in the country'. So this was a particular experience that is regretably missing from this account of unemployed life. Another had moved from a bedsit leaving no forwarding address. The neighbours of a young women told me (six times), with complete disregard to who I was, that she was out strawberry picking, and lastly another consistently made appointments to which she did not turn up.

Some general characterisation of the forty interviewed were as follows - eleven had parents (or a parent) who were unemployed, nineteen came from a manual working class background of which three worked independently as small builders and nine had a non manual family background. One had totally lost contact with her parents. As far as housing situation is concerned, only seven lived in private rented accomodation, although others had had previous experience of this sector, seven lived in the YMCA, four in council accomodation and twenty two with parents or other relatives. Eleven came from small villages, with the rest coming from Norwich. Three of these Norwich dwellers had previous experience of unemployed life in small villages. As far as age is concerned they were between 16 and 22 years old which is distributed as follows -

Age	Nos
16	4
17	6
18	10
19	8
20	4
21	3
22	5
	40

As for duration of unemployment 19 had been unemployed for under six months and 21 for six months and over. However this is misleading, as all but one of those that appeared as short term unemployed had experienced previous periods of unemployment broken by short term temporary work. So this is essentially a sample of those with a good deal of experience of unemployed life.

The question must inevitably be asked - what does this interview sample represent? Firstly the objection may be that the sample is too small to be able to be meaningfully generalised from the results. Anne Oakley's 'Sociology of Housework' (1974) contains a good defence of using a sample of 40 in research of this kind. She argues that large samples of many hundreds should not be automatically accepted as 'good' or a sample under one hundred dismissed.

Inadequate sampling, low response rates, badly worded questions, the interviewer unwittingly influencing response patterns or failing to achieve rapport can just as easily bias large samples as smaller ones. Furthermore, she maintains that these errors are more likely to creep into large surveys, firstly because there may be an assumption that the size of the sample makes attention to detail less important. Secondly because possible occassions for bias are multiplied by the involvement of others, research assistants, coders etc, who may have less comittment to "getting it right"

She goes on to say

> The evolution of the findings of any piece of research must also, of course take into account its nature and aims. Is the research mainly descriptive? Is it hypothesis testing? What claims does it make as to the universal applications of its results? Every research study needs to be assessed on the criteria of whether it measures up to its stated objectives.
>
> For the goals of mapping out an area, describing a field, and connecting events, processes or characteristics which appear to go together, a sample of forty individuals is certainly adequate.This type of taxonomic approach may, perfectly appropriately give rise to 'explanatory hypothesis" p33.

As explained in the introduction, 'mapping out an area' and 'connecting events', as well as exploring in depth a multiplicity of casual connections and interrelated variables, was precisely the aim of this research and so a sample of forty seems adequate. However it would be less than honest not to admit that sample size was dictated more by circumstance than theory. Principally, lack of time was the problem and had it been possible I would certainly have interviewed more people. The research was done in my spare time while holding down a full time job and coping with family commitments. It is worth noting in this context that problems emerged early. In the first ten or so interviews much was learned but, after that, later interviews tended to repeat and confirm points made earlier. I suspect that had a hundred interviews been done the last sixty would have mainly confirmed the first forty.

Of course statistics quoted strictly apply only to the sample and cannot be accurately generalised. I do, however believe that the research uncovers common problems and general factors that will be widely experienced by the young unemployed. It should be possible therefore to describe and analyse these factors and problems but not to rigidly quantify them. There are no statements in the research along the lines of "74.3% of the unemployed feel so and so".

The research also inevitably throws up sub-samples, such as the rural unemployed, and what is a problem for the sample as a whole is obviously more of a problem for these. An extreme example is young women with babies or pregnant, of which there are five. This is too small a number to say anything definiate but interesting points were made in their interviews and it seemed a poor idea to simply leave them out. So the points are made in the text without any claim of having "proved" them. They are considered and speculated about in order to raise food for thought and possible interesting questions and hypotheses for further research. Anne Oakley goes on to quote Moser (1958, p.300):

> There is after all more to research than can be seen from the tables and the researcher, in interpreting his results, is inevitably - and rightly - influenced by all that has gone before, by his aquaintance with the raw materials behind the figures and his own judgement ....
>
> The researcher who cautiously confines his conclusions to those strictly justified by the data may be safe from criticism, but he is not making his own full potential contribution (quoted on p35)

She goes on to add:

> It would be shelving one's responsibilites not to speculate on how ones findings may or may not be generalised beyond the research universe. Important connections to draw are those between one's own findings and the conclusions of other related research.These are broadly the approaches I adopt (p36)

I, too, adopt this approach, relating the findings of this research to others throughout the text. I consider it my duty to speculate on findings, even when the sub-samples are small, in order to generate theory and hypotheses (in the style of Glazer and Strauss) that might stimulate future research.The comments on the interviews with young women with babies are an example of this.

There are a few areas where the sample may not be truly representative. One has already been mentioned, that is the few who declined to be interviewed tended to have arranged to meet people after signing on, that is they were not unwilling to cooperate but busy. Therefore it is possible that the sample is weighted towards those who do have problems filling in time and under-represents those for whom this is less the case. However, the extent of this source of unrepresentativeness seems to be quite limited on the basis of the small number of refusals on the grounds of being too busy.

Under-represented in the sample are young people living with their parents. It proved impossible to discover the percentage of 16-22 year olds in Norfolk who live at home with parents but it is almost certain that it would be more than the 55% found in the sample (ie. 22 out of 40). Willis found in a large scale study of the same age group in Wolverhampton that the figure was 82% and it seems unlikely that the Norfolk position would be very different. Obviously the reverse of this is that there is a higher proportion of people living on their own but, in particular, young people living in the YMCA are over-represented. Six people were living in the YMCA at the time of interview with a further two having moved out fairly recently and at twenty percent this is far higher than that of the general population of young unemployed people. It is impossible to be sure why this should be so but speculation suggests two reasons. Firstly, perhaps those who have been bold enough to strike out an their own are characters who are less likely to fear an interview situation and therefore more likely to say yes. Secondly they may be more lonely than those living in families and more likely to seize on any opportunities for social contact. This might apply particularly for YMCA dwellers who tend to be estranged from their families.

What is the significance of this over representation of people not living in the family home? One advantage is that it enables a more detailed study of people who may have less support and be more vulnerable to the problems unemployment brings. Another point is that the picture of high levels of family support that emerges from the research is strengthened. This is because people who have moved away, or have a background of life "in care", or are estranged from parents as those from the YMCA tend to be, are over represented, with a corresponding under-representation of those most likely to benefit from family support.

Other biases stem from the design of the research.As I mentioned earlier, it was the intention to deliberately select for the sample people living in rural areas in order to investigate these previously under-researched groups.This is particularly interesting in that it adds to the general picture, but the finding may be restricted in application to similar areas, although I believe general problems of youth unemployment are also illustrated. Secondly the sample is deliberately tilted in favour of young women, since the situation of women's unemployment in general has been much neglected.

Interviewing

Interviewing as a method was chosen because of the aims of the project described in the introduction. Social phenomena are often messy and complicated with a mass of interelated factors and variables, and the intention was to explore these in depth. Attitudes were considered important and the desire was to see the experience of the unemployed from their point of view. It seemed that qualitative methods were necessary to probe this level of social reality. Anthony Giddens' preface to Sennett and Cobb's 'The Hidden Injuries of Class"(1972) expresses this well.

> They were interested in portraying in depth the experience of class relationships as expressed in day to day life. Hence they do not employ a conventional survey or sampling approach, depending instead upon a limited number of extended interviews which allows the workers to talk for themselves. This may not endear them to social researchers who consider such techniques indispensable but it allows the author to develop a suptlety of understanding which would be quite impossible to achieve using orthodox methods

Achieving this subtlety of understanding, in this case of what unemployment means, was also the goal of this research. As stated in the introduction one of the tentative hypothesis was that people would be influenced in their desires and expectations by the general working culture and that this would at least partly condition their responses and attitudes to unemployment. The word 'partly' is used because it was also the intention not to neglect the role of conscious thought and strategy. This interest in the interaction of conscious agency and culture puts this research in a similar position to Paul Willis's study of working class boys in 'Learning to Labour' and leads to similar conclusions regarding methods.

> The qualitative methods .... used in the research and the ethnographic format of the presentation were dictated by the nature of my interest in 'the cultural'. These techniques are suited to record this level of meanings and values as well as an ability to represent and interpret symbolic articulations, practices and forms of cultural productions. In particular the ethnographic account can allow a degree of the activity, creativity and human agency within the objective of study to come through into the analysis and the researchers' experience (p3).

So the decision was made to concentrate on qualitative methods capable of coming to grips with and promote an understanding of complex social reality. Observation was impractical as a general method because of time, problems of becoming accepted and, most importantly, because of the degree of geographical dispersal of the respondents. There may well be room for a worthwhile research project undertaken by a younger researcher with more time on his or her hands, who is prepared to spend it 'hanging around' with a group of young unemployed people.

As has been described elsewhere, there was a degree of triangulation by observation, in that valuable clues were often picked up by observing respondents answering questions, as well as listening to their tone of voice and noting the pauses. This was one of the advantages of the method and a strong impression was made by such factors. For example they were taken into account when categorising people as 'depressed', 'dissatisfied' or 'happy with their situation'. Those classified as depressed not only used the word to describe themselves, but also displayed behaviour and symptoms which may be attributed to feeling depressed talking about suicide, crying alone, visiting the doctor for anti depressant drugs for example. They also looked and sounded depressed. Even after much time has passed listening to the tapes and casting my mind back to visualise the person responding creates a strong impression of genuine distress, making it hard to believe they were just saying what they think I wanted to hear. These visual and audible clues set them aside as a group very distinct from those who were classified as 'very dissatisfied'. Taking advantage of such clues has a long history with Lazarsfeld commenting in many of his works from the 1930's on the physical bearing and appearance of the unemployed.

> In studying certain groups one makes a variety of observations: they walk slowly, they loose interest in public affairs, do not keep track of time, express opinions only with hesitation, stop looking for jobs, in short they can best be understood as discouraged resigned beings whose psycological space has been severley contracted
>
> (Lazarsfeld 1944 p43)

This does not mean that quantitative methods have no place in research on the unemployed. Indeed the findings of this research is compared throughout with studies such as those done by Professor Warr's Sheffield Unit (chapter 3). The existence of this Unit with its teams of researchers and research assistants working full time on surveying large numbers of people was another reason for choosing in-depth qualitative methods. Given the limitations of my resources - one person working part time with some help kindly given by 17-18 year old students - competing in this field seemed a pointless excercise. It may not be often mentioned but it is likely that many research projects are conditioned to a large extent by resources or lack of them.

One more reason for choosing to interview young people remains to be stated. I believed I would be good at it! Feeling that years tutoring and counselling young people had given me a feel for the techniques and a greater level of understanding for people in this age group. I am aware that interviewing and counselling are not the same thing exactly but they do have techniques in common. It seemed legitimate to take advantage of this experience and it seems to have paid off in that I believe I did successfully achieve a rapport which enabled the young people to truthfully express their feelings.

The Questionnaire

A detailed questionnaire was also administered as described earlier in this chapter. Use of survey methods as the main line of enquiry was rejected for the reasons described above, it was felt not to be an instrument sensitive enough to map out the complex situations, explore attitudes, opinions, factors qualifying those opinions and so forth. However the questionnaire 'grew' and went through a process of development that went almost full circle and that is worth recounting.

The first idea was to use the questionnaire as a device to record basic information but mostly to get over the most difficult initial problem, that is contacting and obtaining the cooperation of what was a dispersed group of people. The procedure has already been described. The process of using a questionnaire to be administered by people of their own age introduced potential respondents to the project, 'cued' them to the subject matter and appeared a very successful means of overcoming suspicion. This method of gaining access to respondents in otherwise difficult situations can be thoroughly recommended.

The questionnaire generated a considerable amount of data and I soon came under self-imposed pressure to use it as it seemed a waste not to. Some attempt was made to do so particularly in the chapters written earlier, such as the one on 'Time'. The questionnaires were referred to throughout to check the interview data, the parts on how people spend time being particularly interesting. However as time went by I increasingly relied on the interview data, using the questionnaire less and less until I was almost back to the original idea. The reasons were firstly the fact that the interview data was so compelling, rich, interesting and absorbing that there was a tendancy to become immersed in it and to simply forget the questionnaire. Another reason was that the reasons for originally choosing interviews as a main method seemed to be increasingly justified. A rich pattern of interrelated factors making up a complex whole did indeed emerge. Finally, sometimes the two sets of data contradicted one another and there seemed good reasons to believe the interview data. Two examples spring to mind, one of which is quite straightforward. When asked if they had alternative ways of making money many denied this on the form but once rapport had been established were quite happy to describe illegal jobs 'on the side' and so forth.

This relates to the earlier defence of using a smallish sample of forty. The questionnaire, being a much larger sample may be thought to have an advantage but if trust and rapport has to be established before people truthfully answer certain sensitive questions then, larger though it may be, it will be liable to systematic error.

The other example is that often the same people would say they 'never' had problems with time and in the interview talk of nothing else. The reason could be that when 'signing on' they are a least doing something, or it may be that admitting to problems with time in more sensitive than it at first seems. However, if people are prepared to go on at length about problems with time it is unlikely that they are making it all up. In the final analysis all research is dependant on the interprative skills and judgement of the researchers, and I am confident in my judgement that the interview data contains a good deal of truth. All forms of data collection are subject to distortion and I shall go on to discuss this point, arguing that I am justified in having confidence in the finding of the interview.

Interview Questions

When considering how to get at truthful and relevant information and what questions to ask a number of research methods books were consulted. Most useful however was an unpublished PhD thesis by John Cockburn entitled 'The Use of Interviewing in Social Science Research' (UEA 1983). This not only provided a good review of the literature but also includes a number of interviews with experienced interviewers, including Howard Becker, and William Foote Whyte, who discuss the use of interviewing generally and offer advice as to question wording and technique. Such advice provided invaluable guidelines.

The first desire was to allow the unemployed to speak for themselves and to explain their experience and attitudes. Questions then needed to be open ended - encourage them to talk and not to be too directive. Murry Wax (quoted in Cockburn p260) puts the case for open ended questions.

> By open ended I mean that one is interested in, and records the oral responses of the respondants rather than as if we're having to check box's into which you kind of put things and the rationale for doing that is because I want to enter the universe of meaning of the person. Unless one knows the field very well, one doesn't want to impose one's own system of categories on that. It seems to me that so much of so called policy decisions are defined in terms of the authority rather than the way people themselves conceptualise things.

George Homans (Cockburn p260/1) describes his technique for interviewing unemployed steel workers.

> Non-directive interviewing? Well its all described in Roethlisberger and Dicksons' The management and the worker', a classic in the field of industrial research and interviewing method. What it means is you sit down with somebody in an interview and start with some, without any fixed questions, but some topics you'd like to have them talk about if they felt like talking about it, but basically what you do is say 'what do you think about being unemployed' or words to that effect and you pursue any topic that they want to bring up and you encourage them and so on, you know ....
>
> If you're really an investigator of human behaviour your first duty, it may not be your only duty, is to find out what the people concerned consider

their important problems or issues or whatever it may be.

While agreeing with Homans as to the 'first duty', extreme forms of non directive interviewing, such as for example advocated by Stenhouse (1981) who claimed to start the respondent off and then not intervene any more, has problems and is rejected for several reasons, including on grounds of economy. Becker puts this point well (Cockburn p264) "with all due respect to Lawrence thats nonsense I mean you can't. Because if you really do that to the extreme, if you could really accomplish it, you would have mountains of material of absolutely no interest to you"

Time is always a factor and there does not seem to be any reason in principle why respondents should not be directed to areas of interest to the research.

Secondly, interviews are both like and unlike conversations. They have different functions and role expectations about which most respondents are aware. The important point here is the respondent's expectations. They expect and have agreed to participate in a form of talk that is functional for the interviewer, which means they expect to be directed on to topics relevant to the interviewer and for the interviewer to have the main responsibility to direct the talk, keeping it to relevant subjects. If these role expectations are not fulfilled, rather than establishing rapport, the respondent is likely to feel anxious, to want reassurance that she/he is on the right track. Whyte (1960 quoted in Cockburn p32) makes the point, adding that while interviewing may have techniques in common with theraputic interviewing it is not exactly the same thing.

> The interview technique we use is often called non directive. This is a grave misnomer. The non directive interview was a therapeutic development based on a theory that a patient would make progress best if he were left free to express himself or his problems as he wished, stimulated by an interested and sympathetic listener .... While the good research interview may have a therapeutic side effect, it is structured in terms of a research problem. The interview structure is not fixed by predetermined questions as it is in a questionnaire, but is designed to provide the informant with freedom to introduce materials that were not anticipated by the interviewer.
>
> Whatever its merits for therapy, a genuinely non directive interviewing approach is not appropriate for research. Far from putting informants at their ease it actually seems to stir anxieties ....

Lastly, too non-directive an approach would forgo the opportunity to probe. This could mean having to be content with superficial responses or what the respondent might consider the socially acceptable response. Skillful probing holds the promise of getting behind these problems. To quote Cockburn (1988 p31)

> .... such an approach is deep and intensive the interviewer does not rest content with superficial responses but probes skillfully, prolonging the conversation on any subject of his interest until the informational base, the underlying attitudes, the emotional reactions and the intensity of convictions have been fully disclosed. The properly concluded non-directive interview should result in a detailed account which covers the agenda of the project.

This is what was attempted in this research. Questions of the George Homans type such as "What do you think about being unemployed?" were asked and the respondant encouraged to freely express themselves. There were also back up questions that were more specific. For example the question `how do you spend your time? was followed up by asking in detail how they had spent the day before, last weekend, and so on. One general technique was to move from the general to the specific. Becker recommends this technique for getting past rhetoric (particularly when interviewing people paid to 'front' organisation) and the socially accepted answer (Cockburn p303)

Cockburn sums up the problem of achieving truthfull answers by listing likely sources of distortion.

> Individuals idealise their behaviour in the directions of social approval. Secondly, they produce articulations of themselves or behaviours which square with their notions of self as rational, consistant and integrated beings, or with their professional identity. Thirdly that individuals inevitably restructure and interpret their experience with the benefits of hindsight. We saw in a later chapter that the appropriate interviewing technique to restrict these distortions is to ask for concrete examples of behaviour and to restrict the respondant generalising.

As already explained, this research made use of both general open ended questions and the technique of asking for specific examples.

Obviously attention was paid to avoid leading questions or giving any verbal or non verbal clue as to an approved answer. Indirect questions were often productive.Again, ideas were gained from Cockburn's interviews with experienced sociologists. Phillip Jackson provided a useful idea - when asked if he used indirect questions he replied.

> Yes but not by asking them in any flat footed way, like what are the rewards of teaching? But rather by sneaking up on it in ways like 'Everybody, every job has good days and bad days can you describe a

> good day for me?. Or 'lots of people lie awake at night worrying about work - do you lie awake at night? What do you think about? (Cockburn p268)

Questions like these were reshaped to fit the subject, as were those suggested by Maccoby and Maccoby who give this advice.

> Indicate that other people hold what might otherwise be considered a frowned open opinion "some parents feel that it is important to teach a child not to fight with other children. Others feel that in some circumstances a child must learn to fight. How do you feel about this?"
>
> Balance against each other alternatives each having a positive loading "Do you and your family believe in showing affection for each other a lot or are you fairly reserved sort of people?".

So there was an interview schedule but room was left to depart from this and follows up points made by the respondants or to deal with questions in the order they preferred. However all questions were usually asked even if they had already been answered spontaneously, as was often the case. The word 'usually' appears because in long and absorbing interviews it was often hard to remember which questions had been asked, so occasionally one or two were forgotten.

Generally, attempts were made to check answers by asking about the same topic in different ways.

Interviews were tape recorded and respondents were shown the pause button and told that they could stop the tape if they did not want any answers recorded. Of course, they had been assured of anonymity and no one took advantage of this. In general I was amazed at how open and unsuspicious they seemed, talking openly on personally and legally sensitive subjects. On one occassion a respondent's boy friend questioned me after reluctantly sitting out the interview in another room. He seemed satisfied and said "I thought you might be a social security investigator" "Oh" said his girl friend "I hadn't thought of that".Another respondent hesitated when asked about drugs then relaxed and said "OK I'll tell you - sorry to be suspicious but I hardly know you".

Apart from these incidents, everyone was (to me) surprisingly open.

Respondents were asked if the tape recorder put them off and everyone answered words to the effect of 'No I forgot it was there.' I was a bit nervous of it at first, perhaps the younger generations being more used to sophisticated electronic equipment take such things more for granted. The danger is that recording may increase the tendancy for the respondent to go into what Goffman would have called 'on stage behaviour' increasing the distortion described earlier. Also described earlier was techniques for dealing with this, but another was to switch off the tape and say something like "now the tape's off is their anything else you can think of, any area that hasn't been covered?"

People would seriously reflect on this and would often come up with very useful additions. One example was Paul who thought for a moment and then started to describe hiding his Giro when in the queue at the Post Office so that people did not realise he was unemployed. He then spoke at length, without prompting on the feelings of stigma that unemployment brings.

All people were asked "Are there any more questions I should have asked? There may be things about your life that I, as a man, or employed, or older, that I don't know about and so cannot ask about, can you think of anything?

Sometimes new information emerged at this point, mostly I was reassured that I had covered all the main points. (whether this was true and said to please me I can't be absolutely certain).

The first few interviews acted as a pilot but, as only minor changes seemed necessary, they were included in the sample. The question seemed to pass the test that Howard Becker advised (in Cockburn p264/5)

> No, of course what you want to do is be prepared and be open to the possibility that you impose something. Listen for the things that don't fit. Listen for when people have trouble answering, thats always a big thing. If somebody has trouble with your questions its bound to be because some premise that is implied in the question in incorrect.

Gratifyingly, the questions did seem to 'fit.'

In conclusion while it is likely that there was some distortion and exaggerations I believe these were kept to a minimum. The answers were 'true' in the sense that people were not making things up and the problems and strategies described were real. The interviews covered the area while allowing and encouraging the respondants to talk about their own concerns and experiences. Patterns did emerge and theories were generated in the manner described by Glazer and Strauss and these are discussed in the substantive chapters and in both the introductions and conclusions.

While writing this I become aware that I was uncomfortable using terms like, 'respondent' or 'informant' to describe living people struggling to come to terms with a difficult situation. All were helpful and seemed to enjoy the experience (it was sometimes hard to thank them for helping me, because they were thanking me). A very few were inarticulate, most were intelligent people fully capable of reflecting intelligently and honestly on their situation and I am in their debt. Of course as in any research venture, selection from and interpretation of the vast amount of evidence collected has fallen to me.

3 Unemployment: The literature

Kelvin and Jarrett (1985) in their excellent review of the literature on the consequences of unemployment describes this body of research "This material has three main characteristics: it is descriptive, it is diffuse and fragmented, and it is almost entirely concerned with the unemployed man. It is descriptive in the sense that it has concentrated on painting pictures of the unemployed and the situations, and only rarely consider underlying processes and applications..." (p.1) This is accurate but there has been a considerable amount of work done over a long period of time. This tends to be of two types closely related to the levels of unemployment at the time of writing. One branch of the literature emerges during periods of high economic activity and consequent low levels of unemployment.This is concerned with investigating why certain groups, perhaps the disabled or ethnic minorities, or certain geographical areas are missing out on the general prosperity. In other words it reflects the historical period by concentrating on 'special groups' and the problems of integrating them into the labour market. Unsurprisingly this type of research flowered in the 1920's and more particularly in the 1950's - 60's. This chapter is not concerned with this area but with the literature that has developed during times of high unemployment, such as the 1930's and the period since the mid to late 1970's. During this time, unemployment is no longer the province of 'special groups', almost anyone can find themselves out of work and large number of `ordinary people' do so. The point at issue then becomes the experience of unemployment for such people, how it affects them, what being unemployed 'does to people'.

"The unemployed are not simply units of employability who can through the medium of the dole, be put in cold storage and taken out again immediately they are needed. While they are in cold storage things are likely to happen to them".(Pilgrim Trust 1938.)

This chapter will start with a general consideration of research of the 1930's. Then it will describe the research done on the issue of the unemployed's psychological and physical health.After this, topics of concern to this project will be examined in the same order as the chapters of the thesis.

The research of the 1930's

What 'happens' to people was the subject of much research in the 1930's. Some studies concentrated on the poverty and often extreme physical deprivation that accompanied unemployment. The Pilgrim Trust (1938) set up a working party chaired by the Archbishop of York to study this problem. He found that in 1936 three out of ten households lived below a poverty line drawn up by the British Medical Association and based on 'minimum standards for food requirements'. The working party concluded that "There is little doubt that many unemployed men are undernourished" and that further it was often mothers who were in an even worse situation as they made sure that their husbands and children got the majority of what was available. While emphasizing that "none of us had the medical experience required for a thorough study" they reported malnutrition and a variety of related physical problems. Amongst women in unemployed households, they found a increase in anemia, septic hands and skin troubles.This was partly put down to physical aspects of poverty and partly to the closely related aspect - anxiety - which caused 'lowered vitality'.

Official statistics (discussed in Webster 1982 and Macfarlen and Cole in Durward ed 1985) described a rise in both infant and maternal mortality that seemed to parallel the rise in unemployment. Interestingly, then as now government officials denied any connection between unemployment and poverty and ill health of any kind. Sir George Newman the chief medical officer, said in 1936 that "bad housing, slums, insanitation, domestic overcrowding, uncleanliness and poverty" had nothing to do with the rise in mortality. The problem he said was one of personal behaviour that "affected rich and poor alike". Webster (see also Smith 26 Oct 1985) reports that privately Newman admitted that poverty and unemployment were major factors but advised the Department of Health against investigating them because the findings would be embarrassing and would demand action beyond the means of the department. Studies in other countries similarly linked unemployment with poverty and related ill health (described in Smith 26 Oct 1985). Perrott et al found an illness rate 48% higher in unemployed families in the United States and this was supported by the US National Health survey of 1935/36.

Using questioning and physical examination, Marsh in Canada compared the health of 1000 unemployed men with 1000 fully employed. He also looked at 270 employed youths and 600 unemployed families. His conclusion was that the unemployed were underweight, undernourished, had poor teeth and were more likely to suffer from diseases such as tuberculosis.

The other major line of research in the 1930's, which in fact makes up the bulk of the work done, concentrated on psychological effects rather than poverty. Eisenberg and Lazerfield carried out a major review of this work in 1938 citing 112 references. They concluded that

> The general conclusion of practically all workers is that unemployment tends to make people more emotionally unstable ... unemployment represents a personal threat to an individual's economic security, fear plays a major role; the sense of proportion is shattered - that the individual loses his common sense of values ; the individual's value is lost in his own eyes and, as he imagines in the eyes of his fellow men. He develops feelings of inferiority, loses his self confidence and in general loses his morale.

They found general agreement that unemployed men (virtually all this research concentrated solely on men) tended to go through phases. First shock on losing his job, then optimism which often involves an active hunt for work, then pessimism when their efforts fail, lastly they adapt, but at low psychological level, which they describe as a broken attitude. The phase model has had an important and enduring influence on later generations of researchers as has already been discussed in the introduction.

'Marienthal' Marie Jahoda's classic study of an Austrian town devastated by the closure of the one large factory which the majority depended upon for work, was a milestone in research on the effects of unemployment. She later summerised the findings in the following way

> ... the study showed that being unemployed is something very different from having leisure time.The unemployed decreased their attendance of clubs and voluntary organisations, their use of the free library, their reading habits. Their sense of time disintegrated, having nothing to do meant that they were less able to be punctual for meals or other arrangements. Budgeting, so much more necessary than before, was progressively abandoned, while family relations continued in established patterns longer than other relations, there was some evidence that they, too deteriorated and family quarrels increased. (1979, p. 309.)

Marienthal was a one factory village, so that unemployment hit the entire community, a fact which may have mitigated the psychological impact, since the entire significant reference group was in much the same situation. Other studies at that time of unemployed people living amidst employed people showed demoralisation and loss of self respect as the most devastating impact. "The apparently obvious fact that in the depression unemployment was not the fault of an individual became less and less obvious to those who looked for work without success; irrational self-doubt and depressive moods took over". (Jahoda 1979 p309)

The general conclusion of all the 1930's psychological research into unemployment both here and abroad stresses its progressively destructive psychological impact. Resignation, lack of self confidence and depression being the norm. As has been stated elsewhere this was essentially based on the experience of men who had been working for some time.The title of Komarovsky's work 'The unemployed man and his family (1940) is significant. Women did appear but as wives coping with and influenced by their husband's unemployment rather than in their own right. She reported that wives were badly affected but the focus was on the men. Unemployed husbands felt demeaned and their self esteem was lowered by their changed position in the family. Wives tended to blame them for their position rather than impersonal economical forces.

Young people were also not much investigated, an exception being Jahoda and Lazerfield who also found resignation, apathy and depressions to be general. One of their concerns in this and other studies of older people was the political impact of unemployment and this motivated a general concern. Jahoda (1979 p.309) sums up the findings. "The public debate then was divided between those who predicted that mass unemployment would lead to organised revolution and those who foresaw apathy and disintegration. The studies showed resignation as the major response".

To summarise, the research of the 1930's reached a broad consensus. The poverty of unemployment had damaging consequences for the health: it was psychologically damaging and that on losing their job men tended to move through certain almost pre ordained stages - shock, followed by a holiday feeling, optimism, despair, lastly adaption but at a low psychological level.The unemployed experienced problems with time, felt their lives were purposeless and that this was linked with loss of status and problems with identity (see also Jahoda 1982).

The work of the 1930's has been criticized and the limitations of the 'stages' or phase model has been dealt with in the introduction. Other criticisms include that almost all studies were small scale and owed their influence to their emotional persuasiveness and so have been accused of being unscientific. Stokes and Cochran (1984) describe their methodology as 'suspect and imprecise'. Kelvin and Jarrett say that - "Autobiographical and case-history evidence has made a deep impression ... but impact on the imagination however valid in its own right, is not an adequate test of scientific validity ..."However they go on to say that taken together there is too much evidence to dismiss their broad findings (for example for the phase model) but that the limitations of this research should be recognised.

We know a little about the psychological and social psychological

> consequences of unemployment, and we shall be able to contribute to an understanding of their solution as we gradually build up our body of knowledge. No one gains however, when the sense of urgency of the problem means that early findings are presented and treated as if they were established laws. (p.128)

Another criticism might be that the findings are based largely on a sub-group of the unemployed: that is middle aged urban men, made redundant after some years at work. It may not be valid to generalise from this such group to the rest. Youth, women, and ethnic minorities or county dwellers for example may experience unemployment - or at least some aspects of it - differently.

Lastly it might be objected that research done in the 1930's might not necessarily be relevant in the 1980's. Jahoda (1979 + 82) lists some reasons why the situation today might differ from the 1930's. Firstly, unemployment is not as high as it was then and whether the individual perceives others as being in the same situation or not is, as has been stated earlier, important.

Secondly, coming in the wake of 30 years more of less continuous full employment might make it more of a shock. Many in the 1930's may have been forced to get used to previous periods of intermittent unemployment during the 1920's.

Thirdly, the impact may be lessened by the welfare state as unemployment brings hardship but not the same degree of extreme physical deprivation. 'Today physical deprivation is relative rather than absolute.' (Johoda 1979 p. 311).

Fourthly, people today have had more education and the effect of this is uncertain. It may have raised expectation making the situation harder to bear, or it may have equipped them with increased mental resources, making them better able to cope.

Lastly, social values may have altered. Principally there is speculation that the 'Protestant Work Ethnic' may have declined and if this is so then the experience of job loss would be very different. However she doubts that this is the case (1982 p.36-38). Kelvin and Jarrett go further by doubting if the Protestant work ethnic has ever been significant. 'The idea that any substantial body of the working class has at any time worked with a sense of religious calling is arrant nonsense. The vast majority has always done so simply in order to make a living' (p.103)

In Marienthal, Marie Jahoda wrote "we entered Marienthal as scientists; we leave it with only one desire : that the tragic opportunity for such an enquiry may not recur in our life time."

Her desire was not granted and she is still studying the effects of unemployment in the 1980's. For this reason her work does not slot easily into a 1930's contemporary divide. One aspect she has developed from her work then and now is sometimes called her 'deprivation model'. She points out that conditions of work are for many far from a pleasure - conditions may be damaging and alienating (1979+82). Archer and Rhodes (1987) considering Jahoda's work agree, listing the negative effects of work as physical exhaustion, job over load, humiliating social interactions with superiors, boredom, environmental stresses such as noise and air pollution. Further Jahoda quotes Anthony as arguing that the importance of work has been exaggerated for ideological reasons to such an extent that the reality is bound to be a disappointment. "It is an inevitable consequence of the ideological exaggeration of the importance work that the reality of work will fall far short of its promises". (Anthony 1978 quoted in Jahoda 1979). She agrees but goes on to say that "Work has social and psychological implications thatAnthony fails to analyse". (1979. p312). Further she argues that the alienation widely reported is a result of the organisation of work rather than a response to work itself. Overall she says that the research indicates .....'a profound ambivalence: people want to work even while they hate it' (1979 p.312)

To explain this she evolves the concept of work's 'latent functions' that, over and above the obvious function of providing a living, account largely for the motivation to work.

These are:

> Firstly, work imposes a time structure on the working day
>
> Secondly, employment implies regularly shared experiences and contacts with people outside the nuclear family
>
> Thirdly, employment links an individual to goals and purposes which transcend his own.
>
> Fourthly, employment defines aspects of personal status and identity
>
> Finally, employment enforces activity
>
> It is these latent objective consequences of work in complex industrialised societies which help me to understand the motivation to work beyond earning and living: to understand why works is psychologically supportive even when conditions are bad and; by the same token, why unemployment is psychologically destructive". (1979 p.313)

These latent functions fulfill certain human needs, and to be deprived of work is to be presented with the perhaps unrecognised problem of finding alternative means to do so.This is difficult in a world where people expect work to structure their lives and to fail to work is to suffer.

Contemporary Research : Psychological health

Recent Psychological and Social Psychological studies have followed in the footsteps of their 1930's counterparts in detailing despair, depression and psychological damage amongst the unemployed.They have often differed in that rather than using a small scale case study approach they have often opted for large questionnaires, attempting to be more systematic and 'Scientific'. Much use has been made of the General Health Questionnaire in trying to determine the effect on psychological health. This is a measure of psychological health based on questions about lack of confidence, sleep loss through worry, feelings of strain, depression, inability to concentrate and so on. Peter Warr reviewed these studies listing the proportion found to score more than two - this being people judged to have psychological health low enough to give them a moderate chance of becoming a psychiatric case. The results were:

Group size	Groups studied	% in poor psychological health
163	Unemployed school leavers	54%
78	Unemployed Men	62%
399	Unemployed Men	60%
954	Unemployed Men	58%
87	Disabled men	58%
985	Employed recent school leavers	20%
401	Employees in relatively uninvolved organisation	15%
103	Employees in troubled organisation	25%

(Warr in Allen & Van de Vleet eds 1984)

In association with others, Warr has carried out a number of studies throughout the 1980's that confirm this picture of low psychological health associated with unemployment. Others have confirmed this so many times that taken together this can be considered a firm finding.

Of course the problem then, having accepted that unemployment and poor psychological health are associated, is that it could be argued that the individual's low psychological health may be the cause of their unemployment rather than the other way round. There is some longitudinal evidence that this is not the case. Banks and Jackson (1982), for example, studied 1000 school leavers, administering the GHQ both before and after leaving school. The unemployed were found to have poorer psychological health after a period of unemployment yet there had been no significant difference in their GHQ's prior to their leaving school. This tends to indicate that unemployment was indeed the cause of their problem rather than vice versa. Warr (1982) working from the opposite direction found that people improved their GHQ score after they found jobs. Brenner and Bartell (1983) using interviews and the GHQ over a period of time found that psychological health deteriorated overtime - "length of unemployment is significantly negatively correlated with mental health and well being."

In his review article 'Twelve questions about Unemployment and Health' (1985) Warr reviews eight longitudinal studies of this kind and, as measured by the GHQ, psychological health declines after job loss and revives when work is found. He concludes that - at least for men - he considers the case proven.

This tendency for psychological health to decline after becoming unemployed also fits in with the opinions of the unemployed themselves. Jackson and Warr (1984) surveyed 954 men unemployed for an average for five months who reported factors such as nervousness, irritability, and lack of confidence and related these to their loss of job. Those employed for over six months were more likely to express such views.

Another type of evidence has been generated by the American Sociologist Harvey Brenner by what he calls aggregate studies. He used complex mathematical techniques to try to link fluctuations in health statistics to economic fluctuations such as unemployment. He concludes that in New York State between 1841 and 1971, economic instabilities were "the single most important source of fluctuation in mental hospital admissions". (Brenner 1973 quoted in Smith 9.11.85). Brenner's methods have been criticised and Smith comments that 'the consensus among those who have been studying unemployment and health for a long time seems to be that his methods are suspect even if his broad conclusions are right" (9-11-85)

Small scale studies, usually based on case histories and interviews both in the 1930's and more recently have documented the psychological decline of those affected by unemployment. Taken altogether the cumulative result of the evidence is that unemployment is a cause of poor psychological health. There may never be absolute proof but in my view there is so much evidence as to leave very little room for doubt and that this should be the starting point for future research.

To quote Fineman (1987) '.... modern studies that follow individuals in and out of jobs over time have demonstrated beyond reasonable doubt that it is indeed the unemployment or at least a combination of unemployment and relative poverty, that is responsible for the distress rather than vice versa!"

Other general findings on psychological health are that young people also suffer but not as much as middle aged men (See later for consideration of the position of women) (Warr 1984/85/87 Banks and Jackson 1982) and that more work orientated individuals suffer more (Warr 1982/85)

Less work has been done on the reasons for these findings. Kelvin and Jarrett (1985) describe the literature as a whole, both in the 1930's and recently as ..."descriptive in the sense that it has concentrated on painting pictures of the unemployed and their situation, and only rarely considers underlying processes and implications." (p.1)

Warr (1985 in Roberts, Finnegan & Gallie) lists nine possible causes for the poor mental health associated with unemployment

1 Financial worry

2 Restricted behaviours and environments. The unemployed do not get out so much to meet people. They do not go out to a workplace and have less money to go out socially.

3 Loss of 'traction.' Work pulls people along and without it small tasks that are achieved quickly when working take much longer

4 Smaller scope for decision making both at work and because of lack of money to carry decisions out

5 Fewer opportunities to develop new skills or use old ones. Work provides both the money and the motive.

6 An increase in threatening and humiliation experiences. For example attending job interviews and being rejected

7 Anxiety about the future

8 A decline in the quality of interpersonal contacts. For example work relationships are likely to be more satisfying than having to face people at a social security centre

9 A decline in social positions and status.

Physical Health

Dr. Richard Smith writing in the British Medical Journal (7-12-85) considers the research into the psychological effects of unemployment to be vastly superior to that of the physical effects and comments that

> The failure to start a high quality study of this problem is an indictment of politicians, doctor's leaders, and those who decide research priorities. Whether nobody saw the need for such a study or whether a study was proposed and rejected because of the political sensitivity of unemployment, I do not know, but a variety of people around the country have suggested that the government has discouraged rather then encouraged research into unemployment and health.

Studies such as the DHSS Cohort Study (Maglen, Miller and Davies 1984 quoted in Smith) reveal that the unemployed use the health service more than the general population. This is of very little use because it does not deal with the problem that this might be simply because a proportion of the unemployed are unemployed because they are sick. More interesting in so far as this thesis is concerned, is the work of Dr Beal, a general practitioner and Nethercott, a Statistician (1985) of people in his practice in Colne Wiltshire who were affected by the closure of a meat processing factory. They showed a very significant increase in consultation rates compared with a control group. In 1985 they reported a 20% increase in visits to his practice of the affected group and a 60% increase in visits to the hospital outpatient department. Their monitoring of the group continues and was the subject of a television programme in 1988 for the series World in Action. This reported even more dramatic findings; consultation rates and drugs prescribed increased by over 600%. There was also a large increase in very serious illness and even death. Interestingly this rise dates back to the announcement of the plant's closure - two year before it happened.

Their access to medical records concerning the redundant workers and to fully employed neighbours who could act as a control group makes this a very interesting study. It is of course small scale and limited and more research on these lines would be valuable if there is the political will.

A similar study in Miami (Finn, Sandifer and Stein 1985) showed similar results. Thirty men who lost their jobs were compared with a closely matched control group and at the start of the period of study (1979) they showed no significant difference in either physical or psychological health. Within six months both psychological and physical health of the unemployed began to decline resulting in more illness, more visits to the doctor, more medicines prescribed and so on.

An interesting aspect of this research was the strong correlation between measures of psychological and physical health with those showing the greatest degree of social isolation also showing the worse psychological and physical health, Brenner also links them and death to psychological health and claims a link with unemployment. Given that the decline in psychological health seem well established and that physical and psychological well being are linked it would be strange if this deterioration of psychological health did not manifest itself in more illness. Dr Smith's series of articles in the Lancet in 1985 reviews the evidence and he certainly believes this to be the case. However, he concludes by stating that

> there is much we do not know. If I stop to think of the amount of publicity as, for example hypertension or cancer of the colon, I can only conclude that doctors and medical researchers have shamefully neglected the study of how unemployment harms the health of families.

Death on the Dole?

The question of whether unemployment kills has been much debated particularly in medical journals. Dr Smith writing in the British Medical Journal (23-11-85) summing up of the evidence offers an excellent review and this section relies on his writing. Brenner in a number of papers using aggregate studies, sometimes called time series analysis, has linked mortality to unemployment, claiming that an increase of more than one million in five years results in 50000 more deaths from general illness and 167000 from cardiovascular courses. Gravelle has denied this under a heading called 'Lies, damned lies and time series results' (1985 quoted in Smith). Scott Samuel (1985 BMJ 290) has attacked Gravelle for ignoring data and has estimated that British male unemployment causes 3000 extra deaths a year. Interestingly, Morris and Titmus published results similar to Brenner in 1940 and Brenner was unaware of this until after he had done most of his work.

Moser, Fox and Jones (1984) followed up a sample of 5861 men gained from the Office of Population Censuses and Surveys' longtitudinal study and found that in every age and every class mortality was far higher for unemployed than employed.

They made elaborate attempts to exclude those unemployed because of illness so this was a sample of the 'healthy' unemployed and they conclude that, although they could not rule out a selection effect, they consider it unlikely.

Mechanism are uncertain. Unemployment causes poverty and there is a long established link between poverty, illness and death. Unemployment also causes psychological deterioration and the link between this and illness and death is likely but difficult to measure. Smith argues that mental health is an important contributory factor to killing illnesses such as heart disease but goes on to say that measurement problems have led medical researchers to avoid this subject. The result is uncertainty as to exactly how important this factor is. Suicide and parasuicide (defined on deliberate self harm and not simply failed suicide) have been more extensively examined and linked with unemployment so this is one important cause. Platt (1984), has reviewed 156 relevant studies of all types and these point in the direction of unemployment as a causal factor. A report in the Guardian (9-2-90) of as yet unpublished research by Colin Pritchard of Southampton University claims that - "A link between suicide and unemployment is proved conclusively by the analysis of international suicide trends between 1964 and 1986......the unemployment link stands up to broad scrutiny, and that it should serve as a warning to governments"

It is difficult to assess this study prior to publication but it does appear that evidence is mounting. This is not surprising as both suicide and para suicide seem more obviously connected with states of mind than say heart disease and, as we have seen, it is well established that unemployment effects states of mind for the worse.

Smith concludes that it has not been proved that unemployment kills but "The circumstantial evidence is strong and many studies point in the same direction." (23.11.84)

To conclude and sum up this section, the literature from the 1930's and from the work of modern psychologists paints a dismal picture. Unemployment emerges as psychologically and probably physically debilitating. It is likely but not completely proven that this works to create a higher death rate for the unemployed. The strongest findings is that unemployment causes psychological health to worsen. Many writers and researchers from the 1930's and more recently see it as a leveler of individual differences forcing people down an almost preordained route characterised by certain stages that end in adaption at a psychologically low level - a 'broken attitude'.

I will now look at the literature related to the specific chapters on this thesis. Lastly I will look at the literature on womens unemployment.

Time and Leisure

As we have seen Jahoda in Marienthal reported the sad irony that although people had more time on their hands they actually did less, and many modern writers have found the same (eg Miles 1983 Marsden and Duff 1975 Willis 1987 Fagin and Little 1984 and many of the papers by Warr) Jahoda lists the imposition of a time structure as one of the 'latent functions' of work and lack of it as one of the problems of the unemployed.

Difficulties in dealing with this problem, that is filling in time and finding affordable things to do, may be one of the mechanisms for causing the widely reported decline in mental health. The European Centre for Work's study (1983) found that half of the 86 inner city young people they examined had difficulty filling in their time and that they were the most likely to report difficulties in coping with their situation. Miles (1983) chose the problems with the lack of an imposed time structure as his main example when attempting to test Jahoda's latent functions. He also found that those with problems with filling time were likely to be the ones suffering from depression and low psychological health. He concluded from this that these latent functions are powerful predictors of mental health. Hepworth (1980) supports this as does Fineman (1987) who goes on however to criticise Jahoda for neglecting the aspect of fears and hopes for the future. Brenner and Bartell (1983) found that "positive activity" helps to mitigate the worse effects of unemployment, claiming that there is a brief critical period, when if the individual does not adapt by finding meaningful ways of filling their time their mental health goes down hill and this itself tends to prevent or hinder the ability to engage in this positive activity. Kelvin and Jarret also suggest that there are `critical periods where an individual can go one way or the other, that is restructure their lives with purposeful activity or become increasingly listless and depressed. They add however "we have to admit that we have scant evidence for the usefulness of our suggestions". Brenner and Bartell estimate that those who do successfully achieve this meaningful restructuring amount to no more than 5 - 8% of the unemployed population. Again, like most of the research, this estimate concerns middle aged males.

Ray Pahl's study of the Isle of Sheppey found that the unemployed tended not to be the ones that got work in the informal economy as they tended not to have the skills, contacts and small amounts of capital to buy material and transport, (see chapter 7) so one way of filling in time was denied to most. He further discovered they did not even have the money to obtain the material for what he called "self provisioning" - DIY, Beer making and so on. "Our interviewers have documented the despair of those living in their own homes, with their own tools, with time on their hands and with urgent decorating jobs staring them in the face but without the money to buy the paint." (In Roberts et al 1985)

One line of enquiry has revolved round the question - can leisure compensate for lack of work? Can time be meaningfully filled and the days structured around leisure as an alternative? The research suggests an answer for the majority - no! Stokes (1983) Warr (1983) and Kelvin et al (1984) all suggest that while it may help it is at best a palliative rather than a substitute for work.

Sue Glyptis has done a number of studies on this issue; summing up her own work and reviewing that of others she says that leisure does not and cannot became a substitute for work for any but a tiny minority of 'addicts' (Glyptis 1989)

> Unemployment, for the vast majority of people affected by it, is a largely negative experience. We expect to work, by and large we want to work, and we derive psychological as well as financial rewards for doing so. What work removes, leisure cannot replace. ......What leisure cannot provide by its very nature is a sense of compulsion and purpose beyond the pursuit of activity for its own sake. It cannot provide the central core of structure and purpose on which we have come to depend.....Work and leisure are not just a conceptual couplet twinned for the convenience of testing theories. They are experienced as a pair the one deriving meaning from the other. The expectation that large numbers of unemployed people will turn to leisure - especially sport-to use their surplus time and energies is ill founded. Even for the minority of unemployed people who do develop a substantial commitment to leisure activities, leisure does not take on new meanings but it plays its traditional role. Chapter 5 shows that even among committed sports participants, sport played the 'normal' role of a leisure activity, not an additional role of work substitute, a key source of structure, or a central life interest.
>
> For the unemployed leisure is an important ingredient of the quality of life - no more than that and no less...few unemployed people find leisure

easy to believe in as a central purpose of life....

> Leisure will survive as a concept and experience in its own right, if there are sources of structure to surround it, but leisure does not in any sense, signify the end of unemployment" (Glyptis 1989 pp 158-162)

Of course not only sport and organised leisure but also the popular pursuits of drinking, socialising and so on are also curtailed, mainly by lack of money. (This will be dealt with in the next section on money)

As usual Kelvin and Jarrett provide on excellent summing up of the problems related to time.

> Sooner or later however, and mostly perhaps quite soon, the unemployed individual becomes deeply aware of his seemingly unending amount of free time .....much the dominant theme is of an almost obsessive preoccupation with time - the extent of it, with the inability to make use of it, with the sense that one is therefore merely 'killing it'. From the early thirties to the present day, research on unemployment has consistently documented the consciousness of the unemployed of the emptiness of their days (pp 67/8)

No research in the five or so years since these words were written has contradicted this.

Money

Kelvin and Jarrett (1985) pointed out that the studies both in the 1930s and the 1970/80s tended to concentrate either on the poverty of the unemployed or the disastrous psychological effects. What they did not do was make much attempt to relate the two. "There seem to have been very few attempts indeed to trace the interaction of the economic and psychological effects of unemployment (p18/19) adding " we have it seems become too specialised"

This is an important omission as it would seem likely that the two are closely related. As they point out -

> Those concerned with the psychology of work have long stressed that work provides much more than merely money: those of us who are concerned with the psychology of unemployment must now equally stress that to be unemployed is to be poor. Many of the problems of the unemployed stem directly from their hardships and ever those whose origins are in themselves purely social and psychological are made infinitely worse by poverty (p18)

An exception here was Jahoda who, in Marienthal, linked the idea that the unemployed pass through various stages of psychological deterioration to the gradual exhaustion of their material resources. The 'unbroken' and 'optimistic' stages coincide with the period before savings are exhausted while 'despair' comes as the money goes, clothes need repairing, debts rise and so on. Lastly, apathy and resignation but, at a low psychological level, sets in as the individual adapts to living at the very much lower material level. She describes ".... stages of a process of psychological deterioration that runs parallel to the narrowing of economic resources and the wear and tear on personal belongings" (1933/72 p87)

In writing the thesis, it was difficult to decide whether to have a chapter on money at all because it is such a central problem it runs like a common thread through all the problems unemployment brings. It would therefore have been perfectly feasible to integrate it into every section and chapter instead of having a separate one. In practice this has to some extent been unavoidable as it is impossible to exclude money from any chapter or section

Take for example the last section. Perhaps the most important reasons for the tendency for the unemployed to be unable to make use of their time is that they are unable to afford to do the things they want to do. Paul Willis's (1984) large scale study of youth in Wolverhampton confirm this. In a later article summing up this study he puts this well:

> Ironically, those who have most 'spare-time' are excluded, in fact, from 'leisure'. This is because the main forms of modern leisure involve consumption and commercial power - for the young, mobility in cars, drinking in pubs, going to pubs, clubs, commercial discos and dances. Unemployment excludes young people from these things.
>
> Table the example of drinking. Whether we like it a not, this is by far the most common 'leisure' activity among young people of both sexes. Over three quarters of them go drinking, on average nearly four times a week. But only a third of the long term unemployed go to pubs at all and then much less frequently.
>
> ...This does not mean that the commercial forms of leisure do not still exert a powerful pull. Indeed part of the obscenity of unemployment is the great sacrifice of boredom and dead time which can be made just to visit an expensive night club once in a while - with endless nights indoors or hanging about in between" (1986 p160)

Indeed the pervasive importance of lack of money as a problem stimulated Carr Hill (1985 quoted in ch4) to argue poverty is the sole factor that explain the depression and psychological ill health of the majority of the unemployed. He believes that research into psychological factors is nothing more than a diversion from the real problem of poverty and unequal shares. I do not agree. The work of Jahoda, Warr and others provides valuable insights but I do believe that the wage or rather the lack of it is the most important single factor and relates to all other factors even if it is not the only factor.

Relationships - Isolation

That unemployment tends to push people towards isolation has been well documented both in the 1930s (eg Kamarovsky 1940, Bakke 1933 Jahoda - Eisinberg and Lazerfeld 1938) and more recently (For example Marsdan and Duff 1975. The European Centre for Work 1983. Coffield et al 1986. Willis 1984/6 Warr 1985). Jahoda makes the point that work, by its very nature, forces people into regular relationships with others beyond their immediate family. Of course many of these relationships are unsatisfactory or even degrading given the hierarchical nature of much work but most indepth studies find people reporting missing the comradeship of work. Some (eg Kelvin & Jarrett) suggest this may be different for young people who have never experienced work and are used to filling in long summer holidays in the company of friends.

Again the problem of money is very important, Willis (quoted in the section on leisure) points out that most social activities demand commercial power which the unemployed lack. They therefore spend much less time socialising.

For some, there may be a tendency to withdraw from social contacts because of shame and fear of the stigma attached to unemployment. The depression and low psychological health frequently reported may make it more difficult to make the effort to keep in touch with friends.

Willis (1986) describes people meeting unemployed friends and filling their day 'hanging around'. He also found a small minority that were very socially active. However his general conclusion was: "But the dominant experience of the long term unemployed seem to be of very limited sociability, of seeing friends once or twice a week - and this despite their masses of 'free time'." (p161)

Family

The conclusion of most of the literature is that the strains of unemployment badly affect family relationships. Fictional representations such as Bleasdale's "The Boys from the Black Stuff" reinforce this impression. A number of studies have written about difficulties experienced by the wives of unemployed men (see section on Gender below), painting a picture of relationships strained by financial worry and the long hours spent in the company of frustrated and depressed husbands. The tone of a review article on the effects of unemployed on families by Richard Smith (14-12-85) is demonstrated by its title "We get on each other's nerves". He goes on to say

> Unemployment can destroy relationships just as it destroys individuality. The deterioration in the mental health of the unemployed person - be it the father, the mother, or a child - effects his or her relationships with the rest of the family. And in this time of misery the family are likely to be thrown together more, usually in financially reduced circumstances, and sooner or later something may snap.

Willis (1986) in a summary of his study of Wolverhampton's Youths writes:

> It (unemployment) is certainly concentrated in the working class. So many family members may be living on top of each other in restricted accommodation designed for the working nuclear family, competing for the limited conveniences of the home, perhaps recriminating each other for lost potentials and chances. It is no surprise that a third of the young unemployed - half the long term unemployed white working class males - say that unemployment has caused problems in the home (P161)

Hutson and Jenkins (1989) in a study of 58 families containing young unemployed modify this view

> They were, indeed, disrupted and threatened by the long term unemployment of daughters and sons. In a range of situations and to varying degrees their can be little doubt of that. However, there were few cases where unemployment itself actually caused severe family conflict where previously there was none. (p152)

Unemployment caused strains that aggravated existing conflicts. However, in the words of the book's title most families were 'Taking the Strain'.

Coffield et al (1986) - like the present research - found a large amount of family support for unemployed young people. Kelvin and Jarrett (1985) suggest, like Hutson & Jenkins, that the effect of the undoubted strains on family life depend on the quality of relationship prior to the problem. So unemployment can shatter, or at least worsen, shakey relationships but causes strong families to pull together even more - a closing of ranks to help the disadvantaged members.

Family Formation, housing & future progress

There has been considerable speculation about the effects of youth unemployment on family formation since becoming an independent worker and being able to afford a separate household are part of the normal process of becoming an adult. The most common suggestion is that unemployment impedes the process of going out, meeting sexual partners and forming pairs as well as making a separate household unaffordable (eg Gurney 1980 Hendrey et al 1986 Coffield 1986,

Willis 1984/6)

Coffield, for example, makes the point that loss of independence is part of the unintended price paid for the often generous family support -

> . . .the economic advantages to the young person of living at home were obvious. In another sense, however, it can be questioned whether they were advantages at all. To refer to them as economic advantages or benefits suggests that they were preferable to some other economic option in practice, the women and men we knew found no such alternative. Attempts to find jobs and housing in other parts of the country proved unsuccessful.They were staying at home, growing older but hardly more in control of their lives than when they were in primary school. (p146)

> He adds: ....the traditional means of progressing from childhood to adulthood have been broken for hundreds of thousands of working class young men. The social consequences of an ever extending period of dependence on parents and the state will still have to be calculated because the phenomena is so new. The almost endless adolescence which for decades has become the lot of middle class youths, is now the daily experience of their working class contemporaries with one critical distinction for the latter there will be no elite jobs to compensate for the long denial of status. (p205)

Paul Willis (1984/86) has become one of the foremost supporters of this view -

> The young unemployed have, in many ways been thrust into a 'new social condition' of suspended animation between school and work. Many of the old transitions - into work, into the cultures and organisations of work, into being consumers, into independent accommodation - have been frozen or broken. Instead there is a really extended period of relative poverty and dependency on the family and on an increasingly mean and coercive state (1986 p163).

He sees setting up an adult home and family as "almost a universal working class objective" (29-3-84) He stresses the pivitol position of the wage "the golden key" a house, with wage labour the price. Without wage labour, this objective is blocked resulting in a frustrating extended adolescence.

This idea is not however universally accepted. Griffin (1985) suggests that the opposite may be true for at least some young women who may be spurred to redouble their efforts to meet and marry a working partner in order to escape their situation, marriage and motherhood being the traditional route to adulthood for young women. Certainly it may supply an attractive role if the alternative is the role of 'unemployed'

Recently Hutson and Jenkins (1989) have taken issue with Willis.

> A number of commentators, Paul Willis most notably, have argued that one of the most serious consequences of long term unemployment is that it is the social equivalent of a state of suspended animation, preventing young people from reaching adulthood. We did not find any convincing evidence to support this argument. Quite the reverse: despite their unemployment, the overwhelming majority of the young people we interviewed were continuing to claim their adulthood. Being unemployed in the long-term may make transitions to adulthood more problematic; it may also affect the nature of one's claim to adult status, but these are different arguments.

So Hutson and Jenkins do regard unemployment as a problem as far as achieving adult status is concerned but one that is being overcome. They tend to concentrate on being accepted as an adult by parents and others and seeing themselves as adults. They point out that the young people themselves, their parents and society in general want and expect them to become adults. "There is thus a considerable psychological and social head of steam which pushes and pulls young people into adulthood, unemployment notwithstanding." (p154)

Willis is also concerned with this aspect but concentrates more on the practical problems of setting up an independent household in the absence of a wage. This creates problems both in finding a mate, the unemployed in Willis's sample were much less likely to be 'courting', and in being able to afford reasonable permanent accommodation. Reading through Hutson and Jenkins' description of their sample (Appendix pp 161-169) of 17-25 year olds, it is notable that the vast majority are living at home with parents so this issue is not really tackled. It is of course very likely that this problem will be met with varied rather than uniform response. I suspect that Willis is right for the majority of cases (insofar as the practical consequences are concerned) but the issue is far from settled. Hutson and Jenkins note that the concept of adulthood is "multifaceted and unprecise" (p153), which is true enough. It may therefore be possible to achieve some aspects of adulthood (e.g. adult treatment by family and friends) while failing to achieve other aspects such as an independent home and family. Perhaps the result would be a intermediate state of semi adulthood. More research is needed.

Work - The Informal Economy

The literature on the significance of the informal economy and the participation of the unemployed in it, is relevant to this thesis but is fully explored in Chapter 8.

Rural Unemployment

This is an under researched subject. Kasl and Gore (Kasl 1975 Kasl et al 1975 Gore 1978 quoted in Kelvin and Jarrett 1985) studied workers made redundant in a rural area and reported less stress than among those in the same position in an urban area. This was put down to there being a higher level of social support from the rural community. The problem with generalising from this sample is that this was a homogeneous Polish community. The very fact of being a minority community may have created a tradition of group solidarity that changes the community reaction to unemployment.

Other evidence from the United States suggests the opposite - that rural areas are more hostile to their unemployed (Williamson 1974 Osgood 1977 described in Kevin and Jarrett). In these studies the unemployed were found to be an isolated minority and very visible to the community. It may well be that the type of village community may produce different responses. Tight knit pit villages in the industrial North may have traditions of solidarity and group identity that generate social support. In contrast a Norfolk village may not only lack such traditions, but may also be less of a "community" because a high population of residents may have moved in from outside. Further, if the village is more middle class and prosperous with the unemployed a relatively deprived minority then the possibility exists that invidious comparisons will be made both by the community and the unemployed person themselves. The reference group for the individual unemployed person becomes those more fortunate than themselves rather than a community in a similar position.

Most research has concentrated on urban industrial centres with high levels of unemployment. This is not surprising as these areas make up the bulk of the unemployed. However the rural unemployed do exist in quite large numbers and their position deserves further study.

Stigma

The first point to make is that virtually all the smaller scale qualitative studies find unemployed people complaining of feelings of shame and the belief that others look down on them. Most of the larger scale studies (eg Warr 1985-87) confirm this picture. Brakwell's study of 290 school students and 72 young unemployed people concentrates on this aspect and is the source of the quote also reprinted in chapter 10. "The unemployed believed others despise and depreciated them. This is in itself enough to generate discomfort but when reinforced by other trauma associated with unemployment it can threaten the fabric of identity." (1984)

It is a truism that work is a source of status and identity and the unemployed role does not have a high value. Also, how people view themselves is at least partly conditioned by how they believe others see them. If this is one of the factors that conditions their 'self concept' it is not suprising that unemployment will lead people to believe that others despise and depreciate them" and that this will negatively effect their view of themselves.

Kelvin and Jarrett argue that the feelings of humiliation that the unemployed experience are for reasons other than "because of the loss of some mystical dignity of work "(p50) but because they have become dependant not just on the state and its generosity but also an "how he is seen, and perceives himself to be seen by others." (p47)They go on to say: "The feelings of humiliation are a result of the sense of being so very dependant on others, psychologically as well as materially - for it is the condition of childhood, not of mature men. It deeply undermines the self-concept established before becoming unemployed" (p30)

For them, one of the most important psychological consequences is that unemployment makes people self conscious. Normally people are not constantly aware of themselves but unemployment challenges an individual's taken for granted assumptions forcing a reassessment of themselves. The unemployed status is not high and the individual is forced to reassess his or her identity in negative terms.The result is an increased sensitivity to the perceived opinions of others who are suspected of making harsh judgements. It does not matter whether the perception of these opinions is accurate as long as the individual believes them to be. The shift from independent provider to dependant is therefore damaging to the individual's view of him/herself.

Already mentioned in the Introduction it is a general finding that the unemployed tend to blame themselves for their problems and to believe that others are blaming them.They may also feel degraded and humiliated because they cannot join in the general consumerist activities of society, wear the clothes accepted in their peer group or return hospitality by buying rounds of drinks in pubs for example. It is sufficient to say that studies from the 1930s (eg Bakke 1933) to the 1970s and 1980s (Marsden and Duff 75, Hayes and Nutman, 1981, Sinfield, 1981 Willis 1984/6 to list but a few) have stressed the problem of the sense of stigma attached to unemployment.

To quote Willis

> But the final insult and source of separation and depression amongst the unemployed in the fear of other people's accusing fingers. There is a widespread fear that the employed may think that the unemployed do not want to work, or have no interest in working - a precise inversion of their real feelings, and a shifting of blame for their suffering on their own heads .... Whatever the truth of this, the real dilemma is lodged within the unemployed's own experience.The fundamental source of uncertainty and indecisiveness, and perhaps especially for the long term unemployed male is this - that they have to live with the burden of knowing that more effort might improve their chances of finding work, but that 'permanent

> job search' - doomed to failure for the majority - builds in rejection and hopelessness as daily experiences. The long term unemployed are caught between impossible alternatives: doing nothing and blaming themselves; doing something and receiving daily insults to their dignity, worth and intelligence (1986 p162.)

Finally Kelvin and Jarrett ague that the literature suggests that the level of unemployment affects the degree of stigma attached to the unemployed. During periods of low unemployment the majority of the employed feel relaxed enough about the situation to be generous in their attitude. In periods of very high unemployment and in communities where most people are affected it becomes more difficult to blame, and therefore stigmatise the individual rather than wider social political and economic forces. Somewhere inbetween is an optimum level for attributing personal blame.To back this up they claim that the concept of work ethic and stigma were not part of the language, popular or academic, in the worst period of the 1930s.

Politics

Reviewing the literature on the political effect of unemploment on the unemployed, Fraser, Marsh and Joplin (in Roberts et al 1985) describe two views. One is the older traditional view that the unemployed would be attracted towards radicalism either of the left or right, that they would actively challenge the society that had so little to offer them and this would manifest itself in violence, riots etc, perhaps leading to revolutionary challenges to society itself. The other view, which they describe as the 'new orthodoxy' is that unemployment leads to demoralisation with isolated unemployed blaming themselves rather than society, resulting in an apathetic withdrawal from politics.

Most of the research isAmerican. Fraser et al say that empirical evidence from the UK is "close to being non existent" (p358) and argue that, at this stage, description rather than theory building is necessary. What evidence exists on the two views is mixed. Unemployed people have been found to be more radical and critical in their expressed attitudes and more likely to vote for the political parties of high expenditure. Those that are active are more likely to be involved in trade union and other workers organisations, although whether unemployment is a causal factor or whether it is simply a reflection of their class position is unclear. On the other hand they are less likely to vote or participate in political organisations at all. They report in most opinion polls that the unemployed blame both themselves and the government.

British evidence is indeed sparse. Burchell and Devereux (1987) studied 280 teenagers aged 15-18 in Bedford and East London and report finding a strong link between unemploment and radical right wing ideas, claiming that unemployment has a greater influence on their values than their age, sex, socio-economic status or the age at which they left school. This was a common view in the 1930s when Eisenberg and Lazerfield (1938), for example, believed that unemployment had contributed to the rise of fascism.

Francis (1984) carried out a study of unemployed young people staying in Central London YMCA, involving participant observation, in depth interviews but relying mostly on 1805 completed questionnaires. She found two main associations between unemployment and young people.The first being depression, the second, being more relevant for this section, was radicalism.They expressed more lack of respect for conventional institutions and moral values, they tended to support trade unions, dislike the Conservative party and reject religion. However most were not in anyway active, only 8% overall, but interestingly rising to 12% of the long term unemployed. Central London YMCA caters for a very transient population; it is often the first port of call for people coming from Scotland and the North in search of work.They are therefore probably not a very typical sample and what effect this would have is anybody's guess.The European Centre for Work interviewed 86 young people aged 17-21 from the West Midlands. They found that two thirds blamed the government rather than themselves but again hardly any were politically active.

Explanations for this lack of political involvement usually revolve around the isolation of the unemployed - making collective organisation and action difficult and the personally psychologically demoralising nature of the problem. Seabrook (1982) sees the unemployed (and perhaps the working class generally) as stripped of their traditions of collectivity and culturally fragmented by the successful advance of a culture of privatised consumerism. Thus undermined, the unemployed are prey to personal demoralisation when their consumerist dreams collapse and are therefore incapable of a collective political response. Beynon (1982) criticises Seabrook (rightly in my view), seeing his theory as really a moral judgement on the present working class who are catagorised as deteriorated and devalued culturally compared with a previous mythical 'golden age'. This version is negative and hopeless, ignoring possibilities and present struggles. It is a deterministic vision of consumerism dominating all other aspects.

Kelvin and Jarett point out that the catagory "unemployed" is one which people want to escape from rather than idenitfy with, to forget rather than proclaim. It is therefore psychologically difficult for people to organise on the basis of group identity. `The unemployed' form a negative reference group as far as unemployed individuals are concerned. Most do not want to belong to it and want to desert it as quickly as possible rather than fight for it.

"The principal consequence of this, which has repeatedly puzzled commentators (and at times frustrated them) is the negligible political activities of the unemployed as a group." Of course this does not explain the apparent lack of commitment to political parties and causes not identified with the unemployed.

Finally, Hutson and Jenkins (1989) see welfare benefits and, more importantly, family support as mitigating against political activity and in particular explosions of discontent such as riots. By sheltering their offspring from the worst effects they make unemployment bearable if not satisfactory. The young unemployed are getting by, "taking the strain" and their efforts are channelled in this direction rather than politically. The problem is "contained, managed and limited "(p157) and the only solutions to the problem considered are immediate individual ones.

> The result of these minor epics of domestic heroism and perseverance is that unemployment remains, to appropriate C. Wright Mill's famous words, very much more a personal trouble than a public issue. Nobody actually starves (the welfare state sees to that) and the rest takes care of itself. Except in those situations where unemployment is compounded by other problems, such as racism and police harassment, the unemployed are not going to take to the streets, whether in hunger marches or bread riots. Unemployed people are, by and large, not a nuisance to the rest of society, inasmuch as the young unemployed and their families struggle to keep their end up, succeeding - even if only in part - preventing things from becoming too bad, they make their own modest if unintended contribution to the creation of a political climate in which unemployment remains a problem incapable of prodding the rest of the electorate, those who are working, into raising their eyes above the sides of the trough. Precisely because the parents we spoke to cared so much about the plight of their daughters and sons, the rest of us, it seems, feel justified in ignoring it. (p137/8)

Exceptions - Those who enjoy the unemployed life

All evidence suggests that the vast majority of people find unemployment a miserable and damaging experience. However when dealing with human beings there are always exceptions and researching these may throw light on the whole experience of unemployment. Examining what this minority group has that the others do not might offer a useful point of comparison with the majority.

Understandably, people are concerned with suffering and so have concentrated their research efforts on the unhappy majority leaving the exceptions as an unresearched group. Fryer and Payne (1984) have produced one of the only projects on what they call 'proactive behaviour' exhibited by 5% or so of the unemployed population. They discovered that the mental health of this minority improved because they either gave up jobs they considered to be depressing and horrible, and which were having a negative effect on them, or they found something to fill their time in a way that they perceived as more meaningful. Although Warr and colleagues did not concentrate on this group, a similar situation emerges from their studies (1983/84/85 etc).

Most of this research concerns (as usual) redundant unemployed men. The situation for youths may be different although all research suggests that the majority, like their elders, intensely dislike the experience. Evidence from the US (Gaskell and Laserson 1980; Gordan 1979 Freeman and Wise 1982) suggests that a period of 'milling around', going from job to job with periods of unemployment inbetween is considered normal and healthy there. Any piece of research there presenting a 'snap shot' of youth unemployed would very likely produce a larger minority who were not concerned or depressed by their situation. Although it is less accepted here, it is probable that the same situation exists. That is, the majority would still dislike the unemployment but there may be a significant minority who consider it a temporary phase of their life and are therefore not so worried. The situation would repay fuller research.

Women

The neglect of women's unemployment has already been described in chapter one, as has the generally held assumption that women in general suffer less because of different cultural assumptions as to the importance of work. This has been assumed rather than researched and there has been a trickle of research recently that has thrown doubt on this.

Warr and Parry (1982) found that mothers in general and particularly young mothers are protected from psychological ill health resulting from unemployment. They have a purpose, a role and their time constructively filled. Single women and women 'bread winners' they found equally affected as men. Warr, Bankes and Ullah (1982)in a study of 1150 young unemployed found that young women consistently reported more distress, depression and anxiety than young men. Far from being less concerned about work they tended to report greater commitment to work and were significantly more concerned about the stigma of unemployment.

Willis (1984/6) found women less outward going, less involved in hanging around with friends more housebound and less involved in 'spectacular youth cultures' as well as much less involved in sport and other forms of leisure. As outward going activity is a protective factor this result is more unhappiness and depression -

> Unemployment drives women futher into the domestic work and responsibilities. Male unemployment does little to break down the gender divisions of domestic work. Women are generally much more housebound than men and less involved in outside activities. Unemployment heightens this considerably with many unemployed women spending long periods at home during the day. Increased domestic burdens and the collapse of outside activity, especially sport, makes it hard to speak of leisure opportunities for young unemployed

women (1986 p166)

Wallace (1987) found something similar, young men reacted in a more outward going way. Often this was based on fantasy or at least exaggeration as incidence of petty crime or informal economic activity was inflated into 'grand heroic gestures'. This she described as: "masculine romanticisim". Young women who reacted in this way however risked getting a 'bad reputation' and tended instead to retreat into the home and domestic work. She found women just as keen to find work which offered them "a sense of independence and access to money, and offered opportunities to go to dances and pubs, as well as a reprieve from housework. Apart from those very real advantages, employment offered the possibility of travel and meeting new people "(p17 4-12-87)

So they regretted lack of employment just as much as young men and at the same time were denied the street life that seems to offer some relief from boredom. The result in most cases is that they became stuck indoors, burdened with housework, living as 'perpetual juniors' in their parents homes. "Hence, young women resignedly accepted an unappealing and unexciting lifestyle, while young men escaped through fantasy".

This concludes this survey of the literature. This chapter started by quoting Kelvin and Jarrett's description of the literature as descriptive, diffuse and "almost entirely concerned with the unemployed man". This is a fair description and future research will have to go beyond this. Groups other than this much investigated minority group are the prime areas for further study, especially women.

4 'Have you got something to get up for?' – Problems with structuring time

In any study of the effects of unemployment a detailed knowledge of how they spend their time, is of crucial importance. This has been recognised by many researchers both in the fields of Sociology and Psychology. Jahoda, for example, in her classic study of the Austrian town Marienthal in the 1930s, when the closure of a steel works rendered the majority unemployed, discovered that filling in time was indeed a major problem. Ironically although the unemployed had gained many extra hours, there was evidence that they were actually less socially active than they had been in their previously much more restricted leisure time. For example the number of people attending the local library dropped despite the abolition of borrowing charges, newspaper subscriptions dropped by 60%, political organizations and the clubs lost membership and so on. Many modern writers have found the same (eg Sinfield 1981, Warr 1982, Willis 1984, 1986.)

Most psychological studies have shown a strong association between unemployment and poor psychological health. Time management may be important because difficulties in filling in time and in finding (affordable) things to do may contribute to depression and this might be a major mechanism for causing the declining mental health of unemployed people.The European Centre for Work Study (1983) found that half their study of 86 inner city young people had difficulty filling in their time and that these were the most likely to report difficulties in coping with their situation. Brenner and Bartell (1983) found that 'positive activity' helps to mitigate the worst effects of unemployment; they claim that there is a brief 'critical period' and, if the individual does not adapt then, their health goes downhill and this tends to prevent or hinder the ability to engage in this positive activity. Generally, studies seem to suggest that participation in leisure activities does if fact lessen but does not eliminate psychological damage (eg Warr 1983 Stokes 83 Kelvin 1984) See also the useful survey by Warr (1985) of seventy eight studies relating unemployment to psychological health carried out since 1960. (See chapter 3 for a fuller account of these studies.)

Unemployment is bound to profoundly influence use of time, most obviously because, without work there is more unstructured time but less money with which to finance activity. Jahoda (1982) identifies a number of "latent functions" of work, that is things that work does for people over and above the provision of a wage. In particular, it imposes a time structure on the working day.

Although we know that unemployment is bad for people we do not know exactly how they cope, or fail to cope with the lack of an imposed time structure, "how different groups of young people feel, flounder, or cope "(K Roberts 1980). Time is likely to be a major problem because young people in our society are habituated to having their time structured for them from an early age by school, and older people have become used to time structuring through work. On the other hand, it is possible that young people will suffer less in this respect than older people, being used to filling in unstructured time during the long school Summer holidays. There is some evidence that this is true in the short term (eg Warr 1983 M Willis 1979) but further evidence suggests that few take positively to a 'permanent school Summer holiday' in the longer term (eg P Willis 1986 - Fryer and Payne 1984). The evidence of my sample concurs with the findings of the studies I have reviewed that most young unemployed people consider it an ordeal to be endured rather than a positive leisure opportunity.

The first question to consider is, did the unemployed young people in my sample report filling in time as a major problem? Evidence on this subject comes from the direct question on this questionnaire; 'Do you find filling in time a problem?' and, secondly, from comments and statements made during the follow up interviews.

Of 79 responses to the questionnaires, only twenty reported that they found filling in time a problem 'most of the time' (See Table 4.1, overleaf)

Table 4.1
Problems in structuring time: questionnaire

	Female	Male	Total
Most of the time	12	8	20
Occasionally	10	8	18
Rarely	6	4	10
Never	11	20	20
Totals	39	40	79

This was quite a small minority and it may understate the extent of the problem because the question evokes conventional responses. Possibly the results would have been somewhat different had there been a response categorising "Fairly often".

The taped interviews and the interview notes painted a very different picture - particularly for young women. The results are not for exactly the same sample, as the interviews include the pilot interviews and exclude many of the questionnaire people who were not followed up. I listened again to the tapes - read the interview notes and on the basis of their comments and answers categorized them as either having significant problems with time, ambiguous on the subject, or having few problems with time.

Table 4.2
Problems in structuring time: interviews

The results were as follows

Significant problems with Time	27
Ambiguous	6
No Problems	7
Total	40

Clearly use of time featured as a much greater problem in the interview data compared with that provided by the questionnaires. I shall argue that this is because interviews can better reveal the subtle respect in which time structuring is problematic.

Two things stand out when one listens to the tapes. Firstly those reporting problems relating to time are the most likely to report depression, distress, and difficulty in coping and the more serious these problems the more likely this was to be the case. I found listening to all the tapes over a short period of time a grim experience. Much distress was reported but what makes an even greater impact is the tone of voice and long pauses between statements, which reminded me of the poor bearing of the young people. The long pauses - low voices and air of being in some way 'disengaged' are one of the most striking aspects of many of the interviews. These considerations make it hard to doubt their words when they report hardship and distress, hard to believe that they are just saying what is expected of them. The group that reported distress and appeared 'low' were virtually the same as those who reported serious problems with time. In contrast the minority that experience few problems with time not only say they are happy but they also appear livelier and more chatty generally, much more like my college students.

The second point is that time was often the dominant theme of the interviewees. The interviewees would often talk at length with little prompting about this in response to the initial general questions such as "What's it like to be unemployed?" as well as to specific questions about how they fill their time. Time also figured when they were asked to give advice to other unemployed people. Certainly it was the most common subject spontaneously mentioned, more so for example than lack of money, although this was often cited as a cause of having little to do and so is obviously related.

Significant problems with Structuring Time

So what did they say about this subject? The largest category were young women who found filling in time a problem, so I will consider them first. Susan W a 17 year old living in a small village said "I was bored, got depressed easily - most of the time I just sat at home and looked at the paper. I'm one of those people who always needs something to do".

Lack of something to do was the main problem for her, caused by lack of money to join in with her friends consumerist social life and the fact that she was isolated - the only unemployed person out of her friends in the village. When asked about social life she replied "Not at all hardly! I have no money or not enough. I get really bored".

The less she did the more she got depressed, even stopping doing domestic work thus causing rows with her mother.

Jessie aged 18 and living in a shared house in the city recognised, like many, the irony of having free time yet doing less.

> "You can make it good (unemployment) you have a lot of free time and you can use it, but it can get on top of you, you have to work really hard to make unemployment reasonable - if you let unemployment get you down you get depressed a lot, the unemployment gets you down a lot - if you go out and occupy yourself you don't get depressed so much."

(and how about you? SH) "I let it get me down"

> ". . . I lay in a lot, unless I go to see friends and go to pubs when we have money - not much to boast about."

'Doing things' she says is the answer to boredom and depression and she says that she intends to do more, specifically to do the community workshop and learn photography, but she had not done it yet. She finds it hard to get motivated and when I met her in the street months later I asked her about photography and the situation was the same - she was going to start soon! Like many others her way of speaking with a slow quiet voice with very long (painful) pauses, without any of the liveliness I have come to expect from college students including YTS trainees, was as telling as her liberal use of words like 'depressed' .For lack of a better term I use the word 'disengaged' to describe people like her. This condition is quite recognisable even though its symptoms are less easy to specify - no sense of direction and purpose, lack of energy and enthusiasm, unhappiness and a diffuse sense of malaise.

Adrianne, aged 18, mother of a baby who had been fostered temporarily she hopes, was interesting because she claimed to 'never' have problems with time when she answered the questionnaire and then made such problems the main focus of her interview. To the general question 'what is unemployment like for you?' she replied "Boring because there's nothing to do ... God I spend so much time at home its horrible. It really depresses me - sometimes I just sit and cry because there's nothing to do - nowhere to go ... I would like to fill my day with loads and loads of things to do"

Tracy, aged 18, also reported feeling aimless, not having enough to do and frequently crying alone about it.

Julie, aged 19, and living at the YMCA says unemployment is "Right boring quite frankly, most of my time is spent doing nothing quite frankly".

Susan C, aged 20, and living with parents in a small village, said that unemployment is "Boring! It is. I am going up the wall slowly"

She seemed nervous, and depressed and reported recently going through a very low period, sleeping for days at a time, being prescribed anti-depressant drugs. She continued "The main disadvantage is that you have so much time on your hands you don't know what to do with it. That's why you get people turning to drugs and alcohol and all this, just to liven yourself up, else you get completely depressed".

In spite of working in a pub some lunch times and often visiting the same pub in the evenings she made it clear that, as far as she was concerned, time was the major problem. For her this was the most important cause of her depression. When asked to give advice to the unemployed she said. "Keep yourself occupied! keep your brain occupied `cos if you don't you've had it! If you have other things to do and talk about other than just being unemployed then you're alright. If you have a hobby, make it more than a hobby"

Sarah, aged 17, living with parents on a Norwich council estate, described herself as 'a failure' and finished the interview with the words "Sometimes I wonder why I was born". Time was also one of the major problems for her. She said of unemployment "While you are busy its alright, when you are not its terribly depressing, terribly boring".

For the young men whom I categorised as finding time a problem the situation is much the same except that there are fewer of them. Richard, aged 19, and living at home, says unemployment is "Boring! fed up - and I mean really fed up all I do is go round looking for a job, chatting with friends, ain't got no money to go out evenings ...."

James, 18 and living with parents in a small village, said "Time can be a problem; it's no problem if you have something to do".

The money he earned from his few small scale unofficial jobs was important to him but not the most important thing. What he enjoyed was "Something to occupy yourself is as important. You have got something to do. That is nice ..... a really nice thing to wake up to".

Later he said of living in the country "filling in time is the hardest thing - in the city its easier".

Although more quotations could be provided, sufficient have been given to establish the point that many young unemployed people find the lack of a time structure in their lives a severe problem.

Ambiguous about structuring time

Not all of the sample has serious problems with filling time and it will be instructive to consider how some of them organise at least part of their lives so that time does not drag.The following discussion of ambiguous cases begins with the young women. Kate, aged 20 and living independently was not very forthcoming about how she spent her time so she was almost a non-respondent on this issue. However she seemed to fill in her time to some extent by being one of the few involved in politics, that is feminism. She was an 'alternative lifestyle' person who had lived in a squat and, while she wanted to work temporarily to get more money, did not seem committed to the idea of a career or even a permanent job.

Rachel, aged 16, and living in the YWCA, was contradictory on the subject. She was looking energetically for work but on the other hand enjoyed her life hanging around with friends from the YWCA. At one point she said that filling in time was not a problem but later commented that unemployment is "boring - not enough to do".

Frances and David R, two young men categorised as 'ambiguous', were very similar in attitudes, interests and even appearance. Both were semi punk, vaguely aspiring rock musicians with only a loose commitment to working. Frances, aged 20 living in a shared house, said he had adapted to unemployment "because I have no choice" but he was "not desperately unhappy about it".

He fills in time by hanging around with a small group of unemployed friends and by making things take a long time that he would have previously done very quickly. He would like to do more and is looking for a job "but not very hard".

Time is however still something of a problem as he says he values his occasional side job because "it gives me something to get up for - that's become a catch phrase with my friends. `Have you got anything to get up for tomorrow?'".

David R, aged 21 also living independently in a shared house would probably have had more problems with time had it not been for a older sister who visits regularly and pushes him into doing things, such as going to an Arts Centre to make an animated film and to doing an 'O' level in English. He admits that she is a major influence in his life and, without her pressure, he tends to 'vegetate'. He sees this as a constant threat, "always find something to do, always keep active, always keep your brain alive otherwise you become a vegetable".

Unproblematic about the structuring of time

As I previously stated those who claimed to have no problems with time were also those that seemed liveliest and least distressed. Joanne, aged 21 and living at home, hardly considers herself unemployed, she considers herself a dancer. She is a member of a dance troupe that works from time to time at holiday camps and army camps. When she is not employed she rehearses.

Because Susan has a baby, she experiences no problems with filling time with what she considers to be meaningful activity. She identifies with her mothering role and feels her life is invested with purpose. Before becoming pregnant she reports that she had considerable problems with time.

Carl, aged 17 and living in the YMCA, can explain why he has no problems with time with one word - Boxing! It is the driving interest of his life. Of unemployment he says "I don't mind because it gives me more time to train ...... I got something to do. I ain't bored like some people"

Phillip, aged 22 and living independently, appears to be surviving very well and certainly has his time well filled. There are three reasons for this. Firstly, he lives with a working girlfriend who provides company in the evenings and weekends and, probably extra money. Secondly, he has lots of jobs on the side working for a friend who has a small building firm and customising and repairing motor cycles, an extension of his hobby. Thirdly, he is a member of the 'biker' sub-culture, which means he is not concerned with clothes, discos and consumer goods. (He does not own a TV, for example.) Thus his dole money and that earned by his jobs is adequate for his needs, and the sub-culture supplies company in the form of like minded unemployed friends.

Karl is hardly unemployed at all, except officially. The significant point is that his uncle owns a public house where he works whenever he likes, which means almost full time.

These people are exceptions to the rule that unemployment induces misery and will be discussed more fully and in relation to factors other than time in chapter 12.

Main types of activities

Much of the activity of the young people in my sample is lacking in urgency and not directed to any purpose, at the extreme involving staying in bed or lethargic pottering. The following discussion summarises the major forms of activity as described by my sample namely 'hanging around' searching for jobs, personal interest/hobbies and commercial social activities. It looks in more detail at how they spend their time concentrating particularly on those who do find it a problem. One issue is time spent with friends - isolation or lack of it. This is the subject of a chapter in its own right so I shall restrict myself to saying that, while a few are really isolated, more common is a restricted social life that consists of seeing a great deal of a few unemployed friends. 'Hanging around' with a small group of people that share the same problems, either indoors listening to music or watchingTV or outside around the city or parks, emerges as a dominant theme.

Searching for jobs is a significant activity for the majority - following up possible leads, spending time visiting the job centre, and looking in newspapers. A minority would like a job but have become discouraged and so do not pursue this activity vigorously. My research certainly does not support the idea of work-shy youth who could get a job if only they would 'get on their bikes' and look for one. Many are desperate for work, which is consistent with Willis's (1984) contention that lack of work assumes a high importance in the minds of many young unemployed. Both Warr and Willis (1984) believe that those most committed to the idea of working are likely to suffer the most psychological damage as they are constantly rejected and disappointed. My results certainly bear this out. The group categorised as having the most problems with time are also those who most want to work and those reporting the most distress. Endless searching for work and failing, with the accompanying feelings of rejection and disappointment are likely to take a heavy psychological toll. If this is so, then the official view that the unemployed should be engaged in a permanent search for work is a recipe for misery for hundreds and thousands of young people.

"Boring, fed up. I mean really fed up, all I do is go round looking for work" says Richard who visits the job centre at least once a day. His commitment to work has rewarded him by leaving him depressed, lacking confidence and sometimes feeling suicidal.

Unsurprisingly young women were much more likely to report doing domestic work on the questionnaire and very much more likely to include it spontaneously as part of their description of a typical day during the interview. Among those living alone the men's flats and rooms were usually noticeably less tidy and less clean than the women's. Susan's life was devoted to her baby and her flat, which was immaculate. Jacky, aged 19, and living with her unemployed boyfriend, took on all the domestic work. A bad day for her was when "he's under my feet and screeching for something because he's ever so lazy ..... I spend most of my time clearing up after people, doing the domestic work". So, at first sight, it does not appear that these young people are challenging sexual stereotype on this issue, in this case not even though both partners had time on their hands.

Work 'on the side', is important for political and theoretical reasons so this issue will be considered in more detail in chapter 7.

The questionnaire data has to be treated with great caution on this topic because respondents are likely to give misleading or incomplete information on their illegal activities on such a research instrument. The interview data is probably much more valid because the rapport established appears to break down barriers. In fact, I was surprised at their frankness in the interviews. Unsuprisingly only a minority admitted to working 'on the side' in the questionnaires whilst a majority did so in the interviews.

The conclusions reached can be summarised briefly. Firstly, unofficial work both in the number of people engaged and in extent seems mainly a male phenomena. Secondly, this work is mostly small scale, irregular and low paid. For the overwhelming majority, it might provide islands of time-filling activity and a little extra money with which to do things. So it does punctuate otherwise undifferentiated time and thus give it some structuring, but only occasionally.

A minority, more men than women, do some sort of hobby, a smaller minority play sports. Official provisions for the unemployed and for youth generally is hardly used. The most common example was Actionline, a scheme run by the YMCA where the unemployed can learn certain skills such as carpentry and computing. This was relatively popular for YMCA residents as it was on the premises and because a days 'work' earns a meal ticket. Theoretically, it is open to all young unemployed people but I came across no examples of non residents involved and, even for those involved, it was rarely a large part of their lives. One person used the Arts Centre and one the Community Workshop. Religious worship, voluntary work and political activity is the province of a tiny minority. Far more popular were the cheap nights at discos and night clubs, which is indicative of a yearning for a 'normal' social life, that is a commercial one.

Structuring time and coping with unstructured time

A host of psychological studies provide strong evidence that unemployment results in poor mental health. What is less firmly established is the mechanism by which unemployment has this damaging effect and what groups are most at risk. My study suggests that the lack of an imposed time structure is one important factor.

One question posed by researchers is whether leisure activities can compensate for lack of work. (Warr (1983) Miles (1983) and Kelvin (1984) Miles (1984) answers this question with a "yes but",meaning that it can lessen, but not eliminate psychological damage. I would change this to "no but!", meaning that while a very small minority might be happy to spend their time immersed in a sport or hobby, most would not. Few see hobbies as a meaningful substitute for work. Lack of money will anyway limit the ability to take part in many activities and depression may erode the determination to participate. Willis (1986) and Glyptis (1989) confirm this view.

My study suggests that those who successfully find an alternative to the lack of a work imposed time structure cope much better. This is consistent with Jahoda's notion that work fulfils certain 'latent functions', including imposing a time structure, over and above the obvious financial aspects and that if alternatives are not found then the individual will suffer.

It is useful to contrast those who seem to have less problems with time with the rest. Firstly, they are much less likely to be 'good citizens' as conventionally defined. They do more unofficial illegal work, (One factor that protects people against the effects of lack of work is work!) That is, one of the best coping strategies is illegal and more importantly not open to those without skills and or contacts, such as an uncle who owns a pub. Some of those have less problems in filling in time are less likely to be looking for work, more likely to be a member of some kind of 'counter culture' with a weak attachment to the work ethic and less concerned about mainstream consumer goods and leisure. Some are unmarried mothers. By contrast, those who appear to be suffering most, want to work, spend time looking for work, do not like illegal work, dress more conventionally and are likely to refer to themselves as something like 'normal every day people'. In general, they are more conformist so they suffer from their inability to join mainstream society via a job and a wage. We therefore have an odd situation - non-deviants are most punished and the general principle is "Good citizens suffer most".

Davies (Jan 1986) offers advice to the unemployed on the basis of unemployed people he interviewed in Great Yarmouth. The six point guide to survival is as follows

1 Keep your self respect

2 Learn to budget properly - live within your means

3 Avoid changes in your circumstances for fear of confusing the computers and delaying your benefit

4 Guard against 'unemployment psychosis' which manifests itself in lethargy etc.

5 Keep to a daily routine

6 Take every opportunity of jobs that present themselves, even cash in hand jobs

To me numbers 1 and 4 seem merely restatements of the problem and prompt the question how?

Learning to budget is probably good advice but not so easy given the attractions of the general consumerist society and young people, in particular, may find nights out at the pub or disco following Giro day a bigger moral boost than sensible budgeting. People have social needs and these are set by the wider working society. Suggestion 3 may well be good advice but of course changes in circumstances may not be easy to avoid. Would it be fair to add that this could deepen the sense of living in a rut and frustrate job searchers, particularly if they involve moving elsewhere? Lack of an imposed routine is, as my research shows, a major problem but this is a product of the situation in which young unemployed people find themselves and that very situation tends to undermine the willpower to structure one's own time. If, as suggested, calling at the job centre is part of the routine then this could lead to routine rejections and successive blows to self-confidence and self-image. Finally my research endorses the value of unofficial 'cash in hand' work.

Davies approach prompts me to consider what advice I would offer, given the principle "Good citizens suffer most". Is it good advice to join a `deviant' sub culture or lose interest in work consumer goods and consumerist social life? The problem is obvious; the only people who might take advice are the minority that already find such values meaningful. For Susan having a baby provided a role, and meaningfully structured her time, as well as being a route to independent living via council accommodation. Recommending working on the side is of course to recommend illegality, with its attendant risks of getting caught but, in any case it is an option probably open only to a minority who have skills and contacts. Becoming obsessed with a sport or hobby does help to fill time. However one cannot fake obsession; it won't work as a forced response to the difficult situation the unemployed find themselves in. So, if I am critical of some of Davies' 'guidelines for survival' it is not because I have ready answers of my own.

The problem is that most people have been socialized into mainstream values - they want the things that only work and a wage can bring. They are hardly likely to model themselves on those in my survey who are successfully coping with unemployment.

To cope successfully with unemployment is about synonymous with finding successful, meaningful alternative ways of structuring time. This must be done in spite of the long unfilled hours during the day and inspite of the fact that many of the things the unemployed want to do with their time are beyond their means.

5 Poverty and unemployment

An interesting and provocative article by Carr-Hill (in Roberts et al 1985) directs attention to the most obvious factor of unemployment, that of lack of income. He argues that the observed correlation between unemployment and ill health, mental illness and depression is reducible to the well researched effects of poverty and multiple deprivation and not due to any independent effects of unemployment

> Yet there is a wealth of historical evidence to suggest that many occupations are bad for your health and that idleness is good for you. In the former category we can start with Engels (1958), cite countless studies of fishermen, miners and soldiers, and refers to dozens of sociological studies (of some ten years ago) or to any report of the Health and Safety Executive (and some useful summary of recent evidence for the UK is provided by Clutterback 1982). In the latter category, the fact that the British aristocracy who never lifted a finger (literally in some cases) lived far longer than the rest of the population seems to me to be a knockdown argument in favour of unemployment being conducive to good health (p340.)

Carr-Hill is taking issue with those such as Jahoda and Warr, who emphasize the importance of non monetary factors related to unemployment, such as lack of an imposed time structure and so on. This conclusion is not entirely fair in any case since they both also stress the importance of low income. They tend to take it for granted rather than consider it unimportant. (Warr, 1985, Jahoda 1982)

He goes on to say -

> I would claim that poverty and increasingly unequal shares, is what it is all about. The emphasis on employment is myopic ...... it would seem to me to be more parsimonious to rely on the known and repeatedly proven association between low income and other negative life events such as homelessness, family instability and inadequate education for the children, rather than speculate upon the effects of unemployment independent of a drop in income. p341

He goes on to criticise most unemployment research as an 'academic job creation exercise' that detracts attention from the main issues.

> The dominant characteristic for the disabled, those excluded from paid jobs, the low paid, the sick and the unemployed - is their poverty. Instead the present directions of research on the impact of unemployment wrongly emphasizes the work rather than the wage, and thus draws attention away from the fundamental problem of income and wealth in our society. p348

It is doubtful that the lack of income is the only factor but it is a very important one indeed so I will now consider the influence this has on the lives of the young people who make up my sample. A reasonable hypothesis would seem to be that lack of income will be a problem but not so severe as it would be for older unemployed people, because the young will tend to have fewer commitments and may well be subsided by their families. They will also be more used to managing on a restricted income while at school and summer holidays than someone who has got used to the benefits of a wage.

One common finding is that middle aged unemployed men experience greater distress than those who are younger or older (see chapter 3) There may be a number of reasons for this, one of which is the relatively few financial commitments of the young.

I am not arguing that unemployed young people have few money worries: their advantage over the middle aged is only the relative advantage of one poor group over another that experience their poverty even more severely. Unemployed young people are poor relative to employed people of the same age and class background. An important issue will be the effect of wagelessness on their sense of future - of progress to independent adulthood - a process which is heavily dependant on work and wage. Willis (29-3-84) argued that a "separate home is a universal working class objective" and that a wage is the "golden key" to this objective. That is, work is the price of independence and so that, without work, progress to independent adulthood may be blocked.

Perceptions of lack of money

The easiest place to start assessing the impact of lack of money on the lives of the people in my sample is with question 47 on the questionnaire which asks about money problems. The results were as follows:

Q47 Would you say that you have money problems?

	F	M	Total
All the time	11	15	26
Often	10	8	18
Sometimes	9	11	20
Rarely	2	2	4
Never	7	4	11
	39	40	79

Considering that many people in full time work (me for example!) could claim to have money problems at least sometimes and considering also the restricted income offered by unemployment benefit, these results are not particularly clear cut. Although a majority did not report money problems I had expected the proportion to have been even greater.

Why do 31 people on such restricted income indicate on the questionnaire that they do not have severe money problems? One reason could be income from unofficial jobs. Four (of them) claim to be earning at least £30 per week regularly from such work which would, together with the dole, give them an income equal to what most could expect from full time work. This poses the question of whether they are "really" unemployed. Two more earn regularly £5 - £10 pw, which must at least help. A number of the others do unofficial work but so irregularly that the extra money is unlikely to do more than provide the occasional `treat', unlikely to change the general picture of their lives.

Another reason could well be low expectations. People who have never had a job will not have had a chance to get used to a regular wage and so their past experience will have been managing on low income whilst at school and later on the dole.

One indication of expectations is provided by asking how much the unemployed young people would expect from a job (Q21 on the questionnaire) and what would be the least they would accept. Expectations are very modest with most, but not all, willing to accept what I would consider very low wages.

Only twenty three of the questionnaires sample of seventy nine expected to earn £90 per week or more and only eleven indicated that they would not work for less than this sum. In contrast twenty two expected £50 or less and fourty two were prepared to accept this amount. Generally women were markedly more likely to have low expectations than men and were more prepared to accept low wages.

A major difference between younger and older unemployed people is, of course, the former's relative lack of commitments. Few have children, other dependents or mortgages. In fact they are more used to the dependant role and, indeed, many still get help from parents and other adult relatives.

How lack of money is experienced

The interviews confirm that lack of money is commonly identified as a problem but many of them denied that this was their main problem. Shortage of money became a serious concern less as a general anxiety than as a recognition of specific opportunities that have to be foregone. The areas mentioned, in order of intensity of concern, were exclusion from commercial social life, transport, clothes and, less often, basic requirements like heating and shelter.

Given the ages of the samples, it is not surprising that the most frequently mentioned concern seems to be with their social life. There is strong sense of restriction in this area, of being left out in comparison to working friends.

SusanW for example, the twenty year old young woman living with her parents in a small village, said:

> "The problem is you have got no money - your friends will say 'do you want to come out for a meal? do you want to come out for a drink? and you say 'no sorry I can't, I haven't got any money' and I find this is getting more and more common with me now and people are beginning to stop asking now and going out without saying to me first - I find it very hard being unemployed because you need money, and you just don't get enough."

Later she said "There are some good films I would like to go to at the moment but I can't afford it".

Buying drinks and paying ones own way generally is a problem area. Buying drinks for friends is a reciprocal arrangement, which helps cement friendships and people feel degraded if they are unable to take part. Their pride can be hurt to the extent that they avoid social gatherings.

Susan C is a member of a pub darts team but finds this aspect difficult,

> "... you have to buy people drinks because they are buying you drinks and that's a tenner gone straight away. I've got to a stage where I just can't win. I'm saying 'no I don't want a drink'. I'll make one drink, instead of lasting for half an hour I'll make it last an hour or if someone asks I'll just say no because I feel very guilty about them buying me a drink and not being able to buy one back."

One thing I had not expected was that in my sample more young women complained about not being able to pay their way than men. Perhaps the situation has changed since I was their age when men were expected to pay or perhaps it is just the 'luck of the draw' in what is a small sample!

This is not true of every young woman, of course. Wendy told me how boyfriends buy her drinks and clothes and pay for her to enter night clubs. She said

> "They do, they always do, or you alternate. You can't expect them to buy you everything but they are stupid mugs so they do. - You can get away with it. They generally do if you say 'ooh I like them' they will, If they are going to be mugs and buy it that's their trouble not mine."

A more typical attitude expressed considerable ambivalence about being subsidised by a boyfriend. Susan W aged 17, also from a village, said of weekends,

> "Well they weren't too bad because everybody else was usually not working on a Saturday or a Sunday and we just try to forget about work but I couldn't go anywhere. Well I could but that meant my boyfriend paying for me everywhere and I didn't like the idea of that - sometimes he did though."

The feeling of exclusion from an expected normal social life comes out strongly. She continues, when asked about her social life, "not at all hardly .... go to the pub like once a fortnight couldn't go to the pictures because that's two pounds gone and if I went to the pictures I couldn't use my moped that week." (The use of her moped was important, as her isolated village had only irregular and expensive public transport).

It is a measure of her low expectations, that when I met her later she was on a YT scheme and was impressed with what seems to me a miserable wage. She reported that it transformed her social life.

> "This is much better, I've got more of a social life, I don't get depressed so much (why not?) Because I've got money I mean £16 is not much at least £26.50 is - having just that little bit extra helps. I mean I can afford to buy clothes now whereas I couldn't before I get to go out more often. I mean I have been away from home (SH You couldn't have done that before?) Well, I just couldn't afford it. Last weekend I went into Norwich, Friday I went to a disco which I couldn't have done before. Saturday I went to another disco which I certainly couldn't have done before."

Adrienne reported,

> "sometimes people just come round to say "come on we're going for a

> drink" - but it doesn't happen too often because none of us has any money - so we spend too much time at home. Gosh, I spend so much time at home."

Sarah summed it up very briefly when asked what the main disadvantage of unemployment is she replied - "No money so you can't have a good time."

Men, of course, were equally preoccupied by the damage to their social lives. James was concerned that his situation was unhelpful when it came to getting a girlfriend: "The traditional thing is for a bloke to take a girl out buy her lots of drink and everything, a big car ...... well, a car costs money to go to night clubs and everything, which I just cannot do". He also said that he would not be interested in girls who expected such treatment but concluded that in this respect "more money would be helpful".

Certainly, if forming relationships with the opposite sex depends at least partly on access to a commercial social life, then this is going to present a problem to the unemployed. Willis (1985) in his study of young people in Wolverhampton found that unemployed people were less likely to be 'courting'. A larger scale longitudinal study would be needed to assess these effects of unemployment on the process of forming relationships.

Richard complained that lack of money restricted his sporting activities as well as his other social life -

> "I don't do as much as I used to in sport because I can't afford to do it. If I could I would be doing it all the while. I can't go out with mates; they can afford to go out because they work - Disco's! Mind you I wouldn't go there anyway I prefer the old rock and roll music - like the Dial (pub) every Sunday - they have rock and roll. I would like to go there every Sunday but I can't do it."

He went on to describe how in the summer he had wandered down to the pub some Sundays, stood outside listening to the music but did not go in because he could not afford to buy a drink. This strikes me as a metaphor for the sense of social exclusion felt by many of the unemployed people.

To sum up this section - difficulty in having a commercial social life the most common problem concerning money mentioned in the interviews.Almost no one in my sample goes to Youth Clubs, institutions which are not perceived acceptable alternatives. A commercial social life is important to these young people, as the arena for meeting people of the same and opposite sex, pubs, clubs and discos assume a much greater significant than it would for older redundant workers with families of their own. (Drinking and disco's are the activities most ticked on the question in the questionnaire about spending money). Because this is Norfolk and not Newcastle, most of my sample have working friends and compare themselves with the working norm and they feel jealous and degraded if they can't take part in what they consider to be a normal and desirable social life. They feel guilty if friends pay for them or buy them drinks and they cannot reciprocate.

I could continue to quote at great lengths further comments about this area but in the interest of avoiding to much repetition I will leave Richard standing outside the Dial and move on.

Inability to buy the clothes they want worries some,Adrienne when asked how she would spend the extra money if she was working replied "I'd have a car and buy a few things for the house. Oh yes and I'd have some nice clothes, that's it I'd have a decent wardrobe and a car".

She highlighted the link between 'nice clothes' and a desired social life. "It does worry me somehow, if I wanted to go out somewhere nice I couldn't because I couldn't afford it, even if I was invited somewhere nice I couldn't go because I wouldn't have anything to wear." Relatively few, however, stressed buying clothes as a major problem although it was mentioned in passing by many.

Transport is another often mentioned problem, sometimes simply as a desire to own a moped/motorbike/car. Often, comparisons are made between themselves and working friends, as they are with social life and clothes,thus emphasising the strong general sense of exclusion of missing out in comparison to others.

Transport is a bigger practical problem for those living in small villages some distance from the town. Lack of facilities and often companions make trips to the city an attractive proposition but public transport in Norfolk is poor. Buses are expensive and infrequent, making private transport more of a necessity. This was mentioned as a problem by almost all the people from small villages. (The exceptions had fewer money problems and I will write about them later.) This emerges as a major difference between the experience of unemployment in the city and in a small village.

An example would be Susan C who emphasized the expense of going on what have been, for her, fruitless journeys to the city Job Centre

> "... you've got to go to the town to find out about jobs - if you are living in the town its a lot easier - you can just walk it sort of thing. I've got to scrub up money for bus fares or try to persuade my Dad or brother to take me in ..... I know it's expensive it's £1.40 just to go to the job centre, which is a lot of money when you haven't got it."

The cost of travelling to the city also curtailed her social life and she said that if she was working the first thing she would buy would be a moped.

Of course a major difference between the young unemployed and older redundant workers is that for the largest section of the former there are a few worries about food, shelter and rent as these are heavily subsidised, or even provided free by parents. Those living independently still differ from older workers in that most have only themselves to worry about but unsurprisingly they are more concerned about such basics than those living with parents.

An example would be Jessie, a 19 year old young woman living independently. One of the most obviously depressed she answered a question on money problems softly and with long pauses. She was interviewed in the winter; heating was by electric fire and she returned several times to the problem of having to constantly feed the electricity meter with 50p pieces.

> "A problem (pause) yes a problem - I work it out when I get my Giro - divide it up into shopping, electricity and things like that - which doesn't leave a lot for things like drink and things that you enjoy - since its winter I have been putting a hell of a lot in the meter - I only get about £5 - about £5 - £10 a week to spend on myself."

Not many people who lived on their own mentioned heating as a problem but this is hardly surprising because circumstances has dictated that most of the interviews have been done in the summer. However most were in a similar position with regards to heating as Jessie and I would be surprised if they did not have similar problems.

Coping with Poverty

Several strategies emerge for dealing with the problem of living on a restricted income.

One is to get help from parents. Those living at home were the most heavily subsidised.They tend to pay their parents around £10 pw for which they received accommodation, heating and food which amounts to a considerable subsidy. Added to this, most said that their parents gave or lent them money and sometimes bought them clothes. Of those living independently, the majority received some kind of help - money, clothes and furniture. The amount of help given amounted to less than for those living at home, although there were also some people who received no family help at all. So, support from relatives lessens the financial burden that the young unemployed suffer, although this may also have its disadvantages - increased dependency, postponed independence and perhaps a lack of sense of 'having a future', of progress.

Parents are also the main source of borrowing and the majority borrow, at least small amounts, before Giro day. Most debt does appear to be small, temporary, before Giro day appears, generally under £10. However, five said on the questionnaire that they had borrowed more substantial amounts - £70, £75, £90, £440,£450 and unsurprisingly said that they have problems paying it back. On the other hand, as the lenders are generally parents, and more rarely other relatives, they may not really be expected to repay it.

A subsidy that appears to be available only to a minority but is probably very significant to them comes from working boy/friends.

Another is to use catalogues to buy clothes and pay weekly; this has the disadvantage that it is more expensive generally but when a pair of jeans can cost most of a weekly dole money using catalogues can present itself as the only possibility. Certainly, it is a very common practice amongst the young men and women of my survey.

Another is not to worry about it! This strategy is used by the small minority who belong to some sort of youth culture that does not stress the value of new clothes or a consumerist life style generally,such as the biker and semi-punks.

Another is to borrow clothes, a strategy mainly mentioned by women.

A worry often expressed is running out of money before Giro day. Sarah, a 17 years old young woman says of the dole "it ain't a lot but I sort of seem to go through money pretty quickly by Wednesday. That's it and I have nothing until next Wednesday." This is typical of a number of comments made.

Some of the young people attempt to budget very carefully but much more common is a pattern whereby they have a something like a normal social life for a few days after Giro day (pubs, disco's etc) and then have what they consider a dull and miserable existence until the arrival of the next Giro. Of course, this picture is softened for some by regular unofficial work and taking advantage of the willingness of relatives and working girl/boyfriends to lend money. This is not always repaid but many claim to repay their debts, which are usually modest sums of £5 to £10, immediately. Thus makes it even more likely that they will run out before the arrival of the next Giro.

6 Relationships – Restricted social contact

One factor that emerges very strongly from my research is that unemployment leads, if not to complete social isolation certainly to a restriction of social contacts. This is felt to be very important by most of those interviewed and was keenly regretted.

In terms of quantity, ten out of forty interviewed proved to have plenty of friends and to lead a fairly active social life. This did not necessarily mean they were satisfied. In fact five of the six young women in this category and two out of four young men still felt that they would like to meet more people at work or via the more active social life that the presence of a wage would mean.

Twenty mixed mainly with a small number of friends usually two or three, with perhaps a couple of others appearing occasionally. Generally these friends were also unemployed and when this was not the case there were extra problems of isolation during the day and of keeping up with their employed friends' more expensive social life. The majority were unhappy about this situation to varying degrees, only four seeming content.

Ten seemed very isolated and unhappy about their situation, seeing mainly only one other person apart from family. Five were young women, and in each case, the other person was a boyfriend. In contrast, none of the isolated young men had a girlfriend.

It would seem to be a reasonable hypothesis that the more isolated individuals will be more prone to depression and unhappiness and that, conversely, the presence of a supportive network of friends will be a protective factor, mitigating the worse effects of unemployment. This certainly comes over strongly in my research; those with fewer friends complain more of boredom and depression and they are more likely to appear fed up than the minority with lively social lives. Many express the value of friends and they most often said that the advantages of work are in being able to meet people and to earn enough to be able to afford a social life where they could meet people.

The first half of this chapter identifies a number of factors associated with unemployment which interact to limit social contacts. The hypothesised casual link is presented as Figure 6.1.

However, these pressures towards social isolation are not deterministic and other factors intervene to mitigate them. The second half of the chapter will address these considerations, where it will be demonstrated that the majority of my sample succeed in avoiding extremes of isolation - although their situations remain far from satisfactory.

Factors tending to limit social contacts

(i) Wagelessness

The most obvious consequence of lack of work is the absence of a wage, and consequent shortage of money. Participating in a social life costs money, particularly the more commercial forms, pubs and discos etc. and the effect of wagelessness on their social life is a major concern for the people in my survey. (see chapter 5). Lack of money means they cannot go to the pubs and nightclubs as often as they would like, so their opportunities for meeting both old and new

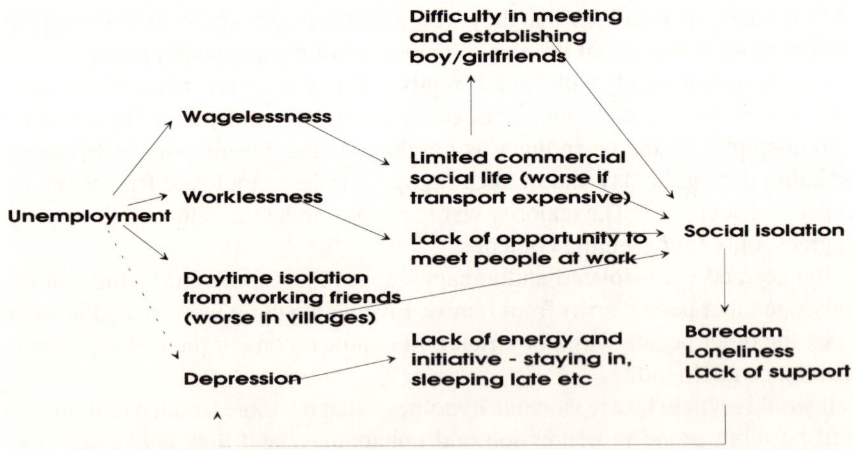

Note: The dotted line indicates casual paths mediated by other factors discussed elsewhere

Fig 6.1 Factors promoting social isolation

friends are restricted.

Many of the people I interviewed feel that their social contacts are limited by lack of money. Some are very isolated because of it. The majority are not totally isolated and are not desperately depressed. Nevertheless they consider this a significant problem and are coping rather than being happy or satisfied. Lack of money cuts down their social activities and means spending more time alone at home and meeting less people less often. Meeting potential boy or girlfriends is a problem mentioned by some. The situation is made worse if parents are poor, or unwilling to help, and is worse for those living in villages where transport costs eat into an already very limited income.

For a minority these factors can lead to extreme isolation. Kevin R, aged 20 and three years unemployed, has lost touch with all of his friends except one unemployed person he met on his YT painters and decorators course. Both his parents are unemployed and cannot afford to subsidize him. He has to pay £15 per week board as well as £7.50 per fortnight to repay bills he ran up on a clothing catalogue, so £37.50 goes from his giro the day he receives it. In a voice which was slow and sounded depressed he described his situation

> "Oh... its really bad... you ain't got no money to go out so I stay in every night - you don't meet people a lot... You meet at work... I just sit and listen to music or write to my penpal - not a lot - I play music a lot get up at 11-12... I got one friend I see nearly every day."

He never goes to pubs. He used to play pool but cannot afford to now and so spends most of his time with a friend who is in much the same position or at home on his own. His main problem is a chronic lack of money - not being able to afford to do things. "There is enough to do if you can afford it but not on what they give you on the social".

Summing up his experience on the dole he said,

> "You don't meet many people- mostly indoors - and if you have to pay a lot of money for board you don't have many friends really - its just-well bad really". Asked if he feels depressed he replied "Yeah all the time I just feel depressed all the time. The only time I feel good is if a friend treats me and that doesn't happen often."

A reduction in social contacts, due to lack of money to engage in an active and desired social life is a problem for most of my sample, even those who are not as desperate, depressed and isolated as is Kevin R.

Jacqueline, who is aged 22 and unemployed, after working at a factory job for five years, is one of five young women who find themselves living with an unemployed boyfriend. She has very few alternative social contacts, a situation best described as "isolated together". Lack of money for the sort of social life she has learned to expect and value, is again her main problem.

> "Horrible! Not used to it. Boring. Nothing to do all day. Night times even less - at least if you work you have your time occupied during the day, at night time you have a bit of extra cash to get out. That's mainly it."

The main disadvantage of unemployment for her is not seeing her friends because they are at work during the day and she cannot afford to meet them during the evening. To compound the problem, she had to give up the car bought while she was working because she could no longer afford to run it, and because of housing problems she had to move to the other side of the city away from people she knows. She and her boyfriend can afford to go to a pub only once a week or a fortnight to meet friends, but this is a great reduction compared with their former social life. She spends much more time alone with her boyfriend, "Yes that's the trouble we are stuck here. I like getting out and about". She argues with her boyfriend much more since becoming unemployed "because we're in each other's way all the time".

Anna, unemployed for nearly 3 years and aged 18, is not desperately depressed. She has half adapted to her situation and has "got used to it" although she still goes to the Job Centre everyday looking for "anything". After paying for board, she has £28 for two weeks and manages to go to a night club and a pub once or twice in that period, partly because she knows the bouncers at the night club who let her in free and because people she knows buy her drinks. The rest of the time she sits at home with her mother watching TV, or occasionally goes to a friend's house or has them round to hers. She sees mostly the same two friends who are employed and so not available during the day. She does not enjoy this situation, would like to go out and meet people "nearly every night" and to be able to afford to buy more clothes and make up to match their more active social life.

Anna also believes that she might have found a boyfriend if she had been able to afford to go out to nightclubs. The same thought occurred to Paul D aged 17. Asked about girlfriends he replied "No I don't get much of a chance to meet them. Perhaps if I could afford to go out more, nightclubs and such it would be different".

Several said that they sometimes avoid going to pubs, and therefore stay in rather than meet people. They are embarrassed because they cannot afford to buy people rounds of drinks. Gary S (aged 18 and unemployed 9 months) said, "I go to the pub in the evenings sometimes - about once a week. More after my Giro - otherwise its hard. People say, have a drink and I say `No I'm okay' because I can't afford to buy one back. It is embarrassing - when I've got my Giro it's OK". He says that he is losing touch with school friends because he cannot afford to go out as often as he would like.

(ii) Worklessness

The next factor has already been mentioned is that many people in the sample consider work not just as a place to earn a wage but as a meeting place in its own right. Asked why they want to work, my sample are slightly more likely to say "to meet people" than they are to mention the money. So another important problem is that the unemployed are denied the opportunity of meeting people at work.

This is considered significant even by those who do not seem to be greatly isolated. Wendy for example received a subsidy from her parents that brings her close to what she could expect to earn from a full time job. She also has a large group of friends inherited from her school days and seems to lead a fairly active social life. Nevertheless, she looks every day for work and her main reason is that she sees work as an important place to meet people. Speaking of the advantages of working, she said, "and when I worked in a shop - you meet different people every day and its a really good way of socializing".

Susan F said that by not working she was missing meeting people. She even went so far as to say that she was not bothered about the money but that the opportunity to meet people at work was much more important. Adrianne made a similar point. What she wants out of work is, "meeting people and things to do. Money doesn't bother me a lot. Julie described the advantages of her two years packing in a factory. "I used to enjoy it meeting people - it was a friendly atmosphere, a right laugh".

Paul D mentions several in the same answer, thus bringing out their interconnection. For him, the disadvantages of unemployment are "money of course, more money would certainly help-it would be nice to have something to do during the day - a reason to get up early and you meet people at work - and money again you meet more people because you can afford to go out more"

James when asked what he was missing by not working similarly linked various factors together. "What am I missing? Making friends at work, the routine and money of course".

(iii) Daytime isolation from working friends

The third factor that tends to limit social contacts for the unemployed is that, although many have a pool of friends, from school, schemes and previous jobs, it is often the case in an area of relatively low unemployment that they are currently working and therefore not available during the day. This also links with the first problem, that of money, because employed friends are likely to have a social life that is difficult or impossible for the unemployed to keep up with.

This is another factor that seems to be worse in small villages when compared with the city. A common problem for village unemployed was that they had few unemployed friends in the vicinity or none at all. So hours spent in the day were likely to be lonely ones. Ten out of fourteen unemployed people who lived in a small village at the time of interview or who had experienced time on the dole in a village complained of loneliness in the day due to lack of unemployed friends locally. Thus one of the most common coping strategies, linking up with and spending a great deal of time with a small group of unemployed friends, was denied to them.

Susan W for example was on her own during the weekdays as her boyfriend and friends were all working. She found it a depressing experience

> "I was on my own (during the day) while he (her boyfriend) was at work. I used to get really ratty as well. He used to come home and say he had a good day at work. I was cheesed off because he was working and I wasn't. I didn't think it was fair. I went right off my food because I wasn't doing anything. I got really depressed. I started catching colds and things because I was staying indoors all the time - sit around all day, read the paper, watch telly. I used to get really bored."

To again demonstrate the inter connections of these problems she adds "but I couldn't go with them - well I could, but that meant my boyfriend paying for me all the time and I didn't like the idea of that".

This was an extreme case as his village is more remote than most and there were no young people around during the day at all. James' situation deteriorated further when his only two unemployed friends in the village got jobs and he found the daytime isolation even more difficult. There were a few other unemployed young people in the village where David R lived but, unfortunately, David did not happen to enjoy the company of these individuals. He complained that they "just sat in the bus shelter and I thought that was a bit useless, and time wasting, so I sat at home". He generally prefers life in the city "Yeah, more to do".

Gary S said of village life "It's bad - there's no one around. Like I said, they're all working or moved away."

In the city this is less of a problem as there is a greater number of unemployed people to interact with, but it is still a problem for some. David R had moved to the city by the time he was interviewed and found an improvement in that he often finds someone to hang around with but, as some of his close friends are students, he finds term time more difficult in this respect.

(iv) Depression

The last factor that tends to limit social contacts is a result of a combination of the other factors listed in this chapter and elsewhere in this thesis. Lack of money, unfilled time, limited friends, lack of a sense of progression and purpose means that people get fed up and depressed. This can paralyse the will and make it harder to feel self-motivated, so that these depressed unemployed people stay in more, sleep late, lack confidence and energy and so make less effort and this, in itself, will tend to limit social contacts.

Unemployed young people commonly recognize this as a danger, a tendency they have to fight by an act of will. It is possible to see this at different stages. Nicola, is aged 19, and has been unemployed for 4 months this time, but has had only temporary jobs over the year since leaving college. She recognizes that she is in the early stages of something that would be better not developed.

> "When I was working I used to cram in things when I wasn't working .... Now I've got no will to get up and do these things. I just think I am less enthusiastic about things I do in my spare time (why?SH) I don't know why that is ..... (is it connected with being unemployed?SH) I think it would be 'cos with being unemployed I think 'what is there left for me to do now'?. I get bored easily. I go out to see my friends but they're all, working and bringing in a good wage and I think, 'is there any hope for me?. I go up the Job Centre regularly but there's nothing there so all hope goes and it takes my enthusiasm away - I do - I do get fed up.

Later summing up she said "I think I've got mixed feelings. I feel I'm getting slightly fed up with life but I'm trying to be optimistic about it ... its a bit of a low time, a time for getting bored".

It is worth repeating the words of Jessie (already quoted in the chapter 4) who seems to me to be further along the spectrum of depression and 'disengagement' than Nicola.

> "You can make it good - you have lots of free time and you can use it, but it can get on top of you, you have got to work really hard to make unemployment reasonable - if you let unemployment get you down you get depressed a lot ...... if you go out and occupy yourself you don't get depressed so much.' ("And how about you?". "I let it get me down."

The danger both Nicola and Jessie recognized is getting less enthusiastic about doing things, making less effort, getting depressed, doing even less, becoming more isolated and so on in a vicious downward spiral. Most of the more depressed people I interviewed had few social contacts and seemed to be in this situation.

Withdrawal, is a matter of degree; it is more likely to be simply making less effort, drawing in, so that the tendency is to meet mostly the same one or two friends.Thus the common pattern of spending a great deal of time with a very few friends who are in a similar position is both a coping strategy and a consequence of the other problems described above.

The factors leading to decreased social contacts can now be summarised. Unemployment results in a narrowing of social contacts to degrees varying from almost total isolation, through reliance on a small restricted group of friends, to simple dissatisfaction with inadequate opportunities to meet new people.

The causes are as follows - firstly, the most obvious result of lack of paid employment is lack of a wage. This results in limited money being available for the kind of social life many of these young people expect and desire. They can afford to go out socially less often and so meet old friends less often and have less chances of making new ones. The chapter on money demonstrates that this is a major subject of concern for many of my sample. Some considered that this cut down their chances of meeting boy/girl friends. This situation is more extreme and severe for those whose parents cannot afford or are unwilling to subsidize them. It is also usually worse for village dwellers as travel expenses cut into what money is available and as many travel to the city most days generally in search of work this can be quite a significant factor.

The second factor is that they are denied the chance of meeting new people at work. This is a very often stated disadvantage of unemployment.

Thirdly, given the above fact and the fact that they have more hours to fill during the day, a significant problem for some is that social contact during the day is cut if school friends are working and so not available. Another point, which is linked to the first factor, is that working ex-school friends will often have an expensive social life that the unemployed cannot match. So on top of the difficulties of meeting new people socially or at work, is the danger of losing touch with old school friends.

Finally the above problems, together with other problems of unemployment, can lead to boredom and loneliness which in turn causes depression and low self esteem. Symptomatic of these states can be lack of energy, "disengagement" - feelings that can cut down the will power and ability to go out and seek more social contacts, thus generating a vicious circle.

These factors quite often appear to work in combination with one another and are all the more potent thereby. The dangers are quite widely recognised by many of the people concerned and they often try to avoid this situation, with varying degrees of success.

Factors tending to mitigate the tendencies towards isolation

I have described factors tending to restrict social contacts but, having noted that few of my sample are highly isolated, the following section addresses the means by which people cope with these factors and identified contervailing factors. These are presented in Fig. 6:2.

(i) Family support

The first and arguably the most important factor is one that is likely to distinguish the young unemployed from any other unemployed age group, and that is the extent of family support. Of course parents are used to supporting their teenage

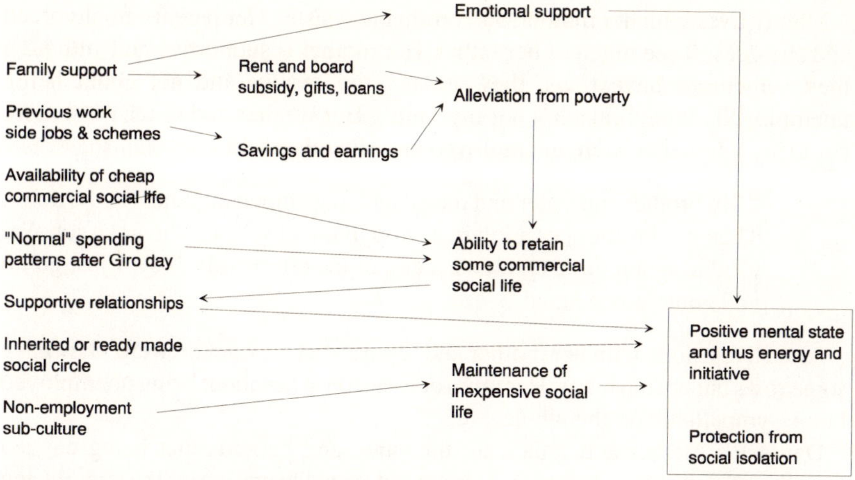

Fig 6.2 Factors mitigating social isolation

children and it might be expected that they should continue to do so. Nevertheless, I was surprised at the extent to which parents supported their children both emotionally and financially, for unemployment can put severe pressure on family bonds. Expectations that teenage children would work and contribute financially to the household are disappointed. Fed up teenagers hanging around the house "getting under parents feet" might cause friction. Parents might tend to blame their children for their unemployment, believing them lazy, and unemployed young people might resent their continued dependency. All of this might be expected to manifest itself in greater family tensions, leading to increased friction and rows. This appears to be the case for a minority of the families of my sample but for a large majority, the families seem to stand up to these pressures extraordinarily well, providing the most important base of support in difficult circumstances. Those living at home are usually subsidised in rent and board and probably also get more emotional support but the practice of giving small quantities of money, buying clothes and offering a sympathetic ear extends to many of those living away.

Family support, mostly but not entirely deriving from parents, can be divided into "emotional" and "financial". Starting with "emotional support", it is clear that there are strains associated with unemployment. The typical response of my sample is to say that parents nag about the subject but, on the whole, are supportive. Brothers, sisters and other relatives were also reported to help.

David R. visits his elder sister regularly and she is an important figure in his life, advising him as to what is going on in Norwich. For example she encouraged him to apply for a "passport to leisure" (i.e. free entrance to the swimming pool and other Council facilities) and he says she helps "just by being there".

Mandy lives with her mother, and brother and sister. Her parents are divorced and she doesn't see much of her father. Her mother is supportive and although they sometimes have rows, they are not too serious and not about being unemployed. "She thinks it's not my fault". Her brother and sister were more company when they were unemployed and she misses this.

> "My brother and sister and me all had to go down together (to the dole). Then my brother got a job in a shop in the city. Then she got a job. We used to go up there and have a cup of tea afterwards. Now I just go up and come home again."

Anna lives alone with her mother and reports that they get on well. They have some rows but not too many. Her mum does get on at her about being unemployed but is sympathetic on the whole.

David P's mother and father are the same and he adds that being nagged occasionally about unemployment is a good thing "keeps me on the straight and narrow", keeps him looking for work and "doing things" rather than hanging round the house watching TV and sleeping late. This is the general picture for the majority, parents get fed up sometimes and complain, for example, about not making enough effort to search for jobs. However, mostly they offer valuable emotional support. Other relatives, such as sisters, brothers, aunts uncles, and grandparents, also play the same role only to a lesser extent.

The practical financial support members of the family provide is also very significant. As described in Chapter 5 most parents give and lend money and often buy their offspring clothes. However, the most significant subsidy goes to those living at home by way of providing accommodation, heating and food free or very cheaply. Board and rent is usually charged in the range £0-£10.

Of course, those living at home are less independent but mostly accept that and appreciate the advantages. Those living at home are usually subsidised in rent and board and probably also get more emotional support but the practice of giving small quantities of money, buying clothes and offering a sympathetic ear extends to many of those living away. David P for example says that he would like to move away but that has to wait on a job. In the mean time he is fairly satisfied at home. His parents do not give him money, except sometimes buy him clothes but they only charge him £5 per week board. "Yeah well its cheap basically". The advantages of still being at home aged 22 are

> "You live in quite a nice place. It's comfortable because some bed sits are pretty shabby ... I get my washing done, its all very handy - meals I certainly get them very cheap. It makes it all very much easier .... It's fairly cushy - It is easier. I'd like to move out but not while I'm on the dole. I couldn't afford it."

He is typical in that most say they wish to become independent at some vague time in the future but are content in the meantime. This poses the question how would these general good family relationships fare if their unemployment was to become permanent? Could they continue indefinitely or would the pressures of lack of independence on one side and financial burden on the other, tell in the long term? A study of very long term young unemployed in their mid-twenties, probably in an area of much higher unemployment, would be necessary to investigate this.

The crucial point about this subsidy, together with giving and lending of money and buying clothes, is that it makes possible what is of grave concern for most of my sample - a commercial social life. This may not be at the level of their employed friends and contemporaries but it does prevent them from being cut off from this area altogether.

Most of my sample do go to pubs and night clubs even though most complain they cannot go as often as they would like. This enables them to keep in touch with old friends, meet new ones and potential sexual partners. This is not to contradict the earlier discussion for they are indeed more restricted in their social lives and therefore their social contacts, but they are not totally cut off. There are a number of factors that prevent this but the first and most important one is this subsidy, and then the fact that the major part of the dole money, of a significant proportions of my sample, is spending money.

Maintaining the type of social life they enjoy, which usually involves pubs, discos and night clubs is important if they are to avoid isolation. Their family is particularly important in this but there may be additional helpful factors.

(ii) Previous work, side jobs and schemes

One of the additional factors is work, by which I mean past jobs, temporary jobs, side jobs and schemes. - Most of my sample have histories that include temporary work and schemes punctuated by spells of unemployment enlivened by the occasional period of low paid illegal side work.

David P, who had saved £1100 before leaving the Inland Revenue for whom he worked for five years, is maintaining his social life by dipping into this weekly over ten months of unemployment. He had £450 left. Mandy had just finished the money she had saved from a temporary Christmas to Easter job at Rowntree Mackintosh and she is looking forward to being taken on over the holiday season again. Jaqueline maintained a healthy social life and ran a car for sometime after leaving a factory job, but eventually it was sold because she could not afford to run it. As indicated above, the car was a protective factor against what did transpire, namely she and her boyfriend slipping into “joint isolation”. Nicola was nearly at the end of the money saved on a six month temporary job and was also using it to subsidise her social life.

(iii) Cheap commercial social life

The next significant factor in maintaining a social life is the existence of cheap nights at discos and night clubs. This is important to a great deal of my sample; most go to discos mid-week when before a certain time it is free to get in and drinks are half price. For example, Francis, Julie and Rachel sometimes go out early, getting completely drunk before 10 pm when drinks are half price then buying no more afterwards.

Certainly this provision is a great deal more used and therefore more important to the unemployed young people in my sample than any official provision such as Actionline (the YMCA), the Community WorkShop or Youth Clubs.

(iv) Short periods of intense social life

Even with half price drinks, going to night clubs is expensive and some will want to go out at weekends with working friends; so this leads to what seems to be a conscious strategy of having a 'normal' social life in the few days after 'Giro Day' and a quiet, often miserable, boring time in the week before. Asked about discos and night clubs Paul D. said "sometimes, every other week after my Giro comes. Its expensive. I would like to go more often".

The strong impression is that most of my sample deliberately organise their money to achieve a 'normal' spending occasionally, even if it means existing on very little later on. Gary W. for example budgets very carefully so that he rarely actually runs out before Giro day but his budget includes £10 for night clubs in the week after Giro and nothing at all for social life in the second week. Many are not so systematic and so run out and borrow before Giro day but they still adopt the same pattern. It is a matter of being "normal" for a few days at least, and "normal" is the spending pattern set by the majority working population. Gary S. often refuses to go to the pub if he cannot keep his self-respect by joining in on a normal basis.

"I go to the pub in the evenings sometimes - (how often?SH) - about once a week, more often after my Giro comes, otherwise its hard - people say 'have a drink' and I say 'no I'm OK because I can't afford to buy back and it is embarrassing. When I've just got my Giro it's OK.

(v) Supporting relationships

It may be harder to meet boy and girlfriends for those whose social contacts are restricted but, as I have said, most are not totally isolated so naturally many do form relationships and these are another mitigating factor. Obviously they ensure that the unemployed person meets at least one other person and this can be a source of emotional support. If the boy/girl friend is working then this helps to maintain a commercial social life as the partner will often pay for entrance to night clubs, visits to the cinema and buy drinks. Not surprisingly given the prevailing social attitudes, young women are more likely to report boyfriends supplying this kind of support, but it also applies to some men in my sample. (See Chapter 5)

This contribution from partners helps but many are not happy with the situation. For example, Mandy says

> "I try to pay my own way - we usually go halves. Sometimes he do, when he's feeling generous he usually do, yeah pay some things, like we went to the pictures the other night and yesterday when you called yesterday we went swimming. He paid for that."

Along the same lines, Nicola reports "He buys two drinks; I buy one. He pays to go into things when I run out of money in the second week. We pay half and half when I've got money".

Karl borrows money from his working girlfriend and she pays for their social life sometimes. He tries to pay her back and feels guilty when he can't.

Not everyone feels guilty. Wendy supports her active social life partly by exploiting traditional attitudes and her attractions for young men. As described in Chapter 5 she manages to find "mugs" who will pay for her admission to night clubs, and buy her drinks.

Many have unemployed boy or girlfriends who are unable to help in this way. Then there is a marked tendency to fall into a pattern of meeting only a very few unemployed close friends or even into joint isolation, that is seeing very few people other than the partner. Indeed, the stress of unemployment may put strains on relationships so that they cease to provide support or even become burdensome.

It seems reasonable to expect that relationships will suffer if people get depressed about unemployment. This happened to Susan W. as described earlier in this Chapter.

When she was interviewed she had started a YT scheme, had cheered up, and their relationship had improved.

(v) Inherited or ready made social circle

One factor that may not apply to older unemployed people is the continued availability of school friends. In some cases this can be a fairly large group and most of the least isolated people in my sample are in this position. However, the pressures described above mean that the longer one is unemployed the more the group is whittled to just a few close friends who are usually in the same position. Retention of a circle of ex-school friends depends on the efforts exerted in this direction and the capacity to maintain an active social life in their company but the factors depend, in turn, on other conditions such as financial and emotional support. Only a quarter of my sample were able to keep in regular touch with ex-school friends.

Six of the sample were in an unusual position in that they live in the YMCA and this supplies a ready made social circle "You meet people the first day" said Gary W. This can be an especially important source of social support as most could not take advantage of the mitigating factor of parental support, having lived all their lives in care or having fallen out with their families. Indeed, it was their family circumstances that were the reasons for their moving to the YMCA in the first place. (See chapter 8)

(vi) Non-employment sub-culture

The last factor to consider is the adoption of a non-employment oriented sub culture. This supplies friendships and emotional support, justification for their position and an alternative non-commercial and therefore less expensive social life. Phillip and Charlotte who adopted this position wholeheartedly are amongst the few people in my sample who have found a satisfactory life on the dole. (See chapter 12). Others, like Frances and David R. seem to have adopted this position less wholeheartedly as a means of coping and would certainly prefer to work if there were satisfactory jobs available. Frances says that he has made an alternative life out of necessity, is "not desperately unhappy about it but then I can't afford to be".

Conclusion

I would like to illustrate and sum up these mitigating factors by describing the case of Fiona who benefits from a number of them to a high degree. Fiona is nearly 17, has been unemployed for five months and lives outside a small village. Firstly, she benefits from family support; her father is a farm worker and although her parents are not wealthy they still subsidise her by charging no rent or board at all. She had worked previously in a supermarket and for a short time on a YT scheme at a fashion shop and while she was working her parents charged £10 per week. Her mother often lends her money when she runs out before her Giro arrives, usually about £5 which she usually pays back. She buys most of her own clothes but again her parents sometimes "splash out" and buy them for her. She also gets help from her grandfather, "I just go round my grandparents. He gives me a couple of quid so if I went round there every day I get more." Generally she visits him two or three times a week.

Her family give her emotional as well as financial support; when asked how she gets on with her parents she replied "Wonderfully! I do get on with them". When asked if she rows she said, "I do with my mum but only about stupid things that last five minutes", not about unemployment about which her parents are sympathetic.

She certainly recognises the advantages of living at home. About leaving she said "I don't really think I could cope honestly ... I spend money so easily - when it comes to little bills floating through the letter box I'd turn a bright red colour - I couldn't work it. I will probably grow into it: not yet though."

She benefits from the previous supermarket job not by living off savings, for she hasn't any, but by qualifying for unemployment benefit at the rate of £31 per week. Because of her fortunate family situation this is all spending money.

She has a boyfriend - a meat cutter in a frozen meat factory - whose company she enjoys. The only thing she says that she would miss about her unemployed life if she found a job would be not seeing him during the day when he works shifts.

He also helps her to maintain a social life

> "I usually go out (to a night club) after my cheque comes - go out on a Saturday then miss the next Saturday to save some money you see - my boyfriend sometimes takes me down anyway and he'll pay for what ever I need. At other times as long as I have the money to get to Norwich and get in he doesn't mind paying for drinks and things. Whatever."

A little work on the work on the side also helps and typically this comes from personal contacts.

> "I do some cleaning for my boyfriend's mum. She's got a big house and her own business. I do two hours work and I get a fiver from that, which I think is pretty decent. I only do that once a week."

She has even done some modelling fixed up with her boyfriend's mother's connections. "I did a bit of poncing around with clothes on." for which she got £50 for two days work. This was a one-off and she is uncertain if the opportunity will recur.

She has friends available still from school and her high spending power relative to others on my sample means that she has a lively enough social life to maintain contact. When her boyfriend is on shift work she often takes advantage of the cheap night at night clubs to socialise with ex-school friends. They also meet about once a week at a pub. This is mostly two regular friends, one unemployed, one on a YT scheme and a larger number of less regular friends.

All this has maintained a good morale. She does not appear depressed and is outward going in her behaviour and attitudes which also helps avoid isolation.

> "I'm quite a happy little person really I don't have no bad days actually. I don't think I do. I do actually if I'm really skint. I suppose that's a bad day but it doesn't happen all that often. I'm really a jolly little creature really I suppose."

Interestingly these factors do not mean she is satisfied with her situation. On the contrary she wants very much to work and so looks every day in the newspapers, goes to the job centre twice a week and has had a number of unsuccessful interviews. So these factors help but do not, in her eyes, make up for not having a job. Unemployment is

> "... boring I suppose - some of the time I'm bored, but it ain't that bad. My unemployment is more than the YT scheme sort of thing, so to that extent its not too bad. I sort of manage all right but that can be very boring ... I don't honestly think there are any advantage. I suppose you can get out more as you aren't tied down by being employed I suppose you can lie in more - well there ain't no actual advantages. (disadvantages?SH) "You haven't got a lot of money to spend have you? You get bored sometimes. If you were working you might stay more cheerful. Well you've got something to do all the while if you're working. You ain't got to worry about what you are doing for the next ten minutes that would be a good thing."

To sum up, these factors do guard against the isolating tendencies described in the first half of this chapter. Where they are present more than average, the young people claim to be and appear more cheerful and with a higher moral than average. Where they are absent or hardly present the opposite applies. Family support seems to be particularly important and where parents are unsympathetic or unable to help this greatly increases the burden. The cases of Kevin, Neil, Sarah and Richard were described at the beginning of this chapter. They exemplify the lack of protection by the mitigating factors described above and, not surprisingly therefore, are highly isolated.

One comment worth mentioning in conclusion is that the advice often given, that the unemployed should move in order to maximise their chances of a job, simply ignores the importance of these protective factors. Family support, school friends and the rest of these supportive networks are very important in helping people through difficult times. So moving away from these networks would be a high risk strategy that would be very likely to result in further isolation and depression. Such advice demonstrates an attitude that does not understand, or is not concerned about the social needs of human beings.

7 Work 'on the side': Participation in the informal economy

The young people in my survey have done considerable amounts of work, that is most of them do not have histories of unbroken unemployment since leaving school. Most of them have participated in schemes such as YT where they have spent little of the time training so that they are just like very low paid temporary jobs. Most have also had short-term jobs. In short, their experience in general is of intermittent work punctuated by periods of unemployment. However it is not this I am going to consider in this chapter; rather it is their involvement in the informal economy, unofficial work done whilst they continue to draw the dole.

The informal economy is sometimes referred to as "irregular", "black", "unofficial" and "hidden" In the sociological literature there are a number of somewhat different definitions describing different phenomena, from giving neighbours excess garden vegetables, "moonlighting", "tax evasions" to working and earning money whilst also claiming unemployment benefit. Ferman and Berndt define the "irregular" economy as "..that sector of economic activity that is not registered by the economic measured techniques of the society but which uses money as a medium of exchange" (in S Henry ed 1981 p26). Gershuny and Paul write of the "underground, hidden or black economy" defined as "production wholly or partly for money or barter which should be declared to some official taxation or regulatory authority but which is wholly or partly concealed" (1980 p7). Henry lists three characteristics which constitute a general definition:

> First the informal economy includes the production, consumption and trading of goods and services, either for cash or kind or for social rewards. Second, these activities take place in ways which are likely to be part-time rather than full-time. Thirdly the activities are unofficial in

the sense that they do not explicitly form part of the state accounting system (1982 p461).

In this chapter I am concerned with ways and means of making extra money while officially unemployed and the significance this activity and the money it generates has for the unemployed. These activities are often illegal but their illegality stems usually not from the act itself but from the fact that it is not declared to the authorities.

Two perspectives on the informal economy

The significance of such activity is an important sociological and political issue and it might be useful to outline various perspectives before seeing what evidence my research provides. Broadly, there are two perspectives. One is that the informal economy is a positive development which absorbs unemployment by presenting alternative forms of work. Some go even further, suggesting that it is a creative movement progressing towards a more human, less alienating post-capitalist society. The second perspective sees it as no more than a survival mechanism for those who have no choice and would prefer social arrangements that would not place people in such predicaments. It also stresses that the informal economy is dependant on, or even parasitic on the main market economy rather than some kind of creative autonomous movement.

The first optimistic perspective emerges from Development studies, the mass of unrecorded small scale enterprises are seen by some as having the potential for labour absorption, ameliorating unemployment and generating alternative employment. (see Bryant 1980, Henry 1982) This idea was applied to the developed world in the 1990s, principally by Gurshuny and Pahl. (Gurshuny and Pahl 1979, 1980 Gurshuny 1977, 1978, 1979) They envisage a move towards a "post-industrial society" where technological changes mean a much reduced formally employed labour force, particularly in manufacturing. Unemployed people would no longer be unable to afford many of the goods and services provided by the formal economy and so would turn to the informal. This informal economy will then grow and offset the decline of the formal economy absorbing much of the unemployment. The role of the State, in this situation, should be to assist this process, to "encourage people to participate simultaneously in both the formal and informal sectors" by such things as "job sharing schemes in the formal economy and training schemes to develop the skills needed for the informal economy" (Gershuny and Pahl 1981)

Grander claims are made by the Ecology Party (1982) and various "alternative movements" (see for example Shanklin 1982). Burns, for example, sees the informal economy taking over, leading to the inevitable decline of the large scale capitalists market economy replacing it with a more humane alternative.

> The instrument for this positive change will be the household - revitalised as a powerful and relatively autonomous productive unit... it is an institution and economy whose growth and strength hold the promise of a democratic, egalitarian society in a stable world. The household economy is the harbinger of revolution the nexus of future culture and experience. (Burns 1977 quoted in Henery 1982)

More recently, writers offering advice to the unemployed, such as Dauncey, (1982, 1986) are motivated by ideas like these, as was the Channel Four television programme broadcast on July 1986 interestingly entitled "Well, you didn't expect us to sit around doing nothing did you?". The idea expressed was that unemployment is not a disaster but can lead to a more fulfilling life outside the formal economy if only the unemployed can be educated about and encouraged to grasp the exciting opportunities available.

The pessimistic alternative interpretation is that for the poor and unemployed the informal economy is nothing more than a survival mechanism, a way of getting by for those who have no choice (Henry 1982). Also, it is linked to and parasitic on, the larger capitalist economy, either by a direct link to larger companies as in the case of casual building work, delivering leaflets and fruit picking or minor services which are paid for by wage earners, and minor jobs done by the tools and material produced by capitalist enterprises. None of this sounds like a newly enpowered labour force let alone an liberating post-industrial society. To quote Bryant

> In contemporary Britain, as in the Third World, most activities of the informal economy have to be understood in relation to the capitalist - industrialist economic system of which they are a part.... The informal economy has no autonomous capacity to provide employment, but has its existence solely through the industrial capitalist economy (1980 p13)

Interestingly, one of the earlier main supporters of the optimistic perspective, that the informal economy can absorb the unemployed, has changed sides. In a large scale study of all forms of work on the Isle of Sheppey in 1984 Pahl discovered a growing polarisation between households where the adults were in formal work compared to households where they were not. He found that work attracts work and that all kinds of informal work, 'moonlighting' (ie holding down a second job), most jobs "on the side" and even "self provisioning" (DIY, beermaking etc) were more likely to be done by people who were formally employed as well, than by the unemployed. His research even qualifies the notion that "side jobs" are a survival strategy for the poor and unemployed as it tended not to be these people that got the work in the informal economy. Money is the key; enterprise and initiative were found to be not enough since the would-be participant in informal work needs a small amount of pump-priming capital to provide the tools, materials and transport required. This money comes from formal employment. Formal jobs also provided the skills and the contacts to find such work. So the unemployed find themselves at an overwhelming disadvantage, competing for informal work with people already employed full-time. Indeed, unemployed people often could not even afford to do their own decorating.

> Our interviewers have documented the despair of those living in their own homes, with their own tools, with time on their hands and with urgent decorating jobs staring them in the face but without the money to buy the paint. (Pahl and Wallace 1985 p381)

The Sheppey study also stresses the dependence of all forms of work on the larger industrial capitalist economy.

> The households which we are able to describe cannot achieve any real independence from market services, their nest centred life style..... can be shattered overnight with an unexpected redundancy. The overwhelming dependence of all forms of informal work, including self provisioning, on the money from formal employment is the basic fact underlining our polarisation thesis.

As well as these sociological perspectives, the idea of unemployed people working "on the side" has attracted attentions from politicians and newspapers of right wing inclination. They give great significance to this phenomenon, maintaining that it is widespread and extensive. The conclusions derived from this can be roughly paraphrased as follows "No sympathy need be wasted on the unemployed as most of them are going very nicely working on the side while illegally fiddling the dole at the same time". "Scroungers" is the word often used by the media to describe this. The remedy is seen as more investigators, and harsher penalties in a bid to "crack down" on these people and this has long been government policy. Media campaigns based on this view discredit the unemployed and defuse concern for them by stigmatizing them for their predicament and labelling them as dishonest and unworthy.

The experience of work in the informal economy

I will now turn to an examination of the experience of my sample in the informal economy and hopefully this will produce some evidence on the above theories.

As far as quantity is concerned, of my forty respondents two have done a relatively large amount of work regularly. A further two work irregularly but still do above average amounts as far as the sample is concerned. Next comes by far the largest category - twenty one have done some illegal irregular small amounts of undeclared work. Twelve have done no work at all. Lastly five do part time work that is legal in that it is declared to the DSS (two of these are counted twice because they also fit into the previous category).

(i) Significant amounts of undeclared work

The two that do relatively large amounts of work on the side are the first category I shall consider. Both are unusual in my sample, in that they have enjoyed life on the dole, although Phillip was looking for a job after five years unemployment in order to buy a flat with his working girlfriend. They will be considered again in chapter 12.

Karl most fits the right wing opinion of the unemployed. His greatest asset is an uncle who owns a pub.

> "At night times I work for my Uncle at the pub serving drinks so I can get quite a bit at the end of the week for that. I don't really want for money yet".

He can work more or less the hours he feels like so he is not really unemployed, except officially. His life-style is helped by his parents supplying free board and his uncle giving his free drinks when he is not working. His work fills in time and, above all, he does not suffer financially.

> "They only give you £27 a week don't they. If I make it up to about £60 or £70 that's about right isn't it for someone of my age. I'm alright. If my mum and dad took board money off me I'll be skint".

He spends his money on "clothes mostly and night clubs. It ain't too bad. It don't restrict me being on the dole. I can do anything I want, practically, within reason".

Phillip has also been an exception in that although he is looking for work now, he spent five years enjoying life on the dole. One major reason for this is that he has been able to keep up what he considers an acceptable standard of living by regular amounts of work "on the side". Firstly he has a friend who owns a small building company and Phillip has worked for him reasonably regularly as general labourer and as a painter and decorator. He has skills in this area partly due to a YOP painting and decorating but mostly learned "on the job" with his friend. He considers himself naturally good with his hands. Secondly he has developed a business out of his hobby - motorbikes. He fixes and resprays bikes. He says he works on bikes "at least once a week. I'll do something earning probably about £30 on average but some weeks I earn a tenner, others £60... (is it regular?:SH) Well as regular as I want it. I sometimes turn things down".

He stresses the importance of contacts; this will appear as a recurrent theme in access to work in the informal economy. An uncle with a pub or a friend with a small building company are valuable assets that set the minority with access to work opportunities off from the rest. Bike work also stems from contacts; Phillip is a member of the biker sub-culture amongst which he says his work has a good reputation. "I'm just known by bikers I suppose. People know about how good I am so they bring me work".

Another theme that emerges from discussing work "on the side" is the fact that, whilst money is important, it is not the only benefit. Phillip is able to say "I don't have money problems as such" and later he adds "There again, I enjoy it - building work - for the money-but it gets me out and about - meet people - acquire new skills - earn money".

Neil and Paul both work more than average but less regularly than Karl or Phillip. The other major difference is that neither fall into the category of exceptions because both want to work officially very much indeed. Neil describes being unemployed as 'Devastating' and spends every day, when he is not working unofficially, job hunting.

He works labouring for a small building firm based in his village and earns £25 - £30 for a full week. The work is very irregular depending on the convenience of the builder "sometimes a full week sometimes not, sometimes nothing". Every morning he also does a paper round for which he receives £4.40 a week and each evening he turns up to the paper shop in case someone doing an evening round is sick; if they are he earns another £1. He looks, sounds and reports being depressed, partly perhaps because he gains little financial advantage from his work. When he has any kind of building work his parents take £20 - £25 per week for board and the rest goes to pay debts and fines. Also he feels stigmatized by being unemployed and worries about the legality of his situation. His parents give him little support, indeed, they blame him for his unemployment and there are constant rows with them.

> "I suppose its alright but you never know what will happen. I mean that job down there - (building) if somebody saw me doing it and reported me I could have my dole stopped and then I'd have nothing, so it can be quite worrying"

But again he reports benefits over and above that of money - keeping occupied, doing varied work and simply the relief of being spared a depressing day of looking for work and failing.

> "If I get work for a day that to me is a good day and if I get a paper round in the evening. It gives me something to do, I mean ohh!! I'm doing something when I go out looking for a job but its the same old thing, whereas if I'm down there (working) I'm doing different things all the time, concreting, pointing, putting up plaster board. It makes a change from just keep going round asking for jobs because that does start to get you down a bit"

Paul is financially much better off than many others in the sample, principally because his family charge him nothing for board when he is not working and only £10 per week when he does. Also, the emotional support he gets from him family has resulted in a much higher morale. However, although he is energetic in his job searching, he often feels bored and frustrated and has a very keen sense of being stigmatized for his unemployment, so he certainly cannot be characterised as happy on the dole.

He works sometimes for a demolition firm and more regularly does gardening for people in and around his village. The demolition firm pays £15 per day and this seems to have conditioned his expectations as it is also how much he charge's for a day's gardening. He has, on average, one day's gardening a week so and perhaps a full week's work for the demolition firm once a month.

Again most work comes via personal contacts, often gained via friends and family. Work comes from

> "just people you know..... its more than often,there's always someone with something to do ... I know a lot of people in ...... I have lived here all my life - its the only way, its not what you know its who you know. If I didn't know a lot of people I'd be skint. I couldn't hack it."Work is important to him for both monetary and non monetary reasons "I wouldn't survive if I didn't do bits of work on the side ..... I want the money. I get bored sitting around. I can't handle it."

(ii) Small amounts of irregular undeclared work

The largest section consisting of twenty one people who do work but on a very small scale, very irregularly. This point needs to be emphasized, that this is very small stuff. I have included everybody here who has done any work at all whilst unemployed, no matter how brief, how badly paid or how long ago. Most is illegal due to the fact it is not declared and those on unemployment benefit should not claim for any day they earn over £2 and those on Supplementary Benefit (now Income Support) should have £1 docked from their benefit for every £1 they earn over £4 p.w. (now £5).

A quick listing of these jobs will illustrate these points. In several periods of unemployment Ian has found work for four or five days delivering and selling soft drinks from door to door. For this he earned between £3 and £5 per day before giving up because he was worried about getting caught. "Five pounds! Getting prosecuted for five pounds! It's not worth it."

John, Tracy, Gary and Paul had done short periods of fruit picking, mostly strawberries, although none of these had done any work for weeks or months prior to interview. One young woman who I never caught up with missed several arranged interviews because, as her neighbours told me with complete disregard as to who I was, that she was strawberry picking. So it could be more widespread than appears from my sample.

Carl had earned £45 for a full week's work labouring for a roofer plus several periods of two or three days working on a removal van and delivering kitchen units. This was very irregular and at the time of the interview, he had not worked for the roofer for over three months or the delivery driver for six months. Kate had done a TOPS course in carpentry which had led to a few small jobs for friends but she had also not worked for months. She explained that she did not actively seek work as she did not feel confident that the six months course had made her sufficiently proficient.

Francis works in his fathers shop earning five pounds or so once every three weeks to a month.

James earns up to eight pounds per week usually gardening and he has the occasional one-off job such as decorating and on one occasion, demolishing a caravan (for which he was paid £5 for a day's work).

Isobelle babysits, earning an average of £7-£10 per week - but not every week.

Charlotte plays in a band and says that her earnings are just a few pounds more than the expenses and mainly she plays for interest and social reasons.

Joanne is trying to form a career as a dancer and has obtained short periods of work most but not all of which have been declared.

Jacqueline has not worked for some months, before that she worked for three weeks in a factory while someone was sick earning £30 per week and before that she did hairdressing. She had to give this up because she found she could not afford to run a car or buy the materials. She says that she is thinking about delivering leaflets.

Kevin R has had three days work in a factory in three years of unemployment. He also used to run a clothing catalogue earning £4-£5 per week taking orders from friends. However, due to lack of money for a social life, he has gradually lost touch with those friends and so no longer does it.

Richard has collected scrap but found it not worth it. For several hours hard work a day he earned £6.

Mandy has done baby sitting and has also had four weeks work filling in for someone who was ill at the shop where her sister works, earning £30 per week. She has had nothing for three months.

David, also filling-in for someone who was ill, earned £30 for one week's work in a restaurant, and also earned £36 for several days digging drainage ditches. He has had nothing for approximately six months.

Fiona's boyfriend's mother employs her for one morning a week as a cleaner, for which she receives five pounds. Her boyfriend's mother also arranged for her two days modelling for a catalogue, for which she was paid £50.

Jacky has worked in stables and done domestic cleaning but, at the time of interview, had done nothing for six months.

Susan and Peter have both done casual bar work. Susan works regularly three times a week and declares this, thus losing her unemployment benefit on those days. However, she also occasionally fills in if someone is sick and this is "discreetly lost in the books". As well as this, she runs a catalogue which earns her about £6 per month. David worked on and off for a month while someone was ill earning £2 per hour averaging £30 per week. However the regular bar man has now recovered and this is the extent of the work he has done in 11 months of unemployment.

Most of this work again illustrates the importance of having contacts in the working world. Ian fixed up his few days work selling soft drinks because he had "known this geezer for a long time". Carl's delivery work came via his boxing trainer and his roofing because of an older boxer. Francis' father owned the shop. James' gardening and bits of decorating and demolition came from people his family know in the village. Mandy filled in for someone who was ill at the shop where her sister worked. Peter knew a publican, so also got work when someone was ill and so on. Having contacts such as an uncle who owns a pub, a friend with a small building firm or simply somebody who knows somebody else with work is a very valuable asset and largely distinguishes those who get reasonable amounts of unofficial work and those who do not.

(iii) Part time declared work

Three of my respondents do only legal, declared part-time work. Sarah works Saturdays in a shoe shop for £10. Nicola works several sessions at a pub and, as her Supplementary Benefit is reduced, in effect she is in fact working for £4 per week. Gary W is paid £4 per week by the YMCA for working several hours a day in the kitchens. He describes it as "voluntary work". Contacts are equally important for those who engage in declared part-time work and, indeed, there were no obvious distinguishing characteristics between those who did and those who did not declare their earnings. In fact, two of my sample declared some but not all of their earnings.

The decision to declare or not to declare work is likely to depend on a number of factors. One is likely to be the visibilty of the work, the likelihood of being discovered. Another factor could be the degree of concern the worker has for 'respectability'; but possibly the most important consideration is the attitude of the employer and the nature of the job. Regular work in a shoe shop for example is more likely to be offered on an official basis than seasonal fruit picking which has a tradition of casual unofficial labour. Other forms of paid work have traditionally been considered personal private arrangements. Declaring them to officialdom is virtually never even considered. Baby sitting and gardening for family friends falls into this category.

Small businesses such as builders wanting a few day's or week's help may find it easier and cheaper to offer 'cash in hand' to an unemployed person than to go through official channels. Some evidence for this lies in the fact that many of the young people interviewed said that they were forced by circumstance to accept unofficial work and that this worried them. The minority that enjoyed their situation by contrast tended to worry less about illegality and respectability. Their freedom from guilt and the absence of a sense of longing for a conventional official job reinforces the maxim coined earlier "good citzens (defined in conventional terms) suffer most."

(iv) No work

The last group to be considered are the twelve that have done no work legal or otherwise whilst unemployed. One fact that immediately strikes the researcher is that ten out of the twelve are young women. At the other end of the scale the four who do the most work on the side are all male so there is a clear sexual division. Males are more likely to do unofficial work, females more likely to do none at all or very small amounts. This is significant and I will return to it in the conclusion.

The value of work in the informal economy

What does this unofficial work mean to the unemployed? Certainly it is usually valued, and is an asset contributing to psychological survival.

Both financial and non-financial advantages are reported; it provides extra money and gives something purposeful and constructive to do. John enjoys the social experience of riding on his bike with unemployed ex-school friends to pick fruit. Carl says

> "I've been and gone six months without working for him or he might give me two or three jobs a week for three or four weeks which is good.It's a bit extra money and I enjoy the job. It's just right. He's one of my boxing trainers. We are in the lorry or car doing whatever we're doing and we drive about and we talk about the boxing and things like that and people who have fought that we know and we just talk about everything and when we stop we do something, deliver something like units. We get out and carry them in for people, then, next thing, your'e driving back and relax. I just enjoy the job. It's friendly. It ain't boring, doing different things all the while"

Francis also enjoys the activity of working in the shop. It structures and gives a point to his day. He explains that work gives "something to get up for. It's become a catch phrase amongst us; we ask each other "have you got something to get up for tomorrow?"

The work is also important to James both because of the extra money and because it fills in boring free time with purposeful activity.

"Yesterday I was helping a bloke. He was paying me for that, that was dismantling a caravan. I do gardening jobs for old people. I've done some decorating work, not much - yesterday I got a fiver (for a days work) which isn't much but then I was quite happy just to get that as it kept me occupied and I got something out of it in the end ..... If I garden twice a week and did a fairly big job for someone, I suppose, I don't know - extra money would be about £8. Eight quid is quite a lot of money if you haven't got much. Eight quid is a lot of money .... Extra money is nice to have but its something to occupy yourself. I think that's the main thing. Just actually getting up and thinking "right today I've got to get up and do such and such in the morning and such and such in the afternoon" rather than thinking "what am I going to do today?" Get up and know that you've got to do something that is nice. That was like the job yesterday, just getting up and thinking ahh! I've got something to do all day, its really good, a really nice thing to wake up to — yeah filling in time is the hardest thing."

Jacqueline and David stressed the difference the extra money made. Mandy liked it because she gets bored doing nothing, so both these factors-the financial aspect and the purposeful activity - are important. Gary is working every day for £4 in the YMCA kitchens and was not concerned mainly for the money, £4 is the most they can pay me, but its not really for the money, its because I'm doing something for a few hours a day. I like - when its all in a mess just getting it nice and clean" He also had a slightly different motivation, or at least he expressed it differently. He was concerned with self-respect and combating his strong feeling that other people looked down on him. He explained that people called him names like "Waster," and, although it was said jokingly, it worried him "because they're earning money, but I don't feel too bad now I'm doing voluntary work. I'm doing it every day for three or four hours a day"

So unofficial work is generally a positive aspect of their life, supplying extra money, filling in time that would otherwise lie heavily, generating a temporary purpose -'something to get up for' - and helping maintain a sense of self-respect when other factors are working in the opposite direction. However, this should not be exaggerated. For all but the minority unofficial work is temporary, very irregular and poorly paid, providing only the occasional treat, only the odd island of activity in an otherwise boring existence. All but a small minority of exceptions would swap it for what they consider 'the real-thing' instantly if they had the chance. For this group the amount of time occupied and money gained is too little to make a major difference to their lives.

Much of the work in the informal economy is, by its nature, very temporary; a builder needs an extra pair of hands for a few days, seasonal fruit needs picking and a shop or a pub needs someone to fill in for a regular employee who is ill. The unemployed then are fitting in when needed and this also applies to much of their bouts of temporary official employment. They are a "reserve army of labour" in a very literal and immediate sense.

Conclusion

To conclude I will briefly sum up the data that emerges from my research and then comment on the theories and reasons outlined at the beginning of this chapter.

Two out of the forty in my sample do a fair amount of paid work regularly and one of these can be considered more or less fully but unofficially employed. Two more also do a fair amount of work on the side but it is more irregular with frequent gaps; unlike the first two they are far from satisfied with this situation and would join the ranks of the fully legally employed the instant they could. Twenty one work illegally, that is they do not declare it to the DSS, but the work is very temporary, erratic and low paid. Three work only legally part time and twelve have not worked while registered unemployed at all.

Some immediate points emerge. Firstly, males are much more likely to work in the unofficial economy than females. Secondly, most work is obtained via working contacts. Thirdly, when unofficial work is done there are both financial and non-financial advantages to the unemployed but, for most people, the amount of work is insufficient to make a radical impact on their lives.

At the beginning of the chapter I outlined two perspectives on the unofficial economy. One, the optimistic view, saw it as having the potential for creating new employment, even progressing towards a more creative form of work in a fulfilling, less exploitative post industrial society. The pessimistic view saw it as merely a survival mechanism for the poor who have no other choice and that it is parasitic on the main capitalist economy with no creative potential.

Obviously my sample cannot provide a definitive resolution to these alternative perspectives but it offers a modicum of evidence, in favour of the pessimistic perspective. As has been demonstrated, most of the work done is trivial and those engaged in it aim to join the main economy just as soon as they can. There are a very few exceptions but I would guess that there always have been and it is hard to see this as evidence in support of the optimistic view. Certainly most of my respondent's work is related to and parasitic on the main economy, particularly the small business sector, (eg. small builders, pubs, shops, etc.) It is difficult to find evidence of any kind of creative movement towards a fulfilled post industrial/capitalist future. Most of the young people involved hate their situation and do not see themselves as part of a creative movement. The right context in which to view this work is probably to link it with the schemes and periods of temporary official employment that most have had. Then we see an army of "fitters in", taken on when there is seasonal work or where an extra labourer is needed and when someone is sick, got rid of when it suits the employer and all the time struggling to join the mainstream. As I said earlier, they are very literally a "reserve army of labour". My research provides some evidence to support Pahl's contentions that the unemployed are the least able to take advantage of opportunities in the unofficial economy. It is true that most find some work occasionally but the fact that 36 out of 40 do either none at all or do very small and irregular amounts, shows minimal involvement in the unofficial economy. The odd lucky exception does not change the overall picture.

The reasons for this low level of participation do not seem hard to find. Firstly, unemployed young people have not had much of a chance to make contacts in the working world and as we have seen, this factor is crucial in obtaining unofficial work. Again the odd person with an uncle who owns a pub does not change the overall picture; some do have contacts, often friends of the family but many have very few and this is the main factor which differentiates between those who do and those who do not get work. This factor is accentuated by the tendency, documented in chapter 6 of the unemployed to become more isolated, to narrow down their social contact to a few friends who are also unemployed and therefore in a poor position to help. Kevin illustrates this point. He became increasingly isolated from school friends by lack of money to participate in a social life, worsened I believe by depression, he therefore lost customers for his mail order agency and had to give it up, therefore further decreasing his money and worsening his position.

The second factor is that the young unemployed have had limited work experience and therefore fewer opportunities to learn the skills that might be useful in the unofficial economy.

Thirdly, like Pahl's unemployed older people, they are not likely to have the small amounts of capital that is often necessary to provide tools, materials and transport. Jacqueline provides a specific example in that she started a small business hairdressing in people's own homes, but it required transport; she had bought a car while she was working, but could not afford to keep it. "I used to do that when I had my car because I could go from place to place but now I can't get my stuff there and I can't really afford to get more stuff for hairdressing". So an opportunity for earning extra money was lost for lack of capital along with the increased chances of social contact and purposeful activity.

Others of course will not even get to this stage due to lack of contacts, skills and capital. So my research does not support the optimistic interpretation of the role of the unofficial economy. It does not seem to me or to the vast majority of the young people I interviewed to be any kind of creative phenomena. As to the theories of the political right that the unemployed are having a wild time working and enjoying a life on the dole, the evidence speaks for itself.

Unofficial work does help make life a little more bearable. With few exceptions, those who have more work seem to have a higher morale and they report valuing it for the extra money it brings and because it helps fill time with purposeful activity. The problem is that there is not enough work to make a major change in the experience of most of their lives. Males do more unofficial work in general, young women are much more likely to do none at all which explains at least partly why they tended to appear to me to be more distressed. It is only possible to speculate on the reasons for the lesser involvement of women in unofficial work. Some research (Willis 1984 and 1986 Wallace 1987) suggests that women react to unemployment in a less outwardly going way than men, becoming more housebound and less involved in outside activities in general. This would tend to isolate them from the contacts necessary to find unofficial work. The explanation is likely therefore to lie in the socialisation process that underpins the position of women in society and results in this less outwardly going response to their situation. So males do have advantages when it comes to coping with unemployment. For the majority of either sex however, the unofficial economy can provide at best a survival mechanism giving the odd bright period in a bleak existence.

8 Housing

I start this chapter on the housing experience of my unemployed sample with two assumptions. The first is qualified agreement with Willis that setting up a separate adult home and family is "almost a universal working class objective" and that the wage is the "golden key" to this and wage labour the price (1984). My sample confirms that there is a near universal desire to have a separate independent home at some time in the future and most see work and the wage as the route. Asked about their vision of their future they either reply that they don't know or more often see it in terms of getting a job and forming an independent home. They then subdivide into optimists or pessimists depending upon how likely they think getting a permanent job is. So one issue is how they will react to this barrier to their progression. Will they remain with their parents indefinitely? Or, in the absence of the expected and socially accepted route, will they seek alternatives? Will they try to become independent in rented accommodation regardless? Will young women see pregnancy as the only route to obtaining state benefits and council housing? Does linking with a working partner provide an alternative to their own employment? It would require a larger longitudinal study to provide definitive answers to these questions so this study can only offer some evidence and suggestions relating to these matters.

The second assumption is that people's living conditions influence their sense of well being; good conditions will have a beneficial effect and bad conditions a depressing influence.

Young unemployed people in the housing market

Before moving on to a consideration of the housing experiences of my sample, I would like to describe the local housing market in relation to the young unemployed. The private sector is the largest, making up an estimated 54% of Norwich's 52,943 dwellings and a larger percentage in the county of Norfolk. The largest part of this - owner occupier dwellings - is closed to the young unemployed because unemployed people cannot get mortgages. In fact, with house prices increasing faster in East Anglia than anywhere else in the country, up 45% in 1987/8, the vast majority of young people, working or not are excluded from this market.

So what options are open to a young unemployed person, apart from living at home with parents? According to Judith Forrest, Senior Housing Advisor Norwich Advice Service, the unemployed are also mostly excluded from that section of the rented private accommodation market that deals with self contained accommodation, because of cost. The DSS will pay up to £35 per week per person direct to the landlord but it is Council policy to refer all high rent accommodation to the rent officer, who may well order it reduced. Because of this most landlords with reasonable property and virtually all accommodation agencies will not deal with the unemployed. Consequently, only those few young unemployed people who have appropriate personal contacts can get self contained accommodation with good facilities and a reasonable state of repair. Much less difficult to find are bedsits that mostly cater for the unemployed. These she described as usually overcrowded with not enough facilities, damp, with coin meters, hard to heat "...run by landlords exploiting the unemployed." She explained that no one chooses to live permanently in a bedsit, they see it as temporary and so drift from bedsit to bedsit with three to six months being the average stay, although people stay longer in the minority of better ones thus making them even less available. Because of the expectation of temporary residence, tenants do not repair or decorate these properties themselves, and also tend not to make such demands on the landlords.

The next largest sector to owner occupiers is council housing which constitutes 42% of Norwich dwellings. Norwich has had in the past a reputation for a good standard of accommodation and relatively short waiting lists, compared to many other cities, but national housing policies in the last 10 years have underminded this. The main problem here is not quality but quantity, there simply is not enough, due to government restrictions on spending and development and council house sales, so waiting lists are long and getting longer. There were 5046 applicants on the Norwich waiting list on 31/3/88. The average wait for single people wanting self contained accommodation was 4 years 11 months before approval of application and a further 9 - 12 months after. For shared accommodation the figure was 3 years 8 months. Should a young couple have a child they would then be categorised as a family and the waiting period would be reduced to about 3 years. A young person could be declared homeless under the Homeless Persons Act if he or she is sleeping rough, on a friend's floor, or under notice to quit - which could be from parents. However this gains them nothing at all as far as the council waiting list is concerned, unless they are also "in priority need", that is they are medically vulnerable, which is interpreted as physically disabled or recently discharged from an institution for mental handicap or illness. Homelessness does, however, help in obtaining a room in the YMCA. Pregnancy also enables access to Housing Association property and women under eighteen may be temporarily housed, usually in the Umbrella Housing Association, and those over eighteen permanently, as soon as a place becomes available. If not homeless, pregnancy would only move someone to the family category, which as stated above would mean about a three year waiting time. A pregnant woman is not counted as homeless if she has any kind of place to live, no matter how unsuitable the conditions.

In Norfolk, County housing is run by the various District Councils and here the situation is worse, waiting lists for single young people longer. Most do not allow people to register on the list until they are eighteen rather than sixteen, as in the case of Norwich City Council. The housing manager of one of the Housing Associations that does deal with young people is now having single people referred to them that have been on the waiting list for seven years. Young people she reported "find it very difficult to find somewhere to live. Councils are taking the view that young people should live at home with their parents. It's not realistic but that's their view." The most complete expressions of this view is the policy of Broadland District Council not to allow people to register with the waiting list until they are twenty five years old and then there is an average five years wait.

The other possibilities are the YMCA/YWCA and Housing Associations. The YMCA/YWCA has been used by a number of my sample. The YMCA was 132 units, the YWCA 51. 10% of the YMCA units are known as "care beds" and are reserved for use by Social Services for young people leaving care. 50% of the YWCA beds are nominated by the Council. For the rest, young people apply themselves, often encouraged by the Housing Advice Centre or social workers. The policy in Norwich, although it varies from area to area, is to help young people by giving them a breathing space, when they leave home, to mature and sort themselves out. There is no strict written criterion; applicants are interviewed and preference is given to those with problems, hence a very large proportion are jobless, experiencing severe problems with their families or having a history of living in the care of the Social Services. It is a large and well known institution and so receives a large number of applications.

Less well known are Housing Associations. The two largest are Broadland and Cotman Housing Associations housing 1400 and 650 units respectively. Both take young unemployed people but no one on my survey had any experience of them. People are referred to Housing Associations by the Advice Centre, the Citizens Advice Bureau, the Council from the waiting list, or hear about them from friends who are residents. They administer hostels, flats and houses. 50% of the units are subject to nomination by the Council and so are administered in the same way as the Council list except that prospective tenants are interviewed by the Association which has the right of veto. Applicants are interviewed on an individual basis. Cotman waiting lists are closed except for "very real priority cases" such as homelessness. The Broadland Housing Manager declined to predict waiting list times except that it would be long!

The rest are more specialist associations, the only one of which that is relevant here is the Umbrella Housing Association for one parent families. Single young women with babies who need social work help are housed by this association whilst they await Council accommodation. The association has 28 flats and four houses and a total of 32 tenants at time of writing. Of my sample one was housed by Umbrella and one was waiting to move in from the YMCA. Prospective tenants can apply direct but most are referred by social workers, health visitors and Council housing departments.

Apart from those agencies mentioned above there are a number of other smaller housing associations and hostels catering for a small number of individuals, none of which appeared in my sample. There is also a night shelter for people totally homeless and sleeping rough. One person using this facility completed a questionnaire but he had moved on before I could contact him for an interview.

The housing market is difficult to enter if you are young and unemployed, so how did my sample deal with this?

The housing situations of young unemployed people

The three types of housing provision that emerge in my sample, are rented accommodation owned by private landlords, collective provision such as the YMCA, the Umbrella scheme for single parents and council housing and, of course, the majority option - the family home. I will look at each in turn concentrating on the views and feelings of the young people concerned. The issue of progression, of moving on, or otherwise, will be considered throughout.

(i) Tenants of Private Landlords

Relatively few were living in rented accommodation owned by private landlords, only three men and four women at the time of interview. Others though were able to talk about past experience in this area and, as there were usually other young unemployed people living in the shared houses or homes divided into bedsits, I had the opportunity to at least observe the living conditions of a wider group while interviewing my respondents.

The first point to make is that, to the eyes of the researcher used to a much higher standard of living, the private sector seems pretty squalid - damp, cold, out of repair, threadbare furnishing, ancient cookers and so on. Perhaps this is not surprising for the young unemployed are unlikely to afford anything but the cheapest end of the accommodation market.

Of course the resident may not see it like this and a number of factors operate that may help young people cope with poor living conditions. These can be summed up briefly. Firstly, there may be membership of some sort of youth culture with a value system that downgrades conventional notions of smartness. Secondly, and very importantly, there are advantages of independence that may outweigh the disadvantages of poor housing conditions, such as being able to come and go as they please and have friends round whenever they feel like it. In short, there is the relief and novelty value of being independent of parental control. Thirdly, they may blame themselves for dirty and untidy conditions. Lastly, and perhaps most importantly, these conditions are often perceived as temporary and expectations for this period in their lives may not be high.

What can be said with certainty is that living conditions in this sector are rather worse than in other areas. However, some were not unhappy about their situation. Francis and David both seemed to accept their housing situation, perhaps partly because both had accepted a 'semi punk' lifestyle which included attitudes that did not lay great stress on convention and so were less concerned with a "nice" appearance or a "smart" house. Francis had at least partly come to terms with his general situation and was "not desperately unhappy about it .... but then again I can't afford to be".

His living conditions in a shared house were not a big issue for him. He acknowledged that the house was in a poor state but this was mainly due to himself and the others living there. "Someone will now and again clean out the bathroom and that but it might get into a bit of a state before its done" .... Otherwise I don't know, I enjoy living here .... its a bit uncomfortable sometimes, its got some really cheap furniture, cheapest you could find".

He adopted a lifestyle that involves spending most of his time with a small group of close friends, doing very little but making it last a long time and at this point in his life he had at least accepted his living conditions.

David, while less adapted to unemployment generally, again does not see his living conditions as a big issue. Although his family is "close knit - we help each other" he values his independence particularly as he comes from a small village where he found himself isolated from friends his own age, (see chapter 6), so he is now enjoying living with friends in the city "It's alright .... its a state - really bad, we get too lazy sometimes to clean it up .... the good things are its fairly close to the city .... two of my friends live here .... (are you satisfied?) Yes mostly".

So two at least are not dissatisfied with their housing situation. Part of the reason seems to be that their membership of an alternative subculture meant that they did not place a heavy emphasis on tidy 'smart' expensive clean surroundings and so did not worry much about poor conditions. Other factors such as independence, proximity to the city centre and the almost constant presence of a few friends were more important to them.

It was not clear to me whether they were likely to remain satisfied with their situation if it continued indefinitely. It could be that they were satisfied because, consciously or otherwise, they considered this a temporary phase of their life.

Francis and David are, anyway, exceptions, as there is considerable dissatisfaction with private accommodation even amongst those who might be categorised as members of non-commercially orientated sub-cultures. Jessie, for example complained about her shared house being cold and expensive to heat in winter and about constantly having to feed the meter with 50p pieces. Few mentioned this aspect but, due to circumstances beyond my control, hers was one of the very few interviews not done in Summer. Most private accommodation looked to me to be draughty. Often there was only electric fires, never central heating. Had I interviewed in winter I feel this would have emerged as an important problem.

Even two people who were otherwise very much exceptions in that they enjoyed their life on the dole objected strongly to their housing conditions. Philip, aged 22, said of his shared house. "Well what's bad about it? What's bad about it is it's falling down - with green streaks around the windows, the shower isn't working the baths and the sink .... (inaudible) it's just been sold and nobody knows who its been sold to". Now living with a working girlfriend he is looking hard for a job after five years unemployment mainly because they want to buy a flat.

Charlotte, aged 22 and unemployed 6 years and living happily in a council house with her unemployed boyfriend and their baby, is very explicit about her previous housing experience. "One of the main problems for people on the dole - it was for me - is that they live in horrible places, in horrible bedsits, and it made me miserable. Accommodation in Norwich is dreadful and we were really lucky to get a house as good as this".

Jacqueline, aged 24 and unemployed for 1 year, is in the position that Charlotte had been previously - pregnant, living with an unemployed boyfriend in rented accommodation, hating it and desperately hoping for a council house soon. (There, the similarities end; they are poles apart in terms of life style and attitudes, particularly to work and unemployment). Housing was one of her main preoccupations, along with boredom, lack of things to do, and money to do things with. One of the first things she mentioned was her housing circumstances,

> "I live with my boyfriend, I'm now seven months pregnant. We live in a bedsit, Huh! £30 each a week, which is something ridiculous. We're now trying to get us a council place but so far we've heard nothing on that and the state of it is diabolical. Me and my boyfriend were happy enough living together but obviously when we get our own place we'll be better off.

Adrienne now living in a room provided by the Umbrella scheme for single parents, also had bad experiences with private rented accommodation.

> "Its alright" she says of her present situation "its better than some places I've lived in. Like I was saying earlier, I rented this converted shed out for £25 a week! This was in Yarmouth. It was on the back of a house. It had a leaky roof and toilet that didn't work. It was damp. It looked nice. The furniture was nice - it looked nice but I caught a really bad case of flu. I was pregnant. I caught the flu. All my clothes were damp. I was coughing and wheezing. This place is brilliant compared with that. I'm on the council list waiting for a council place but its been a year and three months."

Before moving on to collective provision it might be worth summing up the possible reasons why people might move from acceptance or toleration of poor living conditions to feeling resentful and depressed about them. Firstly, some come to resent the high rents and exploitative attitude of landlords.

Where rent was paid directly by the DSS, tenants may not even give any consideration to whether it is excessive, although they may well feel hostility to the landlord about repairs, decoration or even his/her personal behaviour. Secondly, there is concern about the health risks of damp cold housing, as far as they themselves are concerned and, of course, this issue becomes particularly pressing when children are concerned or expected. Thirdly there is the high cost of heating damp and draughty houses. Jessie mentions this and, as stated earlier, I feel that this would have been a very significant problem had I interviewed more people in the winter. Fourthly, people compare their situations with alternative superior housing. This applies to those hoping for council accommodation and those remembering the comforts of the parental home. Lastly, and very important; people may very well be prepared to put up with very poor conditions in order to experience the benefits of independence while this situation is a novelty and the situation can still be considered temporary. However, in time the disadvantages might begin to make themselves felt and, as the situation drags on, it may well start to seem less tolerable. This may become particularly difficult if the person has some notion of progression in their lives; "roughing it" in poor conditions as a single person at 17 might be fun, but at 20+, with several years of experience of this kind of life and a desire to move to a new stage, perhaps involving settling down as a couple and raising children, it may be experienced as acutely frustrating.

(ii) Collective Provision

By collective provision I mean that provided neither by private landlords nor parents so that, in the context of my survey, this means the YMCA/YWCA, Council housing and the Umbrella scheme for single parents. The first and most general point is that my research did not reveal the deep levels of dissatisfaction found amongst those in the private sector. In fact, most people liked where they were living, even if, as in the case of YMCA residents, they tended to view it as temporary and not "real" independence.

The YM/YWCA was generally liked, although with some reservations. Most residents I spoke to liked the staff and particularly the fact that it offers a ready made group of friends all in the same position. Most of all, the YMCA fills a need as it caters mainly for people who have nowhere else - whose families have split up and cannot look after them or who have spent a lifetime "in care" or whose family have moved. It is a religious organisation staffed by committed Christians, although most of the residents stress that this aspect is not forced upon them.

Carl, the would-be professional boxer, ended up at the YMCA because he could not get on with his mother when he lived at home. He had also had trouble, including violence, with his step father. He likes the YMCA, spending most of his time training in the Gymnasium and hanging around with friends he met there. He considers most of the staff "genuine people" who do not trouble him with their religion. Sometimes he finds the rules restrictive but not too much. "I keep to the rules as long as they are nice about it". His main complaint is that the meals are not large enough to sustain a boxer in training. He would like eventually to live independently with his working girlfriend but there's "no hurry really".

Ian's parents had also split up and he lived with his mother in Hereford before moving to live with his father in Norwich. When they did not get on he ended up in the YMCA. He also likes the company of the other residents and spends most of his time with them or with Action Line, a training scheme run by the YMCA where attendances earns a meal ticket. Ian goes partly for this reason but mostly because he gets bored otherwise and has trouble "keeping busy". Unlike Carl, he detests being unemployed but does not mind the YMCA; accommodation is not the major issue for him.

Gary's story was similar - living with his mother in London he left when she remarried because of violent conflict between him and his new step-father. Then he moved to Norwich because his sister and brother, who was working for the YMCA in the kitchens, were here. He explained that he likes the YMCA but considers it temporary. "I like it but it's not home or nothing. It's a stopping station on the motorway of life really - where you can stay just to sort yourself out - but its nice here really. A lot of people complain about it but you get a good room and that .... nice food .... you meet people the first day .... the staff are helpful." He would like to get a flat "obviously its best to do that if you've got a job - money is the problem - buying food and that". The YMCA also helps him with his major preoccupations - difficulty in filling in times and an acute sense of stigma because of unemployment. He works voluntarily in the kitchens, almost full time for the £4 a week it is permissible to gain before his dole is affected. The money is not as important as filling his time and proving that he is not a "waster".

The young women had similar views. Susan graduated to the YWCA after a life time of various forms of "care", foster parents or children's homes. She was the least enthusiastic. The YWCA was "alright", but pregnant, she was looking forward to room in an Umbrella house followed by a Council flat. She was obviously very depressed but accommodation was not the cause. Indeed, she saw some advantages to living there - all her friends were residents and this again went at least some way towards helping one of her major problems - lack of things to do.

Julie was living in a shared house in a small town on the coast, and, when the landlady sold it, she moved to the YWCA in Norwich rather than return to her parents with whom relations were strained. Of the YWCA she says "I like it, there's company, everyone's in the same position .... the rules are the only disadvantages but generally I like it". Again she sees it as temporary, expecting to still be there in one year but hoping to be working with a home of her own in five years.

Rachel left home because she did not get on with her step-father. She moved to her sister's home but had to move to the YWCA when her sister had a baby, because of lack of room.Again she likes the YWCA and spends most of her time, when not energetically searching for work, with friends from there." The rules are not too strict. You can come and go as you like as long as you don't hang around at night". Unlike the YMCA, the YWCA is self catering and her only complaint was that she budgets very carefully and then her food gets "nicked" from the fridge.

The few that had obtained Council houses or flats were very pleased with them and this offers a satisfactory way towards the desired goal of an independent home. There is only one problem; they are too few, and therefore difficult to obtain. Least enthusiastic was Jacky but this had more to do with a desire to return to her small village to be near her family than with dissatisfaction with the flat. Kate was a somewhat special case, living in a cluster unit for young people which she liked but considers temporary.

Charlotte was more than pleased with her council house and was eloquent in her comparisons between the advantages of her present situation and the depressing nature of her previous experiences with the private sector.

Susan moved from the YWCA to a Council flat after she had a baby. She was delighted with her new situation, proudly showing me round her spotless and newly self decorated flat. She had also had a childhood of foster parents and children's homes. Of the YMCA she said

> "That was alright but you got everything done for you. I mean meals and that were done for you. There was nothing to do .... then I got my own place here which I prefer. I mean its best to have your own place isn't it. Oh yeah I'm proud of it, pleased with it. It's what I wanted - I keep it

clean, tidy, I couldn't really ask for more could I? "

Since doing these interviews I have heard that both Susan and Adrienne have moved from Umbrella accommodation to council property, and it is probable that Jacqueline will have done the same. I also met Carl (the boxer) by chance over a year after the interview. He was still unemployed but his girl friend had become pregnant and they had recently moved into a Council flat (Of the flat he said, "It's good! One part of my life is going right") So, like the unemployed partners of Jacqueline and Charlotte he demonstrates that this can also be a route to independence for males. This makes having a child either with a partner like Jacqueline and Charlotte or without likeAdrienne and Susan the most significant means of obtaining council accommodation as far as my sample is concerned. This raises an interesting issue. Does pregnancy become a conscious means to achieving an independent existence via council accommodation and DHSS benefits? Clearly, no definitive answer can be expected on the basis of a small number of interviews but the impression gained is a complex and varied combination of accident, choice, trying to make the best use of one's situation and post hoc rationalisation.

Firstly, all these women with the exception of Charlotte claimed that they did not become pregnant deliberately but, after it happened, they were willing to have the child and were aware of and willing to use the extra possibilities that became available - such as the increased access to Council housing. Pregnancy does offer one route to Willis's "universal working class objective" of an independent home which is open to people denied mortgages or access to "decent" (ie more expensive) private rented accommodation. Unfortunately, it is difficult to discover the extent of such behaviour, the council do not keep statistics on the number of women who are pregnant or have young babies. Norwich Council Housing Research Department told me that the last relevant statistics were collected by the census in 1980 and obviously so much has changed as far as unemployment is concerned as to make them useless. The impression of some concerned with housing seems to be that this route is becoming significant. Judith Forrest, Senior Housing Advisor Norwich Advice Services, said "I do actually believe that girls get pregnant to get a house". She added that it often does not work out to their satisfaction because they are acting on out of date information. The Norwich Housing Department used to have a good reputation and young women would hear of friends and relatives getting housed very quickly after becoming pregnant and assume that this is still the case. Alas, with cuts in Local Authority spending and the sale of Council houses, speedy rehousing is only available to pregnant women if they are also homeless.

Nationally, the birth rate for unmarried young women has risen and is now higher than the birth rate for married women in the under 20s age group but these facts tell us nothing about intentions, including strategies for housing. What research there has been shows that the majority of these were not planned but about 40% said they had intended or did not mind becoming pregnant. (Simon and Smith 1985). There is little real evidence on this issue only speculation.

(iii) Parents home (or other relatives)

The largest group live in their parents' home and these make up two thirds of the young men and half the young women in my sample. The general difference is accounted for at least partly by the fact that it is women who get pregnant and find their way to schemes for single parents and Council accommodation. The young people living at home can be subdivided into two rough groups. Firstly, there are those who take living at home for granted and unsurprisingly, these tend to be younger. Generally they have vague plans to move in the future but usually add that this requires getting a job. From about 19 years of age we find the second group are still at home because they do not have a job and feel that they cannot afford to leave or that leaving would be unacceptably difficult for financial reasons. This group can be seen as having been blocked, their progress halted by their situation. Most of my respondents in both these groups usually get on well with their parents which, to some degree, took the urgency out of their situation. A small minority did not and this makes their situation more depressing.

Fiona, Wendy and Nicola (who lives with her grandparents) are examples of group one. They say they enjoy living at home would like to move away "in a few years time" (Nicola) but are making no detailed plans. They all said that the main problem would be money and that they would need a job. Sarah also takes living at home for granted although she is somewhat different in that her mother is less sympathetic and they row and this adds to her depression. Of the young men John, James , Kevin and Peter fall into this category, content at home but having vague ideas of getting a job and becoming independent sometime in the future.

None of this is surprising, for sixteen and seventeen year olds, used to having lived with parents all their lives, are likely to continue to accept this situation for a while regardless of unemployment or employment. A more interesting issue is whether, as they get older, they are being prevented from achieving independence by their unemployed state. There is evidence that they are.

Moving out is not impossible and offers independence but also offers large disadvantages if home is comfortable, parents supportive and the alternative a "shabby bedsit". As David P. aged 22, says,

> "You live in quite a nice place, its comfortable because some bedsits can be pretty shabby, you have to share bathrooms and kitchens.... I get my washing done. Its all very handy - meals - I certainly get them very cheap, it makes it all very much easier .... it's fairly cushy to be on the dole at home .... I would like to leave but not while I'm on the dole - couldn't afford it."

Paul I had a similar point of view

> "I've already left home once. Me and a friend of mine got a flat and we stayed there for seven weeks and then came back - something to do with the Supplementary wouldn't pay for more than seven and a half weeks or something because that was more like a bed sitter than a flat. We just couldn't afford it .... It's nice to get out and experience living by yourself and coping with this that and the other and coping with bills - just to know you can do it. There again I've got it all on a plate here haven't I?"

Neil is only 17 but has an unhappy home life with parents who he claims are very unsympathetic about his situation, so he would like to move but feels trapped by his situation. He had moved into a bedsit because of these problems but found he could not afford to stay. "If I had a regular wage I'd rather move out of here first and get myself a place because I think that I'd be better off and better off family wise as well, plus if I done that I'd be more self sufficient which I want to get back to being because that's what I was in Attleborough until I started to get some money problems".

Paul D aged 19 does get on with his parents but would like to move if he could afford it "Yes I know I can't live here forever but you need a job really don't you? Flats or even bedsits aren't cheap."

Kevin aged 20 feels trapped, isolated and very depressed. His parents cannot afford to subsidise him so he has to pay £15 a week board. This has curtailed his social life and he has lost touch with most of his friends. He would not like to move at the moment because that would further deepen his isolation. His future hinges on getting a job which he is pessimistic about. In one years time he expects his position to be " just the same". Later he would like to get married, have a house and family but that depends on getting work. "I sort of think I won't get a job at all that much. I'm going to be on the dole for a long time really .... Maybe I might get a job. I don't know really (Would you like to get married have house etc?) I'd like to but I don't think so no." He also feels that the road to being an adult is blocked. Asked if he sees himself as an adult he replied `No not really .... I feel a bit younger, like I ain't twenty." Asked what he thinks makes an adult, he replied, "having a job and being able to do things".

Richard, aged 19, has similar feelings. His relationships are difficult; his parents help him financially but there are a lot of rows mainly about unemployment so he is not happy at home but alternatives and progress in the future depend on work. In one year he said "I'll probably still be living in the same place in my mum's house. I'll probably still be unemployed". In five years,

> "I don't really know, in a way I feel I could get it together (to move) save money - be able to get a job but it's really hard to save money when you're unemployed. You spend it just as quickly as you get it, so in a way I could

be the same .... living at home and being unemployed .... For a start, I'd like to have my own house and my own car and have a dog, and I would like to be working .... I would like to get married and have kids."

To sum up this section. It seems that unemployment is blocking the progress of many young people towards an independent home. Some are prepared to forgo independence because the only alternative they can afford are the "shabby bedsits" described above, which do not seem such a good deal compared to the comforts of home. The younger ones tend to take for granted living with their parents.As they increase in age, more are found whose departure from the family home is blocked by their circumstances. The feelings of frustration start earlier and are more keenly felt by those who do not get on with their parents. However, such feelings will be experienced even by those who have good relations with their parents as they get older and start to perceive a lack of progress in their lives. For, as stated earlier, virtually all (even those who presently take living at home for granted) want to progress towards the conventional idea of a independent home and family at some stage.

One route to an independant house, though not necessarily consiously planned, has already been discussed, namely Council housing for young women with babies or pregnant women.

Mandy had definite plans to move into private accommodation with her working boyfriend. The flat had been arranged by her boyfriend's contact and was being decorated. It would presumably be of a higher standard than could be afforded by those reliant on dole money alone. This might be one possible route to independence as several had working boy or girlfriends. It is probably more likely to be realised by women with working boyfriends because of the generally higher earning capacity of males. However this is the only example of such a couple with definite plans in my sample. I would expect that some of the younger people will take this route later.

Anna had taken the option of sitting out the waiting list for council accommodation. She had been on the list for four years, and hoped to get a flat in about six months.

Conclusion

It can be seen that in my sample, answers to questions about the future reveal that a separate home and family is indeed an almost universal working class objective as Willis has suggested and this presents the young unemployed with a problem - the lack of the "golden key" - the wage. This makes progression towards that objective very much more difficult. Denied access to mortgages, they cannot become part of the "property owning democracy" and their choices are limited, their way blocked. Some opt for independence regardless and gravitate to the private rented sector, but they can afford only the poorest accommodation which the majority find a depressing experience. The general level of dissatisfaction with private accommodation living conditions was high.

Others, usually because of family circumstances, end up in the YMCA which was generally liked but considered temporary. Some get Council housing which they are generally enthusiastic about and this seems the best way of achieving independence in the absence of a decent wage. My research emphasizes the importance of Council accommodation to those who cannot afford to buy. If we are looking for practical policy implications to assist the unemployed then here is an obvious one. Present policy should be reversed and more council houses built for, as far as the unemployed are concerned, the only major problem with council housing, is that there is not enough of it. There is also a need for a secular version of the YMCA and perhaps other local government funded schemes to assist the young unemployeds progress towards independence.

The difficulty of finding Council accommodation means that young women who gain extra housing points by having babies make up the bulk of those achieving this type of accommodation. This raises the issue of whether pregnancy is becoming a deliberate strategy aimed at achieving an independent life. All but one of the young women concerned claimed not to have got pregnant deliberately but once pregnant they were aware of and prepared to exploit the opening possibilities. So perhaps it should be categorised as a semi deliberate strategy. Deliberate or not it is certainly a significant means of achieving the objective of a independent home.

The majority of my sample live still in their parent's homes. For the younger ones this would probably be the case whether they were working or not. For the older ones there is evidence of a postponing of independence because of lack of a wage. Some feel they cannot afford to move away and a minority feel trapped at home although relationships with their parents are strained. This does not seem to be the case for most however. The majority have supportive parents, both financially and emotionally, and postpone independence by choosing the comforts of home, which offer living conditions vastly superior to the cheapest end of the private accommodation market. Just how permanent this situation could be I could only speculate. However my study does offer some evidence to support Carney (1980), Hendrey et al (1984) and Willis (1984/85/86) that unemployment is holding up, or slowing down the process of independence and the formation of a separate family. Employment provides both a source of adult identity and the financial means to achieve adult independence. Without it dependence may be prolonged for some trapping them in a kind of extended adolescence.

9 Depression, boredom and stigma

In chapter 3 I made the point that if anything is firmly established it is that unemployment is associated with poor psychological health. These states of psychological malaise have been measured by the use the General Health Questionnaire (GHQ), which contains questions on lack of confidence, sleep loss through worry, recent experience of strain, inability to concentrate, feelings of depression and a sense of worthlessness. Longitudinal studies have demonstrated, to my satisfaction at least, that people are indeed depressed and generally in poor psychological health because of unemployment rather than vice versa. As with many social phenemona it may not be possible to provide absolute proof but I feel the evidence is so strong that one would have to positively want to disbelieve in order to doubt it.

Some findings are particularly relevant to my study, in particular that young people suffer but not so much as the middle aged who have more commitments and are used to long years of work.

Given that this area has been so well covered, that I am a sociologist not a psychologist and do not have the time and resources of Warr's Sheffield unit, it would have been impertinent as well as pointless to trespass too far into this field. I therefore decided to take their findings as given and not to administer the GHQ. However the young people of my survey were encouraged to express their feelings including those related to depression and boredom. I intend to offer some comments on this area before going on to consider expressed feelings of stigma.

Going back through my notes and re-listening to the tapes, I attempted to visualise each person and to class them into four rough and ready categories that stemmed naturally from the research:

1 The very distressed/depressed.

2 Those that were very fed up with their situation but less distressed

3 Those that did not like their situation but were managing - that is they were semi-adapted

4 Those that were happy with their situation, the exceptions of chapter 12

The results were as follows

Category	Females	Males	
1	Adrienne	Kevin	
	Jessie	Neil	
	Susan C	Richard	
	Sarah		
	Susan F		
	Susan W		
	Tracey		
2	Julie	David	Paul I
	Gillian	Peter	
	Wendy		
	Jacky	Gary W	Gary
	Jacqueline	Gary S	James
	Mandy	Ian	
	Nicola	Paul D	
3	Anna	Francis	
	Fiona	John	
	Rachel	David R	
	Kate		
4	Charlotte	Carl	
	Isobel	Karl	
	Suzanne	Phillip	
	Joanne		

Judgments as to which category to place people were made not only by what they said but also how they looked and their tone of voice. One of the advantages of my methods is that it allows one to do this. Even though this classification is not based on a precise measuring instrument, I have sufficiently rich data to be reasonably confident in the allocation of people to the categories. It is possible that I have been mislead occasionally by catching people on good or bad days and there are undoubtedly some borderline and ambiguous cases in the middle two categories. However, I have documented the "exceptions" in category four in some detail in chapter 12 and would claim that they are quite distinctive. The most depressed and distressed category certainly share certain features; they all reported feeling very depressed most of the time as well as a range of other symptoms, crying alone, visiting the doctor and taking anti-depressants, nerves, feeling lifeless, worthless - lacking in confidence even suicidal. But not only this, they looked and sounded depressed; there were long pauses when they spoke and they had a deadened air about them that I have elsewhere described as 'disengaged'. Readers should take into account that I am trained in neither psychology nor psychiatry and my judgment is that of a lay person. However, I feel very confident about it and I defy anyone who listens to the tapes to disagree. Listening to these tapes is a very distressing experience and in my lay persons opinion these people are in or on the verge of serious psychological trouble.

Looking at this first group, there are a number of points to be made. Firstly, there are a lot of them, ten individuals, that is 25% of the total. Add this to the sixteen in category two, who seem a little better off but are very unhappy with their situation then it can be seen that there is a deep pool of distress. The other chapters will bear this out. It puts into perspective the observation by Warr and others that young people suffer less than the redundant middle aged. It may be true but it is simply the relative advantage of one unfortunate group compared with another.

Secondly, it is immediately noticeable that there is a higher number of young women than men in catagory one. Further, my impression is that, of those people in category two, more of the women than the men were on the borderline between categories one and two. Explanations suggested in earlier chapters for the relatively worse levels of depression and distress among the women than the men include the fact that the former tend to spend more time indoors, more time on domestic work (although mothers still tend to assume the main responsibility), less time in the company of friends in a similar position and less time working in the informal economy.

Mention of work brings me to the third point; the ten in category one are all long term unemployed. Their length of unemployment was as follows: Adrienne two years, Jessie six months but with previous periods of unemployment, Susan over one year, Sarah and Susan F seven months, Tracey two years, Susan W eight months, Kevin three years, Richard over two years and Neil only three months but a history of short term temporary work with previous periods of unemployment. Also, all of these, with the single exception of Neil, had had none or very little unofficial work. So the amount of work done is a significant factor. Most of those in category two had been unemployed for shorter periods and might be expected to move to category one if they continue to fail to find work.

Those in both categories one and two are, with one exception, all work orientated "conventional" individuals who feel keenly the disappointment and humiliation of searching for work and failing. Interestingly those in category three the 'semi adapted' have also mostly been unemployed for some time and with the exception of John have had very little "side work." So perhaps if their unemployment persists, category two will divide into those becoming seriously depressed and those tending to adapt, with I fear, the majority becoming the former.

Boredom

Certainly the most popular word used to describe the experience of unemployment is "boring". This is however a difficult area as young people are apt to make frequent use of the word at school, college and schemes and at work. Boredom and problems with time; having "nothing to do" featured in all the interviews except those in category four. Perhaps I should just restrict myself to the observations that it tended to be much more of a preoccupation with those that seemed to me to be suffering the most.

Stigma

"The unemployed believe others despise them and depreciate them. This in itself is enough to generate discomfort but when reinforced by other trauma associated with unemployment it can threaten the fabric of identity" (G Brakewell 1984)

How true is this statement for my sample? Do young people feel stigmatized by unemployment or has their sense of the work ethic been so weakened that they no longer feel shamed by lack of unemployment? Have they simply become accustomed to it, accepting it without a sense of guilt? My survey reveals that, with a few exceptions, Brakewell's statement holds good. Many in my sample feel that others look down on them and that their situation is "degrading" (Joanne, Neil) and this must add to the pain of their situations. Here is what they had to say on the subject.

It was a major pre-occupation for Gary W.

> "I feel sort of pretty bad because I'm not working. I see other people working and me just sitting there. Well, I do voluntary work but I'm not working for a wage or nothing. I don't know, I mean this man in the (YMCA) restaurant, I go in there and he goes, "here you are you waster" It's all a joke and that, but the names they call you - it makes you feel ah! you shouldn't be sitting here. (So in spite of the fact its a joke it still worries you?:SH) Yeah! I don't know, its because they're working, they're earning their money sort of thing but I don't feel too bad now I'm doing voluntary work.......... If you're working you're doing something and no one can say you're sitting round and that, because you're working you're doing something with your life."

James was similarly concerned.

> "A lot of people, my mum's a particular example, if people, friends, ring up and say 'How's everyone getting on? she will actually say, 'Jamie's looking for a job' as opposed to, 'He is unemployed', which even though it's true, it's really subtle. What she is trying to do is cover up the fact that I am unemployed, scrounger on the state, and so on..... Quite a lot of people think 'He hasn't got a job. It's his fault! He can't be bothered to work, lazy, lazy slob or whatever. I mean, I think, there's quite a lot of that. My friend's dad, he's a funny person like that. My mum, - I know I'm having a go - when I lost my job she said 'You're not staying here unemployed.' I said 'Bloody hell, there's three million others who would like a job.' She said, 'That's not the point; you can find work:' as if, in a sense, they're over there and darling little boy is over here. So she does try to cover it up. I think she doesn't like me being unemployed because I suppose in a sense I'm letting her down and I feel that quite a lot too."

For Tracey and Paul it is felt most strongly when dealing with the DSS and even when cashing a giro. Tracey said "They seem to be looking down on you as if you are, oh! just sort of after money, you know, its so humiliating".

Paul describes his feelings when he cashes his giro

> "Well when you go in there well, you felt like covering your cheque up. You don't want people to know you're not working, because you feel like you're in a different class. It's not like you feel like your lower class. You don't feel lower class; you just feel different from someone who... you feel like you're labelled. You feel like people are saying, you know, 'he's not working' and that sort of thing 'slob!.' When people are not working they think well, 'He's a lazy git. He can't do anything. He don't want to go off after work' That's the basic thing. People don't understand it. I know there are a lot of people who don't want to work, who are on the dole, who are loving it, who are ripping the DSS off left right and centre but ..."

Nicola reports that people in her village, "look down on you if you're unemployed." and, for her, being an adult means

> "Somebody who knows what's going on around them, maybe keep their calm when people are going on about Oh! how the unemployed youths are doing this, that, and the other. You can keep calm and say 'look I'm not like that! you've got to give us a chance.' You've got to keep calm about it."

she said she is in the 'middle stages' between a youth and an adult and that such remarks did worry her.

Quotes like these are typical and commonplace, with even some of the "exceptions" saying they dislike this aspect of their situation. Those involved in subcultures that do not stress the work ethic were less likely to complain of a sense of stigma but not even all of these were immune to it. Most mentioned it at least briefly but of those who made a big issue of it, who seemed very preoccupied with "people looking down on them" what is striking, is that most were from small villages. I have mentioned this in the chapter 10 and tried to explain it there. They are often the only person they know without work and so have no one in the same situation to compare themselves with, no group of unemployed friends to back them up and bolster their self image.

In conclusion, Brakewell's quotation is a valid description of the situation as far as my sample is concerned.

A sense that other people look down on you is one of the problems the young unemployed have to face. In areas where unemployment is not so heavy such as Norfolk compared with the city, Norwich compared with the North, the sense of stigma is worse. It becomes harder, for people to say to themselves "Well, we are all in the same boat. It's not my fault."

People try to cope with the distress caused in a number of ways. Firstly, they may exert a conscious effort, saying to themselves "It's not my fault whatever anyone says". Secondly, they may continue to search for jobs in the hope that their position will change and so that they themselves feel that they do not fit the stereotype "lazy slob" (which of course carries the danger that continual rejection may be even more damaging). Thirdly, they may try to secure their own self-respect and possibly the respect of others by doing voluntary work. Fourthly, they can try to hide the discreditable fact of their unemployment by trying to conceal the giro when cashing it so that others in the queue do not know they are unemployed. Fifthly, they may, seek positive images from the other people in non-work orientated sub-cultures.

For most, however hard they try, a sense of stigma and of being degraded will stick with them adding to the other burdens they must bear.

10 Rural unemployment

Fourteen of my sample lived in small rural villages or had had experience of life on the dole in such places before moving to the city. The special features of rural unemployment have been hardly researched as most attention has been directed towards the large concentrations of unemployed in industrial cities. This chapter is nevertheless brief because most of the points have been mentioned elsewhere as I have tried to integrate the experience of the rural unemployed throughout the text.

Of the fourteen, ten felt there were clear disadvantages to being unemployed in a village rather than the city and they were almost totally united in giving three reasons for this. Firstly, there is "nothing to do" in the village. Of course, this does not apply solely to the unemployed; young people have been moving to cities to find excitement and interest, "things to do", for generations but the unemployed have more time on their hands so lack of opportunity to fill it is felt more keenly. Secondly, they complain of being more isolated at least during the day when others are at work. This is important as hanging around with a small group of friends that are the same position is a very common coping strategy. Also, not having a community of people in the same position, that is being unemployed when most are working, may heighten and reinforce feelings of stigma and personal inadequacy. This might apply to people unemployed in Norwich compared to the Northern industrial cities but will even more so in a small village because, as my interviews show, the unemployed villagers are much more likely to have very few or often no unemployed friends living locally. Thus they are less likely to have the moral support of friends in the same position, more likely to compare themselves only with the employed and find themselves wanting. Thirdly, almost all mentioned the difficulty and high cost of travel both for social reasons and for the purpose of job seeking. When money is already tight, high bus fares can make a great difference.

Most of the ten mentioned all three reasons, running them together although with different emphasis. Susan for example said,

> "I don't think there is enough help going on. Community Programme things, and, all this, they are usually only part time, and its ever so much a way out - we live in the sticks - its a bus drive into the city and they expect you to go in and then go out to Hellesdon or somewhere and its just a bit too much - you've got no transport."

Asked about the difference between being unemployed in the city or village, she continued,

> "Yeah, because you've got to go to the town to find out about jobs, if you are in the town you can walk in whereas I've got to scrub up the bus fare or talk my dad into taking me. It sort of gets very hard. I mean its expensive; its 65p no 70p and that's only one way. That's £1- 40p to go to the job centre and that's a lot of money if you haven't got it..... I can't go round to my friends because they're all out at work."

Nicola was also concerned with the lack of companionship during the day, the stigmatizing nature of being the only unemployed person in the village and the cost of bus fares.

"I think I spend a little bit too much time on my own because all my friends are working so I am on my own not doing anything." Winter, she explained, was worse as she was "very much stuck indoors." She had moved to the village recently with the family. "I don't know people here, most of them have got jobs or are still at school or something I haven't been living here long but the ones I've met seem to be working and look down on you if you're unemployed". Asked directly about the advantages and disadvantages of village compared with city life, she said,

> "In the town there are a lot more people who are unemployed who you can get on with, who can relate to you and see your circumstances but the few people I'm friendly with here have all got jobs and they can't understand it if you say 'I can't go out with you I can't afford it'... Yeah and bus fares. It's 75p into Norwich and 75p out again. That makes your money go very quickly. I can't think of any advantages."

She goes to the Job Centre four times a week as does Neil who also finds it a financial strain. He says,

> "The main disadvantage is getting in and out of the city because of lack of money. Also lack of things to do, that's a big disadvantage... In the city

there is more things to do. It's more of a close knit relationship, if you know what I mean. In a place like this its still a close knit relationship but its a big area and they haven't got so much money - the council and that - to do things with the place, there just isn't as much going on, which is understandable, but ..."

James emphasized lack of company and things to do..

"Filling in time is the hardest thing. In the city, in a sense, its easier. There's more people living there, more people you can go and see. You can get into cinema's cheap and everything, plus there's the library. If I come into the city I see 3 or 4 people and then just go to the library for an hour, which passes quite a bit of time."

He is concerned that in the village there is only one other person in his position.

"Sometimes we see so much of each other little things start to irritate, so to speak... It's a good thing to know that someone else is around. Two of my friends were on the dole and that was really good. They live nearby and we used to muck about all day..At the moment its only Dick. I mean just one person that I can see, whereas with those two as well, I could sort of alternate between the three of them which was a nice break."

Of course like everyone else the unemployed have personal preferences and if there are only one or two people around during the day there may not be the people they would choose to spend time with. Paul D found himself in this position. "Well there was two people my own age in the same boat as me but we didn't get on really so I was on my own more".

David had moved from the country to the city, which he prefers.

"There's more things to do... You don't have to walk so far to see friends and there were no street lights. There wasn't that much to do either. Most of the people in the village sat in the bus shelter, which I thought was a bit useless and time wasting so I sat at home."

Therefore, it can be seen that virtually all of the ten had the same complaints - lack of things to do, increased isolation and the difficulty and high cost of transport. This affects socializing and ability to get a job. They were also much more likely to mention feelings of stigma than those in the city due, I think, to isolation from those in the same position who might bolster their self image. I will deal with this more fully in chapter 9.

What of the minority who do not object to village life? The four people concerned do not see living in the country as an additional burden on top of their dissatisfaction with life on the dole. The rest of the chapter seeks to explain why the minority is content with village life.

Firstly, the three factors the other ten complain about do apply - but not so strongly. Three out of the four, Paul, Fiona and Wendy are not living in such a remote place as the others. They live in small villages but relatively near a small town and, in the town, each know a group of employed and unemployed ex-school friends with whom they spend a great deal of time socializing. Visiting them requires a long but not impossible walk. They therefore suffer less from the isolation than the others.

Paul understands the problem because he experiences it in winter when the 20-30 minute walk is a less attractive prospect but he considers himself relatively fortunate compared to friends who live further out.

> "If its a bad winter you get isolated anyway. You can't go out. You can't get anywhere. That's the worse. They are little roads - but its not so bad for me as I am quite close to town. A lot of my friends live out on the backroads and you don't see them for months - but on the whole its OK for me."

Fiona does not mind living where she is but does see the distances as a minor disadvantage,

> "Can be sometimes. You want to go to Wymondham and you have to scrounge a lift or get on your walking feet. It takes about twenty minutes or half an hour walking to Wymondham, so there's got to be a good reason."

So these people do see disadvantages in their situation but they are not so great as the other ten village dwellers who live further from the nearest town making walking not really a practical possibility.

All three travel to Norwich regularly and here lies another difference. These three are amongst the most heavily subsidized by their parents; they do not pay for board and they are given money so their financial situation is not so desperately balanced as most of the others. This means that £1.30 return bus fare to Norwich does not assume the same significance.

The third attraction of the area for three of them Paul, Fiona and Jacky is that local contacts have enabled them to find a number of side jobs. - Paul with local builders, Fiona cleaning and modelling and Jacky in stables. Having work to fill in time and provide extra money is an important protective factor and very often depends on personal contacts and these three have more than average access to this type of resource. At the time of the interview Jacky had moved to the city to live with her boyfriend six months previously but would like to return to her village. The fact she had not worked since leaving the village was one of her reasons.

Jacky and Fiona also mentioned the traditional attractions of the countryside such as fresh air and pleasant walks. Fiona said

> "What's it like living so far out? That can be quite nice really. I don't mind living where it is. I don't mind just going for a walk outside, I can go up there (pointing) up there, up there, you know its sort of quite good just going for walks."

I am unsure as to why they should appear to appreciate such things more than the others. Perhaps, it is simply personal preference or perhaps the other factors mean that they are less depressed and therefore in a better frame of mind to appreciate the joys of nature.

The last factor is that, as well as getting a significant financial subsidy from parents, all four get on very well with them and enjoy living at home. Wendy and Paul get on "very well", Fiona "wonderfully" and it was Jacky's main reason for wanting to return to the village. Proximity to her family is the important thing to her, asked if she would like to move back she replied

> "Oh yeah! I'll only be 150 yards from my mum then. The village was better than the city. I used to get up in the mornings, help my mum around the house. It was definitely more fun as I say. We used to do the dinner, get that over and done with, do the washing up, spend the afternoon in the garden take the dogs for a walk. My mum and dad have got a boat so sometimes we would spend the afternoon on the broads. I like being with my mum. I'm a mummy's girl; I'm not afraid to admit it either. Being in the city I can't see my friends so often. All my friends are out there. All I can do is run up the phone bill to my sister back home."

She also appreciates the countryside. Summing up she said

> "I prefer to be in the village mainly because there are more animals around me. You wake in the city and breathe in a good breath of carbon monoxide and yes I like living with my mum. I'm not very independent."

So, to conclude, the majority see little but disadvantages in life on the dole in a small village compared with the city. With a great deal of unanimity they complain of there being nothing going on, nothing to do, added to the isolation and feelings of personal inadequacy and stigma owing to the lack of a community of unemployed people. Also, very significant for most, was the difficulty and expense of travel, £1-30 - £1-50, three or four days a week can be very important to those already living on a financial knife edge.

The minority mostly lived fairly close to a small town where more was going on and most importantly there were employed and unemployed ex school friends to meet. They tended to be well subsidized by parents so the cost of bus fares did not loom large. They also enjoyed living with their family and in the country generally.

11 The political influence of unemployment

"On the whole, however, women and men slumped deeper in their chairs rolled their eyes to convey utter boredom, groaned, and muttered at the very mention of the word politics."

This is an indication of the level of political awareness Coffield, Burrill and Marshall found in their study of about fifty young unemployed people living in the North East (aptly entitled "Growing up in the Margins" 1986 p.191). They found them to be apolitical, deeply suspicious and contemptuous of politicians, racist and anti trade union. Most attempts to discuss politics initiated by the researchers met with determined attempts to change the subject. "These young adults reacted in much the same way to our questions as the majority of people respond to a party political broadcast on television, by reaching as quickly as possible for the off switch." (Ibid p191-192)

Although they did not react with such theatrical eye rolling (perhaps because they were interviewed on their own so there was no peer group pressure to ham it up,) my sample were similarly no hot bed of political enthusiasm.

Before going into the political views of my sample it might be worth looking at the other evidence on this subject. Reviewing the literature, Fraser, Marsh and Joplin (in Roberts et al 1985) describe two views. One is the older traditional view that the unemployed would be attracted towards radicalism either of the left or the right, that they would actively challenge the society that had so little to offer them and this would manifest itself in violence and riots perhaps leading to revolutionary challenges to society itself. The other view, which they describe as the "new orthodoxy", is that unemployment leads people to demoralisation with isolated unemployed blaming themselves rather than society, resulting in an apathetic withdrawal from politics.

Most of the research is American. Fraser et al say that empirical evidence from the UK is "close to being non existent" Roberts et al 1985 (p358) agree that at this stage description rather than theory building is necessary. What evidence exists on the two views is mixed. On the one hand, unemployed people have been found to be more radical and critical in their expressed attitudes and more likely to vote for the political parties of high expenditure than the population generally. Those that are active are more likely to be involved in trade union and other workers organisations, although whether unemployment is a causal factor or whether it is simply a reflection of their class position is unclear. On the other hand they are less likely to vote or participate in political organisation at all. They report that in most opinion polls the unemployed blame both themselves and the government.

British evidence is indeed sparse. Burchell and Devereux (1987) studied 280 teenagers aged 15-18 in Bedford and East London and report finding a strong link between unemployment and radical right-wing ideas, claiming that unemployment has a greater influence on their values than their age, sex, socio-economic status or the age at which they left school.

Psychologist Leslie Francis (1984) carried out a study of unemployed young people staying in a central London YMCA, involving participant observation and in depth interviews but relying mostly on 1085 completed questionnaires. She found two main associations between unemployment and young people-depression, and radicalism. They expressed lack of respect for conventional institutions and moral values, tended to support trade unions, dislike the Conservative party and reject religion. However most were not in any way active only 8% overall but interestingly, rising to 12% of the long term unemployed. Central London YMCA caters for a very transient population, often being the first port of call for people coming from Scotland and the North in search of work. They are therefore probably not a very typical sample of young unemployed people so it would not be safe to generalize too widely on the basis of this data.

Finally, the European Centre for Work interviewed 86 young people aged 17-21 from the West Midlands. They found that two thirds blamed the government rather than themselves but, again, hardly any were politically active.

The evidence as to what, if any, effect unemployment has on the politics of those involved, is then unclear. So how does my sample fit into this picture? Evidence as to the state of their political consciousness at the time was gained by direct questions about their interest in and the extent of any political activities, voting intentions, their explanations for their unemployment and unemployment generally and their attitudes to trade unions.

In common with the findings of other studies, political activity was very rare in my sample. Only Kate could be considered an activist. She was heavily involved in feminist politics, working voluntarily at a Women's Centre, active in women's CND and attending demonstrations. Isabelle had left wing views but was not active. However she said that she intended to become involved in Labour party politics when she had more time after her A levels were finished. Paul described himself as "very interested in politics" and was prepared to argue passionately against the Conservatives in favour of Labour and the trade unions, seeing things in class terms Conservatives for the rich, Labour for workers but was in no way active.

Other than these, only a handful expressed a general interest in even keeping up with the political news on TV for example, while the rest were neither interested nor active.

As for voting intentions, Labour would get the biggest vote, with 15 out of 40 going for them, but this figure was exactly matched by 15 "don't knows" who would not vote. 9 plumped for the SDP/Liberals, though this figure may be inflated by the fact that the SDP/Lib Alliance had a high media profile at the time, and only one would vote Conservative. Considering that the Labour Party is the main opposition to a Government which has presided over most of the rise in unemployment I do not consider this an impressive show of support.

"Most were not members, they had no knowledge of their functions or history and so had no views of any kind to express. When pushed by us to say something, a few replied that they thought unions had too much power and Ben added `they make people go on strike when they don't want to' (Coffield, Burrill & Marshall 1986 p192).

Here is where my findings part company with Coffield's, as most of my respondents were supportive to trade unions. A clear majority of 28 said that they would join a trade union if they were working. Only 2 expressed any hostility; the rest said they didn't know or they didn't understand enough about them.

Those that said they would join proved perfectly capable of answering the question why, explaining the basic function of trade unions in terms of the need for collective power and solidarity if workers are to be protected. Voting intentions did not seem to be connected, with most of the Liberal/SDP voters expressing similar pro union views. Most, of course, were not members but this is quite understandable considering that trade unions consist overwhelmingly of people in work, that most join when they start work and that the majority of trade unions do not allow for unemployed members. Sex did not seem to be a significant factor, for both sexes seemed to recognise the advantages equally. Here are a selection of comments on politics and trade unionism:

Anna said, "I suppose I would, yeah (join a T.U.) because if the boss is unfair you've got someone to back you up haven't you".

Jacqueline, who didn't vote last time and considers herself apolitical, would nevertheless join a trade union because, "They can help you out if you're unfairly dismissed or anything. They can help you out. If anything does go wrong they can help you out negotiating wages and everything which is better than you can do on your own."

Kevin, asked if he would join, answered "Yeah I think so. If someone gave you the sack they'll help you."

Nicola "I think I would join a trade union. I think it gives you some sort of security somewhere along the line."

Neil "I suppose I would to give just that little bit more security."

Paul voted SDP but supported the idea of trade unionism . Once he had an industrial accident injuring his hand and had been sacked without compensation "because I wasn't a member ..... I think I would join because then you know what your rights are and you've got someone else arguing for you, you're not by yourself. Last time I was by myself. I went to the Citizens Advice Bureau to find out bits and bobs but! (shrug) but if you've got the rest of the workforce backing you up then you probably stand a bit more chance".

Peter said "I think they are good because they fight for what they believe in - you know workers and stuff, they really help them out. Yeah I'd definitely join a union. I think they are good".

Their comments (and others like them) may not indicate a group willing to dedicate their lives to the labour movement, but they are at considerable variance with the findings of Coffield et al. They show a much deeper well of support for the trade unions as well as a greater understanding of their function. To me this was surprising as my initial hypothesis when considering this question was that the reverse would be true, that the North with its stronger labour movement traditions would produce a generation more sympathetic to and knowledgeable about trade unions than those from the conservative rural South. I am at a loss to account for this. Perhaps Coffield's technique of group interviews produces more pressure to put forward the conventional, that is media inspired view. This is however merely speculation.

The other area that dealt with politics is their explanations for unemployment and they were asked to account both for their own unemployment and for the general problem. The first question was simply "What causes unemployment?" which, significantly, was almost always interpreted as "What caused your unemployment?". To get general answers I had to follow it up with the specific question "What causes unemployment in general".

Plenty were willing to blame the government. In fact, "Margaret Thatcher" was the most popular single response and she was mentioned by name by twenty four people.

"Margaret Thatcher", said Judy, "she's ballsed the country up - everything was all right until she got in".

Jessie blames "old candy floss head! Maggie Thatcher! She's not spending money the way she should be - spending money on weapons to kill us rather than jobs to live on".

Carl blamed "That woman Margaret Thatcher - she's hopeless".

Adrienne "I blame Margaret Thatcher. I'm afraid I just don't like that woman".

Peter, while not quoting her name, blames the Government. "They just use YTS to keep you off the dole figures, they are all for the rich and don't worry about the middle people - its their neglect".

All this sounds radical but two points need bearing in mind. Firstly, as already pointed out, very few; indeed, none of those quoted above are in anyway active.

Secondly, and I think very significantly, hardly any spontaneously mentioned politics first, blaming Margaret Thatcher almost as an after-thought as a result of my probing. They would start off with their personal reasons and only quote political ones when I probed further with such questions as "Is there anything else to blame?". So they would go from the personal to the political as a result of follow up questions. Some typical examples are as follows. Sarah said, "I'm a failure, there's nothing I can do. I just think I'm no good. (probe) Yes Margaret Thatcher" Mandy commented "I don't know there don't seem to be no jobs about, it ain't nothing I've done, for a lot of them you need experience but you're to young to get experiences. I don't know how they work that one out ... lack of qualifications ... the Government not putting enough into industry". Susan - "Employers are too fussy about who they employ, they want experience but you can't get experience. It's catch 22. I'm unemployable I suppose! I've got a inferiority complex I suppose. I don't know, I really don't know". She replied "Maggie Thatcher" only after further prompting.

Personal reasons, were almost always the first offered, of which the most popular, apart from "don't know", were age, and lack of qualifications and experience, followed by general disparaging comments about themselves being "no good", "unemployable" or "bad luck".

Nicola said "I don't know. I've tried for jobs. I've gone for interviews and everything and I've always got a little letter saying sorry, or they didn't contact me at all - maybe the right job for me hasn't come up yet. I've been looking and trying".

There is a strong tendency to blame themselves before the Government, their lack of experience, age, not working hard enough at school, and so on. One said that lack of money to buy smart clothes for interviews was a problem. One saw a disadvantage in living in the YMCA and that employers felt that people living with their families were more reliable.

A few denied their own experience of ceaseless fruitless job search and blamed unemployment on the unemployeds' laziness. Gary saying "so many don't want to work, just sign on and get money and that's it."

Neil, who's life is a constant round of energetic but disappointing job searching, who desperately wants a job, who hates unemployment and seemed to me to be terribly depressed by it said,

> "I would say that in certain respects you can be better off being unemployed, people who when they are in work aren't getting as much as they would on unemployment benefit and also they get money for flats

> and everything, plus their unemployment benefit. They can go out every night. They can have fun. Whereas, if they are working, they lose that. That is one thing that annoys me and I think that one of the reasons for high unemployment ... I don't think the youngsters of today, or most people to tell the truth, don't want to bother going out to look for a job, because one of the people I know up there, he won't bother to go out and look for a job. YTS is quite a bit to blame for youngsters. They find if they get a bedsit they can get more than on YTS ....most people, it makes me sick, because they won't get out and find work and that's why I think most people, quite a few people, are unemployed, they just can't be bothered to find a job."

Finally, Coffield seemed to find most of his sample racist. I did not ask direct questions on this, so my evidence is negative but happily people did not present themselves as racist. The issue did not come up spontaneously although I encouraged them to talk freely about their opinions. In fact, only one person blamed unemployment on black people or immigration.

Conclusion

At the start of this chapter I outlined two views on unemployment and the effect it might have on the political views of the unemployed. The first argues that the unemployed will lose faith in society - be attracted to radicalism either of the left or the right, riot or in other ways actively oppose society. The second view is that unemployment leads to isolation, demoralisation, a tendency to blame themselves, withdrawing into apathy and away from politics.

My evidence such as it is, tends to favour the latter view. They are not active, show few signs of radicalism and tend to blame themselves first, even if they might blame Thatcher second. One contrary and interesting (and for me heartening) finding was the generally high level of support for trade unions.

However, I think my evidence needs to be treated with caution. The sort of study I have carried out can only provide a 'snap shot' of the feelings of the sample at that time and I do not believe that political consciousness is a static phenomena. At the moment they feel isolated and powerless and this generates apathy. If a political movement either of the right or the left could breach the first two feelings then I believe the last would also change. In the late 1980's, unemployed youth rioted in Algeria to such an extent that a state of emergency has been called, troops patrol the streets and the Government is shaken. Later they flocked to the cause of the radical fundamentalist Islamic Party which won an election but was promptly barred and martial law declared. Yet I feel certain that had a survey of the political attitudes of Algerian youth been done two years before it would have found apathy and feelings of powerlessness dominate. I do believe changes in attitudes and activity can come but suspect that if it does it will probably be lead by the young unemployed of the large industrial cities where large numbers mean a greater chance of them experiencing feelings of collective strength, rather than in the less urban areas of my sample.

12 Exceptions: Enjoying life on the dole

Describing the bleak situation of most of my respondents can be depressing for the reader and researcher so it is with the hope of achieving a lighter heart that I turn to consider the exceptions; that minority who do not mind unemployment and who are not depressed, anxious, worried or even just fed up.

The research literature, both sociological and psychological, stresses how awful unemployment is for most people. Psychological and physical health declines and it is considered by the unemployed as an ordeal, or, at best, an unfortunate event to be coped with. Understandably, virtually all the research has dealt with that vast majority who do not enjoy the experience. However, as in all aspects of human behaviour, there are exceptions to the rule. There are people who do not see the fact of unemployment as a disaster, who do more than just cope and their experience might offer a useful point of comparison with that of the majority. The only researchers I have come across who have looked at this issue are Fryer and Payne (1984) who discovered what they called proactive behaviour amongst 5% or so of the unemployed. They discovered that the mental health of this minority improved because they either gave up unpleasant and depressing jobs that were having a negative effect on them, or they found something that filled their time in a way they perceived as more meaningful. Their study was different from mine in that it involved adult redundant people.

I found seven young people who did not object to their unemployment. I now intend to examine the experience of these seven to discover if there are coping strategies that are so successful as to make life on the dole enjoyable.

There are few enough of them to describe each individually and some have been largely dealt with before. Karl for example has been adequately described in chapter 7. The main point about his situation is that he is hardly unemployed at all, except officially. His uncle owns a pub and he can work for him for as many hours as he wishes, so much of his time is occupied and he has few money problems. He is also assisted by a working girlfriend who will lend him money if he needs it and indulgent parents who feed and house him for nothing. It is worth pointing out that his situation is likely to be temporary as he says that when his parents start to ask for board money he will look for a more permanent job and, anyway, this is likely to come via the same uncle who intends to open a night club and has offered him a full time official job.

Phillip was interviewed at the end of his period of enjoying life on the dole as he had started to energetically look for work in order to buy a flat with his working girlfriend. The first factor that made him an exception is again work. He worked "on the side" for a friend who has a small building firm and he fixes and resprays motor bikes, which is really an extension of his hobby. These jobs provide extra money and help fill his time with activity which he positively enjoys. Secondly, he lives with his girlfriend who works and they pool their money as a couple. This helps keep up his financial standards. Thirdly, and very important, he participates in the "biker" subculture, which has a number of benefits. It provides customers for his motor bike work, unemployed friends during the day and this culture puts a low emphasis on consumer goods, smart clothes and night clubs, - which means he needs and is satisfied with less money. He worries less about it "I don't have money problems as such, I don't need much money .... I don't like money." These factors have meant that in the five years he has been unemployed he has had sufficient money, he has had his time well filled with activities he considers meaningful and obtains subcultural support which obviates any sense of shame or stigma.

The subcultural element is a main factor for Charlotte. The other important points are her relationships and her housing situation. She is living with her boyfriend and their baby in a council house and sees this as a huge improvement as her previous life in "horrible bedsits". She moves in a semi hippy music orientated subculture, which is different from Phillip's but carries many of the same benefits. Money, consumer goods, new clothes and night clubs receive a low emphasis-so lack of these things is not considered so important. The work ethic is also downgraded so there is none of the sense of stigma so often reported by the others. The subculture is also a source of friends, "Never a day goes by without someone dropping in". She plays and sings in bands from which she earns a little money but mostly the benefit comes from the social side and the pleasure of the activity itself. Much of her time is taken up with rehearsing. She contrasted her present active social life with an earlier period when she was depressed and apathetic, largely due to living in unsatisfactory accommodation. She would spend

> "lots of time in bed, sometimes never seeing daylight in winter, drinking

> a lot, at one time taking drugs a lot, it gets very nasty, you end up taking drugs just not to feel depressed. Giro day was like the highlight of every fortnight, you would just spend it on stupid things. I would get drunk a lot and I remember being miserable a lot. Now my life is very full. I never just do nothing. I remember doing nothing a lot."

It now adds up to a satisfactory life as far as she is concerned

> "It's a really really good life. I just couldn't conceive of working five or even six days, I don't know how anyone does it. I mean like you have a life on the dole, it may be unfortunate that other people have to pay you but my parents have paid enough tax to keep me on the dole for life. It's wonderful being on the dole, really you have all this free time. Doing a job like washing up or working in a factory that no one really wants to do but you need the money must be a nightmare. I'd love the money sure, but I just couldn't spend 70% of my waking time doing it. I just can't see how it can be worth it."

The joys of subcultural life should not be exaggerated, for other people, like Francis and David, find their membership of a subculture a help but would still rather work for they certainly do not enjoy unemployment. On it's own, the protection afforded by a subculture is insufficient to make life on the dole a pleasant experience. Rather, it is the **combination** of the steady successful relationship, baby, good housing and subcultural activities that is so effective rather than just one factor.

The case of Isobel, can be dealt with very briefly. Like Karl, she is only unemployed officially, for in fact, she is a student. At twenty, after what she describes as an aimless and depressing period on the dole, she has decided to get her A levels and go to University or Art College. She is doing two A levels in the day and one in the evening, for which she is not obliged to inform the DHSS. This arrangement means that she is officially doing only 12 hours so is entitled to claim Supplementary Benefit as long as she declares herself available for work. An optimistic and dedicated student she does her college work all day and expects to get grade A's so, for her, dole is simply a substitute for the discretionary grants that are virtually nonexistent in Norfolk. The situation is strictly temporary and would not exist if there were an adequate system of student grants. Her situation is also helped by supportive parents who do not ask for board money. Her dole is therefore spending money.

Carl and Joanne have a lot in common and so can be considered together. Both have an overwhelming interest and ambition which means they are not really interested in conventional jobs. For Carl it is boxing and he wants to turn professional at some stage. Joanne wants to be a dancer. Both fill their time with training and life on the dole gives them time to do this. Periods of unemployment can therefore be considered part of their apprenticeship.

Joanne is further along her particular road. She has an agent and has dancing jobs lasting from one day to three weeks in holiday centres and entertaining the troops in Northern Ireland. Usually, she signs off while she is working. Her time is pleasantly filled with training and rehearsing with the other young women from her dance troupe. She says that she is starting to feel like a dancer rather than unemployed.

Carl lived in the YMCA and trains in the Gym everyday, of unemployment he says "I don't mind because it gives me more time to train.... I got something to do. I ain't bored like some people."

His vision of the future is of a successful boxing career with a prosperous life style. He would not mind a job but makes it clear that boxing would have to come first. The job would have to be a heavy labouring type job to build up his muscles for boxing. He has other advantages, such as the odd irregular job on the side organised by contacts made through boxing and he is subsidised financially in a small way by his working girl friend, but it is his enjoyment of boxing and his boxing ambitions that make the difference.

I have met him several times in the two years since the interview and domestic responsibilities have caught up with him. His girl friend became pregnant and was classified as homeless so they received a council flat, all of which he is pleased about. "At least one part of my life is going OK." Motivated by the responsibilities, he has found a factory job and is waiting for a job on the oil rigs, which he was offered but it has been postponed since the Piper Alpha disaster, as several rigs have been shut down for safety refits. He retains his boxing ambitions training regularly in the evenings.

Susan L's situation was changed by the arrival of a baby. She had been unemployed for two years and spent the first year or so living in the YMCA and now has a council flat. Her interview is full of comparisons between what she considers an aimless boring life before her baby and the vastly more satisfactory situation after. Specifically the baby bought her a routine, "something to do", a sense of purpose and a feeling of being needed. She now has independence in a flat, which she showed me round with obvious pride. The following are just a sample of the quotes that demonstrate this.

> "I've got a flat, I've got a baby, I'm on my own. I find it hard looking after him but I am getting in a routine now. I like looking after him, I like what I've got, I've done well, the flat I am pleased with the baby and that" Friends (met at the YMCA) come round and see me, I go out when I want to .... I like it, I like doing what I'm doing now. I've got my own place, I do what I want". "Yeah there is a big difference, yeah well now you've always got something to do. I can't turn round and say I'm bored, I've got hoovering to do, look after him, I'm not wandering round doing nothing

> if you know what I mean, I cook for myself, I can have anything I want to eat, it's better than being in a bedsit or any thing like that."

Asked about her feelings about being unemployed she replied

> "It can get boring (laugh!), like it all depends. I've now got a baby. It's alright if you've got something to do. I do house work, I look after him but if I was living like I used to live in the YM and things like that, it does get boring. Yeah, I wish I had had a job then but I got my own flat and a baby - you're doing things all the time."

She described a typical day before the arrival of her baby, putting on a bored voice

> "go down the city look about the shops, didn't have much money, just do that sort of general thing, just go to the YM for tea, go out for a drink at night, get up to do the same old thing everyday, that's what everyone does nowadays. I mean go out now and everyone's down Chapelfield Park, its just one of them things."

This is a huge contrast with the way she sees her present situation.

> "Do I prefer now? Yes I do I know I've got someone who needs me, if you know what I mean" Of the YMCA she said "It was alright but you got everything done for you, there's nothing to do ... its just a sort of bed and breakfast place. I mean everyone just sit there you can't cook or nothing, everything, everything's just done for you I mean I got my own place, which I prefer. Its best to have your own place isn't it". Of her flat she said 'Oh yeah I'm proud of it. I am pleased with it. I keep it clean and tidy I can't really ask for more can I."

She seemed very lively, cheerful and generally on top of things, the flat was spotless and friends were helping her to decorate. Her flat had become something of a meeting place for friends still living in the YMCA who chipped in to hire videos and pay the video machine rental, so she was not isolated. There was no signs of the vague "disengaged" look or manner of speaking that characterised many of the other young people in my sample. Although she said she did not get pregnant deliberately, having a baby does seem to her to be an acceptable solution to the problems of unemployment, providing a role, a routine, independence and a sense of meaning in her life. Of course this would not be the case for everyone. Adrienne for example found that the strains of lone parenthood depressed her and eventually the baby was taken into care. Susan F, pregnant at the time of interview, and very depressed, was looking forward to the baby's birth hoping that it would also answer her problems. At least it had got her a room in the Umbrella housing association, a half-way house to an independent council flat.

Conclusion

Seven people out of the forty interviewed were exceptions in that they have had periods on the dole when they are not looking for work and have been fairly happy with their situation. At nearly 20% of the sample this is much higher than the 5% found by Fryer and Payne (1984). This does not strike me as surprising as Fryer and Payne's research centred on adults who had more commitments, had got used to the working routine and whose feelings of self identity would more likely to have been conditioned by long years at work. Temporary periods of unemployment without worrying too much about it are therefore much more likely to be associated with young people and apparently, in the USA, a period of 'Milling around' going from job to job with intermittent periods of unemployment is considered normal or even healthy for young people before they decide on which career to settle in (Gaskell and Jameson 1980, Freeman & Wise 1982).

It is worth emphasizing that, for most, this is a temporary period. Most will work eventually if it is available. Karl is likely to be working officially for his uncle. Phillip wants to move to the next stage of his life by buying a home with his girlfriend and so is energetically looking for work. The birth of his child has prompted Carl to find work in a factory and his immediate goal has become higher paid employment on the oil rigs. Isobel will undoubtedly go to university or art school and find a middle class job. "Straight down the line to success", was her assessment of her future.

So do these seven have answers to the problems of unemployment, of living fulfilled lives on the dole? A number of points emerge. Firstly, plenty of illegal work helps; it provides money, fills time with purposeful activities, provides interest and the opportunity to learn useful new skills. Secondly, social and financial support of family, friends or a partner can help make for a good life. It was notable that all the male exceptions had employed girlfriends. Thirdly, the unemployed could become part of a subculture that does not value work and the material benefits of work. They would thus worry much less about consumer goods, clothes, going to night clubs and the sub culture provides for the social support offered by like minded people. A burning interest in something such as Carl's boxing, Joanne's dancing and Charlotte's music is an enormous help particularly if there is an ambition to make it a career. Then a routine can be constructed around training and practising, filling in time in an enjoyable and constructive way and so removing feelings of boredom and aimlessness.

Then, there is the prospect of having a baby, either with a partner as in Charlotte's case, or without as in Susan's. This provides a routine of meaningful activity, a role to replace the stigmatized one of "unemployed", a feeling of being needed, and tangible benefits like an independent flat.

The problem is that such solutions are not generally applicable. Work "on the side" is not easy to find, as I indicated in chapter 7, it depends largely on contacts, who can not just be invented. I also suspect that interest in dancing, boxing or youth sub culture cannot be forced, that without a genuine interest it will not seem meaningful. Also, not every young women would relish Susan's approach; for Adrienne having a baby is not so much a solution as a problem in itself.

Finally, studying the exceptions and comparing them with the others further illustrates the maxim coined earlier "Good citizens suffer most". Those who are "Good citizens" as defined in conventional terms, who want a regular legal job rather than side work, who hold mainstream values rather than sub cultural ones, who want to work hard and reap rewards in terms of consumer goods, smart clothes and later a house and family and who want to do this in the conventional job and married way are the ones who will suffer most. In other words unemployment is odd in that it punishes the conformist rather than the deviant.

13 An emerging underclass?

"'Underclass' is an ugly word" writes Charles Murray in his famous polemic *The Emerging British Underclass* and it is easy to agree with him on this point at least. However, since he has done so much to popularise the term and because it has been taken up by other writers from different political standpoints, such as Frank Field (1989) and J K Gailbraith (1994), as well as gaining some general usage, it has become a difficult one to avoid. Writers and researchers and anybody else trying to come to grips with the reality of large scale youth unemployment seem bound to consider it as a concept.

Before discussing what light this study can throw on the emergence or otherwise of an underclass, it has to be admitted that the evidence provided here is inevitably limited. This is firstly because of the limited size of the sample and the area in which it took place. On this last point it might be objected that high youth unemployment in the formerly comparatively prosperous South East of England is of relatively recent origin, being a product of the recession of the early 1980s and more particularly the early 1990s. While making the evidence up to date as this is the area most hard hit recently, it could mean that the process is not as advanced as elsewhere. Further unemployment is still not as high or as concentrated as in areas such as parts of London or the industrial North and this could mean that the situation is different. However Murray (1990 p68-82) urges researchers to engage in face to contact with the unemployed and as this is exactly what has been done in this study, it would perhaps seem permissible to comment. Further few studies can be expected to stand alone and give definitive answers to difficult and complex social questions. Most fit into a body of research adding a piece of evidence that helps make up the general picture. This is the case here. As shall be demonstrated below there have been other researchers, some from areas of traditionally high long term unemployment, that both strengthen the evidence of this study and are strengthened by it.

One problem posed by this area is that there is no unanimity as to definitions of the 'underclass' or as to what groups it might be comprised of. Sometimes the 'underclass' is seen as those groups at the bottom of the class structure, who are separated from the rest by 'income, life chances and aspirations' (Field 1989). Or as Gary Ruciman (quoted in D Smith 1992) describes them:

> Those members of British Society whose roles place them more or less permanently at the economic level where benefits are paid by the State to those unable to participate in the labour market at all.

This view sees the creation of such a class, or group, as mainly the result of social and economic changes. Behavioural and culture factors are secondary. However, they do edge in with Field for example, (inAnalysis 1992) adding that these groups:

> ... are not prepared to rejoin Great Britain Ltd. Not on the terms on offer. Those terms. Should these jobs become available. Now that group is different from the vast majority of the unemployed. Most of whom are anxious to join the world of work on almost any terms.

Murray is more forthright in attributing the growth of the underclass which he claims to detect, largely to one factor: their behaviour. The 'early warning signals' are 'illegitimacy, violent crime and drop out from the labour force' and it is not all the poor or all the unemployed who qualify for inclusion but those who include themselves by their behaviour. *The Emerging Underclass* makes this clear. That the underclass has different value and, of particular relevance here, these values would cause them to reject work even if it were to be available. They are not simply unemployed but 'unemployable'- a term ironically most used when there are few jobs to be had - but more about that later. To quote Murray (1990):

> When I use the term 'underclass' I am indeed focusing on a certain type of poor person defined not by his condition eg long term unemployed, but by his deplorable behaviour in response to that condition, eg unwilling to take the jobs available to him.

I am not talking here about an unemployment problem that can be solved by more jobs, not about a poverty problem that can be solved by higher benefit.

> . . . the definitive proof that an underclass has arrived is that large numbers of young, healthy, low income males choose not to take jobs.

Twice Murray offers a challenge: create a few hundred well paid jobs and offer them to young men from a poor neighbourhood. It is predicted that these men will either refuse to take them, or quite quickly fail to cope with the work discipline. (Along I am sure with many others, I deeply regret that such an experiment is likely to fall outside my means.) Thus proving they are undoubtedly unemployable members of a dangerous underclass. The benefit system is implicated in this reluctance to work. Benefits are said to make it rational for young people to refuse work. The same argument is applied to young single mothers who are seen as rationally choosing to rely on the state.

The notion of deserving and undeserving is explicitly stated. An idea stemming from his background.

> I was taught by my middle class parents that there were two kinds of poor people. One class of poor people was never even called 'poor'. I came to understand that they simply lived with low incomes, as my own parents had done when they were young. Then there were another set of poor people, just a handful of them. These poor people didn't just lack money. They were defined by their behaviour. Their homes were littered and unkempt. The men in their families were unable to hold down a job for more than a few weeks at a time. Drunkenness was common. (1990 p1)

A Sunday Times editorial (26/11/1989) emphasises the negative connotations associated with this view.

> The underclass spawns illegitimate children without a care for tomorrow and feed on a crime rate that rivals the United States in property offences. Its able-bodied youths see no point in working and feel no compulsion either. They reject society while feeding off it. They are becoming a lost generation giving the cycle of deprivation a new spur . . . No amount of income redistribution or social engineering can solve their problem. Their sub-lifestyles are beyond welfare benefit rises and job creation schemes. They exist as active social outcasts, wedded to an anti-social system. (quoted in Oppenheim 1990 p24/25)

David Green ends the preface to Murray's work by suggesting a new rallying cry 'Bring back stigma all is forgiven'.

In all cases, this is seen as a growing and qualitatively new phenomena.

Murray's views are, of course, contested with many comments either defining the 'underclass' differently or denying its existence at all. It is often objected that approaches such as Murray's in effect involve 'blaming the victim'. Kirk Mann (1992) sums this up well.

> What Murray does illustrate is the fact that it is all too easy to slide from the identification of a social group who suffer social problems, into the position where the victim is regarded *as* the social problem.

What light can this research throw on these problems? Firstly the overall impression of the vast majority of the interviews is of a group often isolated and excluded from the activities of their working counterpart. However, it clearly emerges that this is because of their *condition* ie unemployment, rather than their *behaviour*. The isolating factors are practical problems such as lack of money for a social life, and the other problems described in Chapter 6 and elsewhere. Behaviour only becomes relevant when these factors cause demoralisation which itself aggravates the situation. They are not a matter of values and it has been emphasised throughout that the majority hold mainstream values, conventional opinion and desire and envisage a conventional life pattern. They want a 'proper job' and the things that this makes possible, smart clothes, a commercial social life and in the longer term a separate independent home, marriage and a family. The source of their pain is that they are denied these. They are the conventional 'good citizens' who suffer most. The non-deviants who are nevertheless punished. They will join the working majority the moment they are able to.

What about the exception of the last chapter? Two points need to be repeated. The first is that most would have probably been in the same position whatever the job market and similar people have existed in every historical period. However, this is not because they make up some kind of eternal 'underclass'. Some are going through a sort of 'apprenticeship' while they attempt to build an alternative career, in boxing or dancing for example. Others are enjoying an alternative life style but this is not new and cannot be seen as part of a qualitative different phenomena.

This leads to the second point. For most this is a temporary state of affairs, linked to their youth. They will re-enter the job market after an interval, should this prove possible.

Certainly there may be some individuals who choose differently but this would be a genuinely residual problem were it not for the fact that the employment situation is so poor. On this 'problem' I would agree with Gailbraith (1994) when he says:

> There will be seeming abuse, to be sure. Some will always choose to live in idleness on the safety net. That we must accept: people are not perfect. A preference for leisure is not wholly unknown to the rich.

As stated earlier it is possible that things may be different in areas of higher, more concentrated, longer established unemployment but the evidence points to the situation being not so very different. Bradshaw and Holmes (1989), for example, found that people living on benefit in Tyne and Wear little different in their values than working people.

> At a time when British poverty is again being discussed in terms of an underclass, it is of crucial importance to recognise that these familiar and probably millions more like them living on social security benefits, are in no sense a detached and isolate group cut off from the rest of society. They are just the same people as the rest of the population, with the same culture and aspirations but simply too little money to be able to share in the activities and possession of everyday life with the rest of the population. ('Living on the Edge' quoted in Oppenheim 1993 p24)

Heath (in D Smith 1992) reports similar findings. McRae and Young (reported by A Walker in Murray 1990) reports that the young unemployed placed great importance on having jobs. My research found precisely the same attitudes, so limited though it is, it does offer a small piece of supporting evidence to a larger body of findings.

'Illegitimacy' is another factor central to Murray's analysis. Because of the limited size of the sample the possibility that young women might become pregnant in order to gain access to housing and benefits has to be left open. However, to 'come clean' I do not believe that this happens - at least certainly not on any significant scale. Where unemployment may be a factor is in that motherhood offers a role other than the stigmatised one of 'unemployment' for those left with few alternatives. That they have been left with no alternatives is the result of a predicament not their own choosing but one which they are forced to survive. The concept of 'blame' seems hardly applicable. The young women concerned said that they had not become pregnant deliberately. The element of choice came in having the baby and this may well have been influenced by the perceived emptiness of their lives.

Murray argues cogently in favour of the concept of 'blame'. He has an attractive point to make about reducing our readiness to call people victims (p71) and crediting people with individual responsibility. Describing what would be his own attitude should a daughter of his come home pregnant, he says:

> I am not obliged to throw her out of the house. But I will think what she did is wrong. Not just a mistake, not just a miscalculation, but wrong. I will tell her so. I will love her, help her and think hard thoughts about the male who collaborated and find fault with myself as a father . . . but none of this will change the underlying reaction that is in my view essential for the sustenance of a civilised society. I will blame her.

Who one blames and for what is essentially a matter of values and it might well be wise to think twice about labelling people as helpless victims. However so much depends on work in our society, from immediate avoidances of poverty, through establishing adult status and identity, to achieving a desired life plan, that in long periods of mass unemployment, it does not seem unreasonable to regard the unemployed as 'victims'. Even if, and it seems unlikely, it could be proved that young women were getting pregnant in order to get council housing and benefits, or to find an acceptable role for themselves, it would seem harsh to blame them rather than a society that offers so little in the way of alternatives.

The crux of the matter is attitude to job creation. Murray and others are clear. For them the major problem is voluntary drop out from the labour market, so training initiative and job creation will not solve the problem of the underclass. This research suggests otherwise Kirk Mann (1992 p 107) details attempt in previous historical periods to identify groups of unemployables. Of Murray's polemic he writes:

> Murray correctly points out that historically there have been numerous attempts at identifying an underclass. What he fails to mention is that while each generation has seen a sub-status within the working class, each period has also witness the rehabilitisation of that stratum. The Victorian residuum appears to have evaporated in the heat of the First WorldWar. Likewise, the class of unemployables of the inter-war period failed to survive the Second World War. Why, we must ask, have these disappeared if the values of the underclass are transmitted across generations.

Mann is substantially correct. Certainly this sample of unemployed young people would be quickly reabsorbed into the labour market should adequate numbers of decent jobs materialise. It might be wise to qualify this by admitting that some long term unemployed might have initial problems with adapting to work, but past experience does not suggest extended difficulties.

One further qualification is that many might reject employment if the jobs created are low paid and exploitative. Murray refers to 'decent' jobs but it is not clear if he and I would agree on what this means. The same argument goes for training schemes. If these are perceived as unlikely to lead to jobs and more concerned with massaging the unemployment figures than providing genuine training, then some may well reject them. Paul Connery (Analysis 1992) puts this well.

> While there is a very high level of disillusionment about the range of initiatives that are on offer through the employment services, through other government agencies. There will have to be a qualitative change in what's on offer to people like that to bring them back into employment. The nature of job growth over the last 10-15 years consists of highly

> insecure, unsafe, low paid jobs. Jobs that are paying £50-60 per week gross, particularly where people have got dependants. Paying a net income below what benefit entitlement would pay . . . clearly an expansion of those kinds of jobs is not going to tempt people back into the labour force.

He may well be right. The problem here is the quality as well as the quantity of jobs. Is a refusal to accept abject gross exploitation to be the qualification for underclass membership? My own view is that the issue is not over generous benefits tempting people to adopt underclass lives, but unemployment or low paid, miserable exploitative jobs. Jobs that condemn people to relative poverty even when in full time employment.

Finally, however, it might not be wise to totally reject all the views of Murray, Field and other supporters of the underclass thesis. People are affected by their social situation and unemployment dominates the lives of most of those unfortunate enough to experience it. In Chapter 3 The Pilgrim Trust (1938) was quoted.

> The unemployed are not simply units of employability who can through the medium of the dole, be put into cold storage and taken out again immediately they are needed. While they are in cold storage things are likely to happen to them.

This could be correct. Unemployment is a miserable and alienating experience and should it continue indefinitely it would not be surprising if alienated groups were produced. One reason for the popularity of the belief that there is a large underclass in existence now is the fears of the more fortunate section of society. This has been true at least since the time of the early industrial revolution which produced a preoccupation with the 'problem of order'. If we condemn groups of young people to perpetual unemployment with no hope and no chance to participate, there may be much to fear. Already there is strong evidence that links growing property crime to unemployment. Dickerson (reported in the Guardian 1994) for example has demonstrated that the figures for burglary almost exactly match the rise and fall of the unemployment of young males.

Does this contradict the earlier part of this chapter? Not really, it leads to a conclusion similar to that of Hawsley (Analysis 1992) that there is a danger of creating an alienated group (which I would prefer not to call an underclass) if unemployment should continue indefinitely but 'the evidence at the moment is that this process is not yet very far advanced'.

What would be dangerous would be if the stress on behaviour and in particular voluntary rejection of work should be accepted. This could easily be used to justify inaction in the face of unemployment. Equally it could lead to justification for cutting benefits, a project more likely to force people into crime than into non-existent jobs. All this would be tempting for a government ideologically committed to leaving such matters to the market alone. Yet, as we have seen, past 'underclasses' mostly dissolved once unemployment returned. This one would too, if enough decent jobs were created. Murray sees job creation as largely irrelevant to solving the problem of the 'underclass'. On the contrary it is the key.

14 Conclusion: Living a predicament

In the first chapter, the core model of casually-related factors was introduced (here reproduced as Fig.13.1) as well as a number of ameliorating and exacerbating factors, such as family support, work 'on the side', and so on.The conclusion will present a summary of the findings and a re-examination of these factors and the interrelationship between them. Some statistical correlations from a data summary will be presented.The paper will conclude by evaluating the overall model which has been used to analyse the research. The statistical correlations presented below may be misleading as they only present analysis of two variables at a time and the situation is a good deal more complex.This will be explained in the text.

All factors are correlated against the depression/dissatisfaction categories. This is divided into four sections as described in the introduction and in chapter 9. These are rough and ready categories which stemmed naturally from the research. These categories and the correlations constructed below are intended as a convenient means to organise a discussion of causal factors rather than provide a basis for statistically significant multi-variable analysis.

Category One describes people who not only reported feeling very depressed and having a range of symptoms such as crying alone, being prescribed anti-depressant drugs, feeling worthless, lacking in confidence and even suicidal. They also looked and sounded depressed. Category Two describes those who expressed strong dissatisfaction with their situation.They reported often feeling 'down' about being unemployed or sometimes 'depressed', to use their own words but their answers - and their bearing indicated - that dissatisfaction rather than depression was the more accurate description and, although most could be described as very dissatisfied, the distinction between Categories One and Two seems marked. Category Three were also dissatisfied, but were cheerful and optimistic. Category Four are those described in the chapter 12 as enjoying a life of unemployment. Categories Two and Three represent a continuum of dissatisfaction arbitrarily separated. This is in contrast to Categories One and Four, which seem much more distinct with a wider gulf separating them from the next category, and appeared to the interviewer as much more obviously separate categories.

The breakdown into these categories was as follows:

Category One	Severely Depressed	10
Category Two	Strongly dissatisfied and sometimes depressed	16
Category Three	Dissatisfied	7
Category Four	Exceptions	7

So what factors correlate with depression, dissatisfaction or the lack of it? It is important to realise that one factor may tend to exacerbate or ameliorate the situation, but no factor works in isolation. Any factor may be important or even dominant; on the other hand it might be overwhelmed by contrary factors. These interrelations between factors are very important and the methodology was designed to discover these interrelationships. This is then an 'other things being equal' approach. For example, having access to above average amounts of illegal work in the informal economy is a protective factor, other things being equal, but they may not be, so the protective power of this factor may be lost.

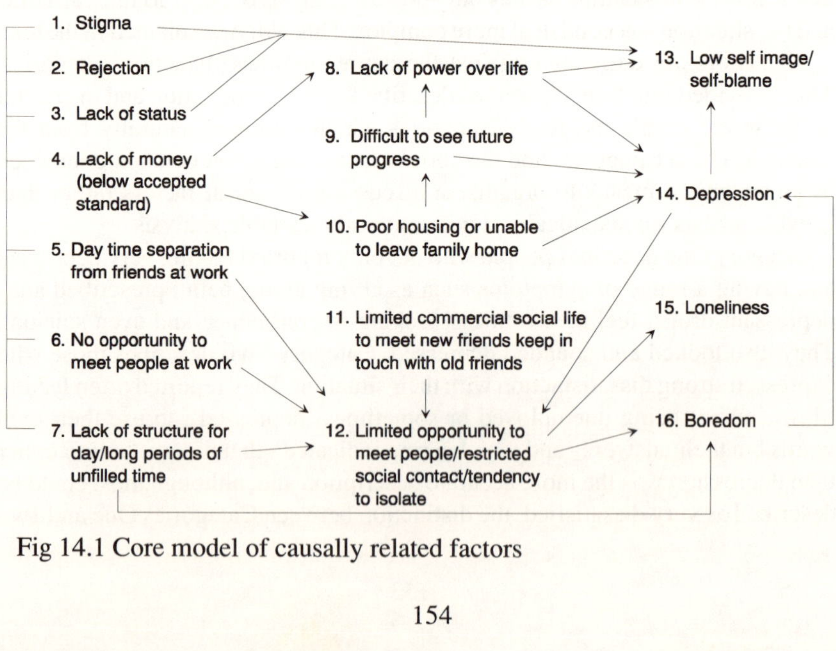

Fig 14.1 Core model of causally related factors

Findings

Rural/urban

One of the most distinctive features about this piece of research is that it looks not only at the situation of those in a city of relatively low unemployment, but also it deals with people from small villages. Both groups, but particularly the latter, have hardly been researched. So how does life in tiny rural villages compare for the unemployed with that in Norwich City?The statistical correlation is as follows:

Table 14.1
Rural Residence correlating with Depression

	Depressed	Very Dissatisfied	Dissatisfied	Exceptions
Rural	3	6	2	0
Urban	7	8	2	0
Ex. of both	0	2	0	1

This does not demonstrate a very clear-cut relationship, which is interesting because ten out of fourteen people who lived or had lived in villages whilst unemployed could see nothing but disadvantages in the rural unemployment situation. There was a large measure of agreement as to why. Firstly, there was a lack of 'things to do' and while this does not apply only to the unemployed, the unemployed have more time on their hands and so this tends to become a more pressing problem. Secondly, difficulty and cost of travel was also a problem. They travel to Norwich both for the purpose of job-seeking and for leisure, and the cost of £1.40 - £1.50 several times a week can severely strain an overstretched meagre budget.Thirdly, and very importantly, there were very few, and sometimes no other unemployed people in the village. This led to isolation and loneliness during the day, as well as increasing their visibility as unemployed which leads to the feelings of personal inadequacy and stigma, the lack of a community of unemployed people being a particular problem.

The minority that did not see rural living as a disadvantage mostly lived close to a small town where there was more going on and a community of employed and unemployed ex-school-friends, so they were not as isolated.They were also above averagely subsidised by their parents and so did not see the expense and travel as such an issue.

What strongly emerges from the interview data is that for these reasons, the situation of the unemployed is worse in small villages than it is in cities.That they are not all depressed is due to other factors.A general theory can be devised from this. Due to a lack of a community of unemployed to provide support (i.e. 'we're all in the same boat' attitude), being unemployed where the unemployment rate is low is an extra burden. This creates a feeling of being more visible as unemployed, a feeling of standing out as a failure, and this invites comparisons with employed friends and neighbours. These comparisons are damaging to one's self-image and there is a hightened sense of stigma. Although this is particularly strong in small villages where there are only a few, or even only one person unemployed, it should also hold true in cities like Norwich compared with areas of high youth unemployment. People ask themselves questions like 'why me?' 'why have I failed?' 'what is wrong with me?'. In other words, a hightened sense of self-blame is likely where unemployment rates are relatively low. There should also be a greater tendency to use the employed culture, especially other young adults such as friends from school, as a reference group when the individual assesses his or her success or failure in life, rather than using others in the same position. If this is the case, then judgements made about the self are likely to be negative.

More research is needed comparing areas of high and low unemployment. Rural unemployment in any case has hardly been researched. Kasl and Gore (Kasl, 1975; Kasl et al, 1975; Gore, 1978) have compared the situation of unemployment in rural and industrial areas, and found the opposite of my conclusions. They found that the rural unemployed showed less stress, and they explain this by suggesting they receive more social support. However, the situation was completely different. They researched adults; unemployment levels were higher; and very significantly, this was a homogeneous minority group, a Polish community. It is not difficult to imagine why traditions of solidarity derived from minority status might alter the situation. More in tune with my findings are those ofWilliamson (1974) and Osgood (1977) in the USA. They found rural areas to be more hostile to the unemployed and this was a situation where unemployed people were more isolated and visible.

A complicating factor emerges from Jahoda's famous work, 'Marienthal' (1933 & 1972), the study of an Austrian town hit by unemployment. This was a one-industry town, where nearly everyone was thrown out of work when that industry collapsed. This caused a decline in all communal and social life, with the community unable to support individuals. This raises the possibility that several situations are possible, each related to the level of unemployment. The first is the situation I have described with unemployed people feeling visible, comparing themselves to the employed and finding themselves wanting. Here, there would be a tendency for both the community and the unemployed individual to blame that individual. The second would be a situation where unemployment is high, and most people's friends are unemployed.The tendency here would be to use other unemployed as a reference group, making it difficult to feel a sense of blame. In the third situation, the unemployed rate is so high that community morale collapses. Kelvin and Jarrett (1985) speculate along similar lines:

"Taken together, these various findings suggest that there may be an optimal level of unemployment for any one community, such that the community may then have both the resources and the will to support the jobless. That however is a matter for further research." (p.59)

Time

As described in chapter 4, problems with finding meaningful 'things to do', with filling long hours of unstructured time dominate many of the interviews. Other researchers have found links with problems of filling in time and poor psychological health, and have found that 'positive activities' can help but not eliminate the worse effects of unemployment. (See chapters 3 and 4)

Unsurprisingly, there is a strong correlation with reported depression/ dissatisfaction and reported problems with time:

Table 14.2
Problems with Time correlated with Depression

	Depressed	Very Dissatisfied	Dissatisfied	Exceptions
Severe	9	2	0	0
Often	1	11	4	0
Occasional	0	3	3	0
None	0	0	0	7

The most striking thing about the table is the extremes: most people who seem depressed and report depression and stress also report severe problems with time, and conversely, all the 'exceptions', those who enjoy their lives on the dole, have their time well-filled with meaningful activities. People may, of course, reflect upon their situation and the study shows that many of them recognise the problem and the effect on them: 'You can make it good', says Jessie, '... If you let unemployment get you down, you get depressed a lot, the unemployment gets you down a lot. If you go out and occupy yourself you don't get depressed so much'.

Others spoke in the same vein about having to make a conscious effort of the will to 'do things', which may be job-seeking, or hobbies or past-times, or you 'vegetate' (David). In other words, the need is to guard against falling into apathy and depression by making an effort to be active. Avoiding this vicious circle is no easy task. Jessie had decided to attend photographic classes to 'get into photography', using the new camera she had received for Christmas but, when I met her six months later, she still had not done so as she felt too 'down' to make the effort.

Problems with time have been noted by a number of researchers and this study confirms it is a major problem. (see the various works of Jahoda, Warr and the European Centre for Work, 1983; Brenner and Bartell, 1983; Stokes, 1983; Kelvin, 1984) However, it is not a completely independent variable; it is strongly linked to lack of money, which results from being without a wage. The central fact about the unemployed is that their spending power falls below what they consider an acceptable minimum - so they cannot afford to fill their time by doing the things they want to do. In other words, their cultural expectations have taught them to want to do things they cannot afford and, for this age group, this tends to mean a commercial social life.

On the other hand, this factor is not totally reducible to lack of money. Extra unstructured hours during the day need to be filled: most young people are used to that time being structured by school, and expect work to do the same. These hours therefore drag and appear purposeless. To some extent, school summer holidays will have accustomed them to this situation and this may be one of the reasons why so many psychologists' studies report that the psychological health as measured by the GHQ of unemployed youth is poorer than that of employed in the same age group, but not so bad as that of the older redundant worker. (See, for example, Warr's 1985 review of these studies). Twenty years of work will have conditioned a greater reliance on work to fill and structure time during the day. However, this is only the relative advantage of one unfortunate group over another; very few relish a 'permanent summer holiday'.

Time also relates to the tendency towards isolation which makes it more difficult to fill in time by meeting and 'going round with' friends. Extreme situations like being the only unemployed person in a village make time harder to fill. As already stated, if friends help fill time, then time must be more of a problem for the more isolated people unemployed in areas of relatively low unemployment. Even in such areas, of course, some will have friends they met at school for example, with whom they are used to filling in holiday time, and this continued availability of friends may be another advantage over the redundant older person.

Friends/Isolation

Chapter 6 stated that unemployment tends to restrict social contacts and that a reasonable hypothesis would be that the more isolated individuals would be more prone to depression and unhappiness and that conversely, the presence of a supportive network of friends will be a protective factor, mitigating the worst effects of unemployment. This comes over strongly. The correlation with depression/dissatisfaction is as follows:

Table 14.3

Isolation or lack of it correlated with Depression/Dissatisfaction

	Depressed	Very Dissatisfied	Dissatisfied	Exceptions
Isolated: one or no friends	5	5	0	0
Small group of friends	5	7	4	4
Wide circle of friends.	0	4	3	3

The first point is that those isolated individuals are concentrated in the categories that indicate depression or strong dissatisfaction. However, the table also highlights the observation made in chapter 6,that while having friends may be protective, it does not lead to a happy situation for most.This is best illustrated by the fact that seven out of ten who have been classified as having a wide circle of friends are still dissatisfied or strongly dissatisfied. Again this is only one factor to consider.

The ways that unemployment restricts social contacts and tends to propel people towards isolation can be summarised briefly. Lack of a wage limits the ability to join in with the desired commercial social life, pubs and nightclubs for example, and so opportunities to meet new friends and help keep in touch with old friends are lost. This may make it harder to meet sexual partners. There are no opportunities to meet new people at work, and it is difficult to keep up with the social life of employed friends from school, who are also not likely to be available during the day. The result is a drift towards restricting the level of social contacts and this is a central concern of many of those interviewed. Even many of those with a seemingly wide circle of friends stated that they would like to go out and socialise more and that a main reason for wanting to work was to 'meet people'. What can be said is that the tendency of unemployment to restrict social contact outside of the family is one of the main causes of the problems associated with unemployment. This may hold true for any age group, but the argument is that the general working culture as it applies to young people is what is influencing the expectations of the young unemployed, and this culture stresses the desirability of a commercial social life for the young. They expect to be able to go to pubs, nightclubs and discos and, consequently, feel deprived and excluded if this is denied to them. Such feelings were strongest for the minority of very lonely, isolated individuals, but were also expressed by others for whom the situation appeared less extreme.

Finally, YMCA dwellers are a special case as the institution provides a ready-made circle of friends: 'You meet people on the first day', and most hang around mainly with others from the YMCA. Again, this does not mean they are satisfied with their situation; most still very much want to meet more people through work and a commercial social life made possible by work.

Family Support

The fact that really sets the younger unemployed person apart from other age groups is the degree of family support they receive. This study reveals significant levels of emotional and financial support, mainly from parents but also sometimes from other relatives. It is worth noting that people living in the YMCA who tend to be there because they do not have families or are estranged from them, are over-represented in the sample. So, if anything, this research underestimates the levels of family support.

That parents should support their children many not seem surprising, but it has been a theme of the literature that family bonds are put under stress by unemployment (Kamorovsky, 1940; Marsden and Duff, 1975; Fagin, 1980; Popov, 1985). Drama series such as 'The Boys from the Blackstuff' (Bleasdale, 1982) have presented a picture of families buckling under the strain of their situation. It is easy to suggest reasons why this might be so. Parents might blame their children for their unemployment; they might expect them to 'pay their way' once they have left school; children might resent their continued dependency; the other strains of unemployment might make them hard to live with; and of course, having teenagers 'hanging around, getting under their feet' might be difficult for parents. However, as explained in chapter 6, most families seem to survive this remarkably well, providing the major prop to the young unemployed person. Conversely, the minority who do not have such a prop and in particular the smaller minority whose parents are actively hostile (Neil, Sarah and Richard for example) are considerably more vulnerable.

Fig 13.V (reprinted from chapter 6) indicates the manner in which family support functions to mitigate the worst aspects of unemployment.

To take emotional support first, families directly provide company, try to boost their children's self-image and so on. The correlation with parental emotional support and depression/dissatisfaction is as follows:

Table 14.4
Degree of Parental Support correlated with Depression/Dissatisfaction

	Depressed	Very Dissatisfied	Dissatisfied	Exceptions
Parents hostile no support	3	0	0	0
No parents	2	4	1	3
Some support	4	5	1	0
Very supportive	1	7	5	4

Of course, in each case other factors are in play, but the table does demonstrate that 'other things being equal', parental emotional support is an important protective factor although for most it is not sufficient to make people satisfied. Conversely, a hostile blaming attitude can be seen to be very destructive. All this is borne out in the interviews.

Perhaps even more important is the financial aspect of parental help, as this is one of the main factors that help young people maintain their desired commercial social life. This in turn helps them keep in touch with people outside the family circle and is very important for morale. The two are often the same, for emotionally supportive parents tend to be financially supportive; but not always, as it depends on the parents' means. This is one advantage of being young and unemployed in an area of relatively low unemployment, to set aside the disadvantages stated earlier; their parents are more likely to be able to support them financially. The interviews confirm that those with unemployed parents (or parent) often still get some financial subsidy, but much less.

The table correlating family financial support is as follows:

Table 14.5
Degree of Family Financial Support correlated with Depression/ Dissatisfaction

	Depressed	Very Dissatisfied	Dissatisfied	Exceptions
Little or no support	5	5	1	3
Average support	3	2	1	0
Above average support	2	9	5	4

Those without support can be seen to be concentrated under the depressed and very dissatisfied categories while those with regular support concentrated in the very dissatisfied and less dissatisfied categories. The table shows that parental financial support helps but, like all single factors, it is not sufficient to equal a satisfactory life for most.

The largest family financial subsidy goes to those living at home, consisting of cheap or free rent and board, so that a large proportion of their benefit money is spending money. Also the family may buy them clothes or lend/give them money. All this makes a very significant difference to the lives of many young unemployed, enabling them to have some semblance of a 'normal' (as defined by their cultural expectations) social life, albeit at a lower level than they consider satisfactory.

Partners

Partners (boy/girlfriend) are another source of support, providing emotional help and, if the partner is working, financial help. The financial help can be significant for a small number and unsurprisingly consists of paying for social life - drinks, entrance to discos, for example. Interestingly this support was given by both males and females, and both male and female unemployed reported feeling guilty about receiving such assistance without being able to reciprocate. There was one notable exception, Wendy, who boasted of getting young men - 'mugs' - to pay for her social life and to buy her clothes.

Significantly, all male 'exceptions' had working partners who helped subsidise their social life, while none of the 'depressed' males had partners. Where people had unemployed partners there was a tendency to fall into 'joint isolation', that is, to see almost no one except that partner. This happened to four of the sample of young women.

Finally, it was argued earlier that unemployment tends to make it harder to find boy or girlfriends, and this is reflected in the fact that twenty-seven did not have a partner. This is a result of the tendency to isolation, and the lower level of social life. Willis (1984) also found this in a study of both unemployed and employed youths in Wolverhampton. He concluded that unemployed people are less likely to be 'courting'. There has been some speculation on the effect of unemployment on family formation, with Gurney (1980) and Hendry (1984) suggesting that the problems of unemployment are delaying this. On the other hand, Griffin (1985) suggests the opposite, with girls in particular looking for a working male to settle down with more quickly than when employment offers an alternative. Both may be possible: the sample includes people with working partners, so that route may be open to them. However, the problems described earlier of meeting people, and the fact that lack of a wage makes finding an independent home more difficult, suggest that the phenomena of delayed family formation may be significantly more common. Of course one small sample is hardly conclusive, so there is room for more research here.

Work

Illegal work, savings from past work and legal part-time work are other sources of extra income for some. It was argued that for most however, there was too little of it to make a major difference to their lives. Work was valued both for the money it brings in but also for non-monetary reasons: it fills in time with purposeful activity; it can offer opportunities to meet people; learn new skills, and so on. Very importantly, it offers variety, something different from the drab sameness of life on the dole. It gives 'something to get up for' (Francis). It is worth repeating part of what James said:

> "Extra money is nice to have but it's something to occupy yourself. I think that's the main thing. Just actually getting up in the morning and thinking 'right, today I've got to get up and do such-and-such in the morning and such-and-such in the afternoon', and to know that you've got something to do all day. That **is** nice - like that job yesterday, just

getting up and thinking 'Ahhh! I've got something to do **all** day'. It's really good, and a really nice thing to wake up to - yeah, filling in time is the hardest thing."

Work correlates with depression/dissatisfaction as follows (overleaf):

Table 14.6
Amount of work correlated with Depression/Dissatisfaction

	Depressed	Very Dissatisfied	Dissatisfied	Exceptions
Little or none	5	5	3	1
Very irregular	2	8	2	1
Fairly reg/less than £15	2	2	2	3
Reg more than £15	1	1	0	2

(Note these categories are not the same as those in chapter 7: they include legal part-time work whereas chapter 7 concentrated on illegal work.)

Like other factors, work emerges as protective 'other things being equal'. But other factors can singly or in combination negate its protective influence. Alternatively, other protective factors can make up for lack of work. To cite two examples, Neil is the person who has a lot of work 'on the side', yet is still depressed. The largest contributory factors here are the hostile and blaming attitude of his parents; the fact that they take almost all his money for board, so his spending power is lower than most; and his desire for a 'proper job' and fear of the consequences of illegality. At the other extreme, the person in the top right hand corner of the table, Susan, has no work of any kind but she has structured her life around her baby and council flat, and is an 'exception' in that she is not unhappy on the dole. In general, however, the table shows that work is a protective factor.

This study also offers a modicum of evidence on the significance of the unofficial economy. Chapter 7: illustrates two views on this subject. One is optimistic, seeing it as having the power to absorb surplus labour and even as a creative phenomenon, leading to a less exploitative, post industrial society. The second perspective sees it merely as a survival mechanism for the poor who have no other choice, and emphasizes that it is parasitic on the main economy with little creative potential. The evidence of this study is unequivocally in favour of the second perspective. Most of the work done was trivial - irregular, merely filling the gaps in parts of the official economy and done by people who would join the main economy the moment they could. These arguments are dealt with at length in chapter 7 but, obviously, this is a small sample so cannot be definitive. More research is needed.

Other points made, were that work 'on the side' depended on contacts - an uncle who owns a pub, a friend who owns a small business, a father who knows the right people, and so on, and this sets aside those who are lucky enough to get regular unofficial work and those who are not. The other thing that sets them apart is gender: women are much more likely to do little or no unofficial work. I will explore the significance of this later.

Housing

The points made in chapter 8 can be briefly summed up. As far as private accommodation is concerned, there was much dissatisfaction with living in 'horrible bedsits' (Charlotte) or shared houses. Not everyone was dissatisfied, however, and the factors which outweigh the dislike of poor conditions are clear. These are: the novelty of being independent of parents; living with friends close to the city; and perhaps, most importantly, the feeling that this is only a temporary phase of life. (There is a parallel with students who are often prepared to put up with relatively poor conditions because they rightly consider this only a temporary phase of their life.) Dissatisfaction is likely to grow with time when the novelty wears off and the young people start to think in terms of settling down and forming a family. Membership of a subculture that does not emphasise smart houses and furniture also helps lessen dissatisfaction with poor conditions.

The YMCA provides an invaluable function, catering for those who for various reasons do not have family support. It was generally appreciated, staff were liked and individuals who might have otherwise been vulnerable to isolation (no family to support them, emotionally or financially) find a ready-made group of friends, sharing the same fortunes. However it is considered temporary both for the young people concerned, and by the rules and aims of the establishment ('a stopping station on the motorway of life', according to Gary). In the difficult housing situation in Norwich discussed in chapter 8, this prompts the question: 'What next?' The answer is probably depressingly poor bedsit accommodation.

As for the largest section - those living with parents, most have good relations with their parents, and enjoy emotional and financial support. Of course this means that the minority (Neil, Sarah, Richard), those who are living at home but not 'getting on' with their parents, or those whose parents cannot afford to subsidise them (Kevin), are at a considerable disadvantage. In general, though, the option of living with parents provides an easy, subsidised alternative. There is evidence of an age difference - those up to the age of 18 or 19 accept the situation as a normal continuation of their life-long situation, and thinking only roughly of becoming independent 'someday', which means when they are older and hopefully working. Above this age group, people begin to realise that their situation is holding them back; they become dissatisfied but prefer the easy option to life at the poor end of the private housing sector. Several had tried independence, enjoyed the novelty for a while, and then, often after getting into debt, moved back to the family home. As already argued, this factor and the extra difficulties of meeting sexual partners means a delay in family formation for a significant number.

Council accommodation was generally felt to be very satisfactory but, in this sample at least, was restricted to those who had babies. The major problem with council housing as far as the unemployed are concerned is that there isn't enough of it.

The difficult housing situation of the Norwich area is another feature in which the research is distinctive. If helping the unemployed is the aim, there is a need to reverse the current policies restricting the building of council flats and houses. This type of accommodation is the only reasonable option for those wishing to move to the next stage of life, independent family formation, without Willis's (March 1984) 'Golden Key', the wage. Such a reverse of policy would of course not only benefit the jobless but also many working young people, because the rise in house prices and interest rates in the last years of the 1980s had also pushed home ownership beyond their reach.

Returning to the unemployed, there is also a need for an expansion of the YMCA-type accommodation in the area. The YMCA does a vital job, but demand outstrips supply. As to correlating housing with depression/dissatisfaction, the results are not particularly helpful: (see over)

Table 14.7

Housing situation correlated with Depression/Dissatisfaction

Housing	Depressed	Very Dissatisfied	Dissatisfied	Exceptions
Private	2	3	1	1
Ymca/Umbrella	2	3	1	1
Council	0	2	0	2
Parents	6	8	5	3

The table is fairly ambiguous and the interview data reveals that many are not in their 'boxes' due to housing. Phillip for example is the person in the private sector who is also an 'exception'. He enjoys the unemployed life but hates his housing situation. The two 'depressed' people who live in the YMCA are depressed for other reasons than their housing situation. Similarly, housing is not an issue for three out of the six 'depressed' people living with their parents. For the other three it is, in the sense that a large part of their problem is living with unsympathetic parents. So clearly, while sometimes useful as a device of explanation, these kinds of two-variable correlations do not reflect the complexity of the situation. This is attempted in the text 'core model', and the explanations concerning ameliorating and exacerbating factors and strategies chart this complexity of factors and their interrelationships.

Interest

There has been some investigation into whether hobbies, sports and other interests can make up for some of the problems of unemployment, particularly problems with finding meaningful ways to use and structure time. Most have concluded that leisure interests can help but not make up for lack of work (See chapters 3 and 4). In general, this research supports these findings - most young unemployed people want work and the benefits of a wage, with other interests secondary. Some reported deliberate attempts to 'do things'; for example Paul attempted to fix up a derelict car; David made an animated film at the art centre; Jessie did not quite make it to the community workshop for photography lessons. The problem is that many start to see this as a second class way of time-filling rather than something they really want to do, explaining that they wouldn't bother if they had a 'proper' job to fill their time.

The ever-present problem of money intrudes here, with several reporting that they had to abandon sports and hobbies due to lack of money. Richard for example gave up karate and Susanne abandoned first tennis lessons and then the game itself.

The largest interest was unsurprisingly what could be categorised as 'general social interests'; drinking, dancing, socialising, and so on, and as has been already explained, lack of money and other factors functioned to limit this.

What can be added is that a genuinely strong (or even obsessive) interest can have a very positive effect on a minority. The only significant correlation in this area that this was true for, was six out of seven of the 'exceptions'. Especially effective at ameliorating the effects of unemployment are a burning interest that the person concerned wants to make into a career. Carl's boxing and Joanne's dancing are the examples here and these two would probably have been unemployed while they pursued those interests whatever the employment situation. There has probably always been people for whom periods of unemployment form part of a kind of apprenticeship, where they use this extra time to perfect their skills and pursue their goals. Many would-be actors, artists and sportsmen/women probably go through periods like this.

Linked to these are the two 'subcultural' persons - Phillip and Charlotte. Phillip's passion for motor bikes and Charlotte's for music, fills time in an absorbing and meaningful way, whilst also forming the basis for part-time jobs 'on the side'. They also have considerable social benefits, encouraging mixing with other like-minded individuals.

Isabelle's interest in her studies is likely to pave the way to a middle-class career ('straight down the road to success' was her assessment of her future) and given a rational system, she would have been on a grant and not appeared in this sample at all. Susan's main interest is her baby which has supplied her with a role and feeling of importance and self-worth, as well as access to a council flat.

The problem for the majority, is that it is difficult, perhaps impossible, to manufacture 'obsessive' interests. So mitigating the effects of unemployment by use of leisure activities would not be an effective strategy for most. The majority want to work and perceive other ways of time-filling as less meaningful than full-time work.

Subcultural membership

The term 'subculture' is here used very loosely to describe anyone who appears to be or describes themselves as members of a youth group such as punks, hippies, bikers and so on. Seven members of the sample could be so categorised. The rest describe themselves in terms such as 'normal' or 'ordinary everyday person' when asked.

These seven were divided fairly evenly into the depression/dissatisfaction categories with no real correlations:

Table 14.8
Subcultural membership correlated with Depression/Dissatisfaction

	Depressed	Very Dissatisfied	Dissatisfied	Exceptions
Subcul.Mem.	2	1	2	2

For the four in Categories Three and Four, there does however seem to be some advantage according to the interview data. Firstly, the subcultures (perhaps best described as semi-punk, hippy and biker) do not put a high emphasis on the conventional things our society values: career, smart expensive clothes, 'nice' housing, or a commercial social life, so they are less likely to worry about not being able to afford them. There is anyway more money available for the things they do want to do because their budgets are not strained by trying to afford new clothes or entrance to nightclubs.

Secondly, there is usually a social circle of like-minded individuals available for company. Thirdly, as many of these groups do not stress the desirability of work and provide social support for this view, there is less likelihood of group members feeling a sense of stigma associated with their unemployment. Lastly, for the two 'exceptions' (Category Four), the subcultural life and contacts provided extra work, with its attendant benefits of money and time satisfyingly filled. In Charlotte's case, this was playing music and for Phillip, repairing and respraying the motorbikes of 'biker' friends and contacts.

So for some people subcultural life helps, but not for all. Charlotte's description of the dangers of the life is worth repeating. At an earlier stage in her life she remembers living in 'horrible places in horrible bedsits, which made her miserable. Life came to seem empty, and she spent:

> lots of time in bed, sometimes never seeing daylight in winter, drinking a lot, taking drugs a lot. It gets very nasty, you end up taking drugs first

> not to feel depressed. Giro day was like the highlight of every fortnight, you would spend it on stupid things. I would get drunk a lot and I remember being miserable a lot. Now my life is very full. I never just do nothing. I remember doing nothing a lot.

As argued earlier, in chapter 12 she enjoys life because of a combination of factors, not just one. She has a baby and a successful relationship, a good council house and financial and emotional support from parents, in spite of living away.

These two are more active and wholeheartedly involved in subcultural life, compared with the two who could be classified as 'depressed'. Jessie and Tracy seemed more like fringe members; both lacked parental support, and both were isolated, with Tracy seeing virtually no one apart from her boyfriend who was going to college, and so not available during the day

Taking everything into consideration, membership of a subculture is protective for some, although hardly any kind of general solution to the problem of coping with unemployment. Most unemployed young people think conventionally, want conventional things, and so subcultural life would not be meaningful for them. Like passionate interests, subcultural values cannot be faked.

Obviously, this can work the other way: the depressed and dissatisfied individuals tend to be those that adhere to conventional norms and values. This does not simply mean an absence of subcultural allegiances, but a positive desire for an 'ordinary' normal life. They want a legal job rather than work in the illegal, unofficial economy; they would like to wear smart new clothes; go to nightclubs; buy a motorbike or car or stereo; go on holiday; and have plans, or at least hopes of one day meeting someone and settling down to form an independent household. They tend, by conventional, conservative (with a small 'c') judgements, to be 'good citizens', and unemployment is odd in that such people are punished rather than 'deviants'. Hence the phrase coined earlier 'good citizens suffer most'. Other research has correlated work commitment with psychological health, concluding that those unemployed people with the strongest commitment to work are those that suffer most. This is true, but it is likely that what they are really measuring is not simply desire to work for the sake of it, but commitment to a culturally conventional life career that is made possible only by the presence of a wage.

Stigma

Chapter 9 started with the following quote:

> The unemployed believe others despise them and depreciate them. This is in itself enough to generate discontent, but when reinforced by other trauma associated with unemployment it can threaten the fabric of identity. (Brakwell, 1984)

The text demonstrated that for this sample, there was a good deal of truth in this statement.

A sense of stigma correlates well with depression and dissatisfaction (Categories One and Two of depression/dissatisfaction Index): (see over)

Table 14.9

Sense of Stigma correlated with Depression/Dissatisfaction

	Depressed	Very Dissatisfied	Dissatisfied	Exceptions
Strong	4	6	0	0
Less strong	6	9	5	2
None	0	1	2	5

The opposite also holds true; those without any apparent sense of stigma tend to be less dissatisfied or 'exceptions', enjoying their life of unemployment.

The sense of being degraded in relation to others; that others look down on them or do not give them the status or acceptance that they feel is their due, is felt to be very important to many of the young people in the sample. (see Goffman, 1988, for a discussion of the nature of stigma). Such feelings pervade the literature of the 1930s and 1970s/1980s. Little seems to have changed in this respect. This is important, for if a person's views of his/her self-concept are at least partly conditioned by how they perceive others view them, then this will be destructive to the unemployed individual's self-image (see for example Goffman, 1969). Judgements made by them about their own status are likely to be disturbingly negative.

It was argued earlier that the work ethic is something of a myth. That the most pressing reason why people work is to make a living, rather than out of any sense of 'calling'; that the wage and what it means both in the short term (i.e. social life, not feeling ashamed at being unable to return hospitality or buy friends drinks, not being able to buy clothes, and so on) and in the long term (being unable to afford a separate home and support a family) are more important. Non-monetary benefits of work, such as Jahoda's 'latent functions' can be accepted without involving such a thing as a deep-seated work ethic. However, the concept can be applied here. If it is a myth, it is a generally accepted one and the belief (which does not have to be true) that others are judging one harshly in the light of such an ethic must be disturbing.

Given the idea that high visibility as unemployed heightens the sense of stigma, then it should come as no surprise that all those living in small villages expressed a sense of stigma. In fact, eight out of ten people who appeared to have a strong sense of stigma, lived in rural villages. This is a very clear majority of villagers - eight out of eleven and so a minority of the sample make up the majority of those expressing a strong sense of stigma.

With the large majority expressing some sense of stigma, this emerges as a significant problem. It would be interesting to compare this with areas of very high youth unemployment. The expectation should be that in these areas such feelings would be less strong and less widespread, but more research would be needed to validate this.

Views of the future

Reservations about the future also correlates with depression and strong dissatisfaction.

Table 14.10
Views of the Future correlated with Depression/Dissatisfaction

	Depressed	Very Dissatisfied	Dissatisfied	Exceptions
Pessimistic	8	4	0	0
Uncertain/fearful	2	9	2	0
Optimistic	0	3	5	7

'Uncertainty' correlates with the two categories of dissatisfaction rather than depression.

Apart from the 'exceptions' who were all optimistic, all expressed optimism or pessimism in terms of getting a job as a means to a future adult independent life.

It is hardly surprising that those pessimistic about the future prospects should tend to depression. It is difficult to know whether this causes depression directly, or whether the other effects of unemployment cause the depression, which then psychologically inclines them to pessimism. Alternatively, the experience of rejection when job-seeking may have conditioned them to expect failure. It is not possible to resolve this definitely with my limited data and it is possible that the truth is a mixture of all these.

Money

Money can be dealt with very briefly - not because this most important of factors should be neglected, but because a lack of it impinges on many other factors and it has been largely dealt with already.

Money is the most important factor involved in achieving desired objectives such as a commercial social life in the short term and an independent household in the longer term. The various factors that boost spending power have been analysed separately and it remains to correlate overall spending power with depression/dissatisfaction. This takes into account all the factors that boost spending power; family subsidies, 'side' and part-time work, savings from past work and so on, as well as negative factors such as repayment of debts and rent/ board to family.

Table 14.11
Spending power correlated with Depression/Dissatisfaction

	Depressed	Very Dissatisfied	Dissatisfied	Excepts.
Very low	4	3	0	0
Low but slightly increased	5	7	3	2
Higher	1	6	3	3
High for sample	0	0	1	2

The correlation is clear: the depressed are mostly in the two lowest categories concerning spending power of the unemployed. Boosts to the spending power of the unemployed helps their situation but the table makes it obvious that this does not equal satisfaction for most. Again other factors are involved.

Duration

Duration of unemployment is likely to be significant if a somewhat ambiguous factor. If long-term unemployment means six months or over, this is a sample of the long-term unemployed. Eleven have been signed on for less than six months, but with a single exception (Peter who had left school four months earlier), this is the length of time 'signed on' **on this occasion**, so they had had previous periods of unemployment.This complicates matters as periods of unemployment punctuated by short-term temporary jobs is a common pattern and because of this, it is difficult to interpret the statistical correlation:

Table 14.12
Duration of unemployment correlated with Depress/Dissatisfaction

	Depressed	Very Dissatisfied	Dissatisfied	Exceptions
0 - 6 months	1	8	6	1
7 - 12 months	5	6	0	2
above 12 months	4	2	1	4

Certainly this demonstrates that most of those in the depressed or very dissatisfied categories have been unemployed on this occasion for seven months or more. Also, those who have been signed on for six months or less, mostly fell into the two dissatisfied categories. None of this is at all surprising as all the other problems such as lack of money, worries about the future, particularly optimism about the chances of finding employment, and so on, are likely to wear people down as the time spent living with such factors drags on. This thesis has tried to explain the causal factors that shape the experience of unemployment, but of course these factors will not operate at full strength from day one. Lack of money is the obvious example. As time goes on, living on a budget may become more wearisome.

On the other hand, people may become adapted to their situation over a period of time. However, the correlation does not show much evidence of that. It is true that the exceptions, those that enjoy life on the dole, are overwhelmingly long-term unemployed, but they have not adapted; they have for reasons already explained, mostly achieved a satisfactory life from the start. Two of them are not really unemployed at all, except in the official sense. The others are long-term unemployed precisely because they have achieved a satisfactory life and so do not wish for a job.

Gender

This thesis is unusual in not having neglected the position of women: in fact, as the interview sample contains twenty-two women compared to eighteen men, it reflects the experience of young women rather more than men. This section can however be brief, not because gender is unimportant, but because the different experiences of women and men are integrated throughout the text.

Some points can be explained: firstly, there was absolutely no sign that women suffered less then men. Quite the contrary, they tended to express more distress and dissatisfaction than men.

The correlation is as follows:

Table 14.13
Gender correlated with Depression/Dissatisfaction

	Depressed	Very Dissatissfied	Dissatisfied	Exceptions
Male	3	9	3	3
Female	7	7	4	4

The tone of the interviews indicates that unemployment is at least as difficult for young women as for young men. This is surprising, as conventional wisdom and research suggests that women have been socialised into seeing work as less central to their identity. It is worth repairing Kelvin and Jarrett's (1985) summary of the literature: "Unemployment does not seem to induce in women a sense of failure as a woman in the way it so frequently seems to produce a sense of failure as a man amongst men" (p.66)

and later: "... to hold a job still does not seem to be as central to the social psychological situation of a woman as to a man ... who is much more likely to see his situation as personally deeply demeaning" (p.66)

If this is true, and if women continue to see work as less central to the course of their lives, then it would be expected that they would not worry so much about the lack of it. This does not seem to be the case at all. Listening to the interview tapes creates a strong impression that the women generally are experiencing more distress. It is of course impossible to make firm statements such as 'women suffer from unemployment more than men' for a number of reasons. Firstly, the sample is too small and secondly it is possible that it may simply reflect the end result of a socialisation process that has enabled women to express emotion and distress more freely than their male counterparts. Whether or not this is the case, the distress expressed is real, and according to this research, young women dislike and suffer from unemployment at least as much as young men. This is an unusual finding which contradicts the usual view and which deserves further research to discover how general this is and to further explore the reasons for it.

As to the reasons, it is possible to make some suggestions. It is possible that the greater penetration of women into the workforce has altered the situation so that for young women at least, work has become more central to their identity in ways similar to the case of males. There is scope here for further research by psychologists and social psychologists. Alternatively, the psychological commitment of women to work may indeed be less but this factor may be outweighed by others. This would fit in with the general view of this thesis, that responses to unemployment are the result of interrelationships of a wealth of causal factors, some of which can overwhelm and negate others, depending on the circumstance.

What might these factors be? Warr and Ullah (1984) have reached similar conclusions. In a study, of 1,150 unemployed 17 year olds they found that young women 'consistently reported more distress, depression and anxiety' than young men and were 'significantly more concerned about the stigma of being unemployed'. The young women tended to report more commitment to work and perhaps more significantly, spend less time out of the house, less time with friends and were less likely to be members of 'groups, clubs or teams'. Willis (1984/86) and Wallace (1987) found something similar. That young women tended to become more housebound and generally reacted in a less outward going way. As outward going activity appears to be protective the result is more unhappiness and depression. While supporting this, this research can add a very important point: young women are much less likely to be involved in work in the informal economy and, as has been demonstrated, this is a strongly protective factor.

All this seems to suggest a simple theory; regardless of the psychological commitment of women to work, other factors may be operating that make unemployment a distressing experience for women, over and above the general ones such as lack of money and so on. Put generally, Warr's findings and this research suggest that the socialisation process has had the effect of inducing men and women to approach unemployment differently. Practically, this means men tending to react in a more outward-going manner: getting out of the house, hanging around with friends, seeking work in the informal economy, and so on. In contrast, young women tend to confine themselves more to the family home or more to the company of a single partner thus missing out on a range of protective factors such as group support and unofficial work.

Another issue concerning women and unemployment is the question of whether some may choose to have babies as a means of achieving a meaningful role for themselves as well as more tangible benefits such as access to council housing. This will be dealt with in the next section. Finally, it is worth repeating that the area of women's unemployment is a neglected one characterised by assumptions rather than research. It is therefore the prime area for further investigation.

Strategies of dealing with unemployment

A look at these issues in terms of the strategies that young unemployed people could and do take advantage of, in order to deal with the potential problems of unemployment, will conclude this thesis. The term 'strategy' is a difficult concept, it implies rational decision-making and choosing of options, and there is always the possibility that people may respond to an interview situation by imputing more rational significance to their actions than is actually the case. In other words, they may be 'muddling through', scarcely in control, but not liking to admit this to an interviewer, or perhaps even to themselves, so they could justify their actions by putting an unjustified rational gloss over them.

There is also the issue of structural constraints. When speaking of strategies, it is not intended to imply too much freedom of choice and action; lack of money and so on decreases the scope for rational action. Indeed, unemployment is a direct constraint emerging from economic factors beyond their control: given freedom of choice, most would be spending much of their daylight hours working and their evenings using their wage to engage in a commercial social life. However they are rational human beings and will attempt to influence the events in their lives even under difficult constraining circumstances. To misquote, they may be trying to make their own history but they can certainly not do so as they please and definitely not under circumstances chosen by themselves. (Apologies to Karl Marx! For a discussion on the concept of strategy see Crow, Feb 1989)

So what strategies emerge from the data? Most are conscious attempts to take advantage of the ameliorating factors described earlier. The 'exceptions' are particularly interesting as they may demonstrate successful strategies. In general, they throw light on the situation of the others by posing the questions, 'What is different about them?' 'What do they have that the others do not?' They provide a kind of reverse proof of the pressures of the majority because their situation is simply the opposite: they have alternative ways of making money; they have friends and their time is meaningfully filled, and so on. Strategies revolve around dealing with the problems, trying to achieve at least some social life for example, or attempting to fill in the long and unstructured hours that others fill by work.

Continuing to live with the family

While the sixteen year olds may take this for granted, some of the older people report choosing to continue living at home for longer than they would ideally like, or giving up attempts at independence because they find the advantages outweigh the disadvantages: conditions are more pleasant and the emotional support and financial subsidies higher. Examples of people discussing this option can be found in chapter 8.

As the family is the most important ameliorating factor, attempts to move away are fraught with risks. The often-stated advice to the unemployed that they should 'get on their bikes' and move in search of work ignores this. Moving would be a higher risk strategy as for many it involves abandoning their most crucial support system.

Seeking work in the unofficial economy

This can be a helpful strategy but depends largely on contacts and not everyone has an uncle who owns a pub. For most it is not possible to use this strategy to achieve anything other than very occasional irregular relief from the problems of a life of unemployment.

Cheap nights at nightclubs and discos

Taking advantage of what are often called 'student nights' at nightclubs where drinks are half-price for a certain period and entrance is free, usually up until about 10pm, was commonly reported. This kind of opportunity does not appear in any of the literature that I have come across but is very significant to a number of those interviewed. It enables them to socialise in the kind of commercial setting they prefer. To experience the kind of social life that the general working culture experiences, as young workers also go to these events, and where entrance is free and drinks only 50p, the unemployed can participate on something like equal terms. Some reported getting completely drunk during the period of cheap drinks and then buying no more afterwards. Certainly 'student nights' are used far more than official provision for the young unemployed: youth clubs, the community workshops and so on.

Careful budgeting versus the 'big night out'

Careful budgeting is one strategy but given the low level of Unemployment Benefit, it leads to a uniformly dull life and a sense of exclusion from the socially accepted forms of social life. Some choose instead to 'blow' their money on a 'normal' social life after Giro day. This results in a pattern of pubs and night clubs the weekend after they receive their Giro, followed by a drab period before the arrival of the next cheque. It has been argued throughout that the unemployed's expectations are conditioned by the general working culture and this strategy means they can have what they consider a normal desirable social life for at least some of the time, whereas the superficially 'sensible' strategy of careful budgeting means this can never be achieved.

This illustrates the problem of the concept of strategy mentioned earlier. It may be that this pattern may indeed represent a strategy or it may simply be an 'after the fact' justification of a way of life they have fallen into. The likelihood is that it could be either of these things for different people. Some described a careful budgeting system that set money aside for the weekend after Giro day, in the same way as money was set aside for clothes and food, with nothing for a social life the weekend before the Giro was due. Conscious strategy or not, the big social weekend may be more of a morale boost than more even budgeting.

Joining a subculture that does not emphasise material gain

This has the advantages described earlier but it is doubtful if it could be described as a strategy to deal with unemployment. It could in come cases be a response to unemployment, but it is more likely that the minority who join such subcultures do so because they find the subculture value system meaningful or perhaps simply to follow fashion, or the lead of friends. The advantages that subcultures have in relation to unemployment can probably better be understood as a 'latent function' of the subculture. As a strategy it is unlikely to appeal to the majority of conventionally-minded individuals who do not find subcultural values meaningful and so is hardly likely to be any kind of general answer.

Conscious attempts to 'do something'

In response to the questions on which advice they would give to other unemployed young people, most answered that they should, by acts of will, go out and 'do things' rather than 'vegetate' or 'let it get you down'. Their own attempts to 'do things' run through the body of the interview.

This usually means one of two things - either constantly forcing themselves to search for jobs, or taking up some kind of interest. A pattern emerges whereby activity declines, and with it, morale. The individual realises this and by an effort of will takes up a hobby or interest or renews the search for work. The increased activity improves morale until the interest comes to be perceived as a mere time filler or as rejection in the job market saps confidence. Then activity and morale decrease again until the next attempt to 'do something'. Expressed as a graph, it would look something like this: (see overleaf)

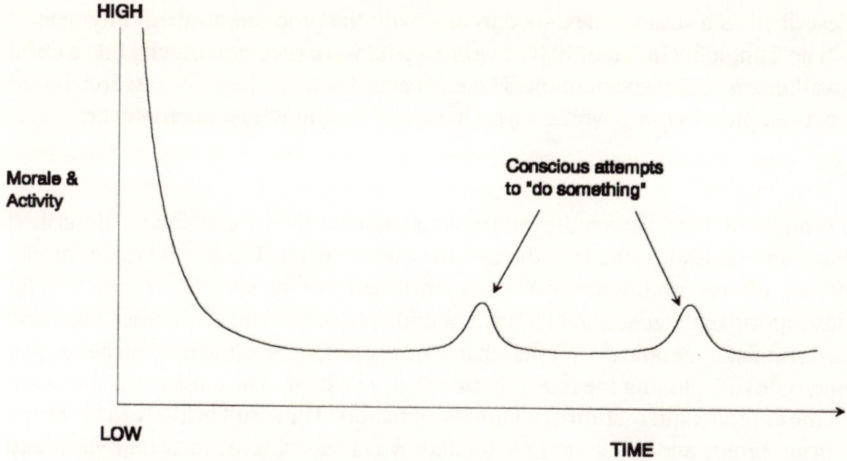

Fig 14.2 Morale and activity over time

Having an obsessive interest such as Carl's boxing and Joanne's dancing does not fall into this category. Nor can this be described as a strategy to deal with the problems of unemployment, for both want to be professionals and unemployment provides time to train and practice. They would therefore have probably been unemployed at any time as periods of unemployment for them can be seen as part of a kind of apprenticeship. Such obsessiveness cannot be forced and so cannot be adopted as a strategy by just anyone. It is however possible that a small number may be prompted by unemployment to try to make a genuine interest a career, or to make a hobby more than a hobby if other options are closed.

Having a baby

The possibility that young women are getting pregnant in order to qualify for benefits and council accommodation is a controversial area. Certainly in the opinion of the senior housing advice officer in Norwich, this does happen and the only people who found their way into council housing in the sample were women with babies. However, most (all the single mothers) said that they did not become pregnant deliberately so probably the element of strategy starts after the fact.That is, once finding themselves pregnant they are aware of the new possibilities in the situation and are willing to take advantage of them.

As well as material advantages, at least one single mother found life better for many reasons. She had a purpose; someone to love; a role less stigmatised than the role of unemployed as well as having her day filled with meaningful activity. Another woman who was pregnant was hoping for similar advantages but yet another had found the strains of unsupported motherhood too much and had got depressed, with the result that the child was taken into care. Again, all these said they did not get pregnant deliberately so actually getting pregnant cannot be described as a strategy designed to deal with the problem of unemployment.

The sample included only five women who were pregnant or who had a child so all this is really speculation. There is certainly scope here for research based on a sample of young women who have had a child whilst unemployed.

Final comment

Throughout this research the interrelated nature of the various factors described has been stressed. In the Introduction the Eisenberg and Lazarsfeld stages model of the effects of unemployed was criticised not because it is not a valid description of the reaction of many unemployed but because it is descriptive and deterministic. People do not march uniformly down the same road on becoming unemployed, passing inexcusably from stage to stage. The outcome is the result of the complex interaction of a number of factors. The result is likely to be varied - from suicide and psychological breakdown at one extreme to an enjoyable and satisfactory life at the other. That unemployment is an ordeal for most is well documented by this and all other researchers. It is hoped that this research has gone beyond description and charted some of the factors that make it so. However there are also ameliorating factors that mean that most are dissatisfied but not broken or totally despairing and it is also hoped that this research throws some light on these.

In this chapter, subcultural membership was used as an example of this interrelationship of factors. In the interviews it is revealed as a protective factor but one that could be supported by others but also overruled by a combination of adverse factors. The same applies throughout; all the factors are real in their effects but are more paramount. Research which attempts to isolate and test variables mislead because of this fact, foundering because of the 'messy' complexity of real life.

Outcomes are also affected by that the fact employed are conscious beings albeit severely constrained by circumstances. Therefore, the strategies they adopt and the actions they take are an important consideration. Graham Crow (8 Feb 1990) has discussed the problems of using the concept 'strategy'. He raises a number of issues but the one that is of concern here is the problem of rationality "In theory, strategic analysis applies to only certain types of action, ones which must amongst other things be at least in some senses rational, and take place within broadly predictable social situations" (p2) Later referring to Goffman's work he writes "Much can be gained by searching for rationality in actions that so not obviously and immediately advertise its presence .... the general point is clear, that it is possible to understand as rational behaviour that which seems to the untutored observer unthinking (p14/15).

Some responses to unemployment can be seen in this way. One example already given is the tendency to concentrate on the 'big night (or weekend) out' after Giro day. This is when they attempt to examine the constraints of their relative poverty by having a 'normal' social life, going to night clubs perhaps, leaving them with very little money and a miserable existence until the arrival of the next Giro. This is often presented by some of the young people themselves as a better morale booster than the alternative strategy of careful even budgeting which means they can never achieve what they consider a normal social life. However Crow goes on to say ...."it is important to bear in mind that not all actions are rational...." (p15) It is therefore possible to see this pattern as the result not of calculation but of 'muddling through' given a spurious rationality by hindsight.

It is hard to be sure but it is my impression that for some at least this pattern is a rational decision. Coffield (1986) and Willis (1984/86) back this up.

Continual job search is the most obvious strategy since it offers the hope of an end to the problems of unemployment but it is a high risk one carrying the danger of continual rejection and further blows to the self confidence. Might then it not be possible to regard apathy and resignation as a strategy to avoid these risks? Morgan (Feb 1989) in his comment on Crow's article points out that some have even referred to 'unconscious' strategies". The concept is indeed a difficult one that deserves further consideration.

Policy Implications

The policy implications emerge naturally from this research. Readers can, of course, make their own judgements so this issue shall be considered only briefly. Before doing so however I would like to argue against the fashionable assumption that unemployment is in some way 'inevitable'. Unemployment is not a natural disaster, it does not come from heaven like rain and snow but is the consequence of the actions, decisions and policies of human beings - not, of course, of human beings in general but of the minority that hold political and above all economic power. Until for example everyone has decent housing, until there are adequate hospitals, and schools in good condition, until there are well repaired sewers and an extensive public transport system it is absurd to argue that there is no work to be done. Whether we put money and resources into doing these things, or into tax cuts for the wealthy or into creating ever more efficient means for killing people is the question. In my personal view unemployment is an unnecessary evil and the first priority is to end this waste of lives and talent and find these people useful work to do.

If however we were to do what we should not, that is assume that high levels of unemployment are here to stay, then what can be done? Firstly, it should be remembered that most wish for a fairly conventional pattern of life. They want to progress via a commercial social life through 'courting' to marriage and a separate home, children and so on. It is important to remember that those who suffer most are those that want to lead conventional, hard working lives. They are the 'non-deviants' who do not want to work 'on the side', who do not wish to join exotic sub-cultures and so on, who are good citizens as judged in conventional terms. Policies should bear this in mind. It will not be enough to try to fill in time via subsidising sporting and leisure activities, although this may help and could form one part of the strategy. Improving their financial standards via higher benefits would help avoid some of the sense of exclusion and isolation that unemployment brings. Above all, if any government is to be judged as serious in wanting to help the unemployed (and those with low incomes generally) there must be a return to a programme to build large numbers of council homes and these must be affordable. This would allow the foundation of a separate family for those who cannot hope to get mortgages.

In other words the minimum necessary would demand the complete reversal of government policies followed throughout the 1980s.

Appendix: The sample

Anna

Anna was 19 and living at home with her mother, who is divorced and unemployed. Her mother still manages to support her emotionally and by subsidising her board and lodgings. Anna has been unemployed for three years and has no jobs 'on the side' or other forms of income at all. She is dissatisfied with her situation but not depressed having to some extent 'got used to it'. She would like to have money to spend on clothes, make up and going to Night Clubs. Although she gets on well with her mother she would like to live independently. In spite of feeling discouraged about her chances of work she still visits the Job Centre and has had two interviews shortly before being contacted for this research. She said she was choosy at first but now would take anything, expecting no more than £40 pw.

Adrienne

Adrienne was 18 and living in accommodation provided by a HousingAssociation for single parents. Her baby was temporarily fostered as her situation had become "too much" for her and she hoped to have her back fairly soon. She had been unemployed for two years. Her parents are divorced - her mother unemployed, her father a painter and decorator. She feels very isolated and depressed and would like to work in order to meet people and have 'things to do' but is not looking for jobs because she feels the need to prove she is available to look after her daughter. She returns again and again to the problems of isolation and having 'nothing to do'. She has a boyfriend but has fallen into a pattern of seeing only him - a situation she keenly regrets.

Charlotte

Charlotte was 22 and had been unemployed for some years. In fact she had never had more than short temporary work since leaving school at 16. She lives in a council house with her boyfriend who is also unemployed and their baby. Her father is in lower management her mother a physiotherapists assistant. Charlotte is an exception in that she enjoys her unemployed life and does not wish to work. She finds her family and social life very satisfactory and dislikes the idea of spending hours at work day after day. She and her boyfriend play in successful local bands and have a supportive group of like minded friends. Her lively and cheerful manner set her apart from the more conventional work orientated individuals.

Carl

Carl was aged 17 and unemployed for one year. He lived in the YMCA having become estranged from his mother because of conflict with his step father. He has never known his natural father.

Like Charlotte, he is an exception, enjoying his unemployed life but for different reasons. His reason is his obsession with boxing. The training fills his time enjoyably, gives him a purpose and a vision of the future as a wealthy, successful professional sportsman. He would like to work but this comes second to his training. Contacts made via the boxing club have provided occasional work "on the side" as a roofer and house removal person.

He also had a supportive working girlfriend. However later his situation changed when she became pregnant and he felt obliged to find work - a temporary job in a factory. He seems confident that he would shortly get a job on the oil rigs via contacts from the boxing world. He continues to box in his spare time.

David P

David was aged 22 and had been unemployed for one year after working for five years for the Inland Revenue. He left voluntarily because he hated the work but had hoped to find another job fairly quickly. He lives at home with his parents, his father works nights as a switch board operator, and his mother does not work.

He is somewhat cushioned from financial hardship by supportive parents, occasional bar work and savings from his previous employment (£1100 down to under £400 when interviewed). He describes himself as bored and dissatisfied but less unhappy than when working at his previous job.

David R

David, aged 21, had been unemployed for six months. He had had only temporary work in a holiday camp since leaving school and some very irregular work on a farm, digging ditches, and kitchen work in a restaurant. He lives independently in a shared house but before that he lived with his parents in a small village. His mother is a cook and his father a technician in the RAF.

He describes his situation as "sometimes alright, sometimes depressing", and feels that he is "vegetating". He is looking for work but much less than before, feeling somewhat discouraged. His parents are fairly supportive but the significant figure in his life seems to be his older sister who constantly visits, encourages him to do things', look for jobs, enroll on courses, and so on.

Fiona

Fiona, aged 17, has been unemployed for four months, with previous short periods of unemployment. She lives with her parents in a small village. Her father is a farm worker and her mother is not working. Fiona is in a fortunate position compared to many unemployed people. Financial subsidies from parents, grandparents and her boyfriend, as well as having unofficial part-time work, means that she is only marginally worse off than many young workers. She gets on 'marvellously' with her parents and enjoys a good social life describing herself as 'a happy little person really'. Nevertheless she is energetically seeking work and attending interviews and is very dissatisfied with this aspect of her life.

Francis

Francis has been unemployed for two years since leaving the RAF. He is 20 and lives independently in a shared house. His parents are shopkeepers.

He is a member of a sub-culture that could perhaps best be described as 'semi punk'. Francis's main survival tactic is to spend almost all his time in the company of a close-knit group of friends. He is not however satisfied - rather semi-adapted; saying that he has had no choice but to 'get used to it'. He still looks for work but not as much as when he was first unemployed. He worries about the effect unemployment is having on him - that is achieving little and finding that things he would previously have done quickly now take a long time.

Gary S

Gary aged 20 lives with his older brother in a council flat. Both were brought up in various foster homes and hardly know their parents. Gary is very dependant on his brother who lends and sometimes gives him money, as well as supplying subsidised accommodation and food (£10 per week).

Unemployed for over two years since completing a YTS painting and decorating scheme, Gary is a work oriented 'conventional' person. He is looking for any unskilled manual work, and although he feels discouraged sometimes, he intends to 'keep trying until I find a job'. Unemployment he finds boring with no advantages.

Gary W

Gary is 16 and lives in the YMCA, which has the advantages of supplying a group of friends in a similar position. He is in the YMCA because his unemployed mother remarried and he did not get on with her new husband. He has been unemployed for three months.

He is conventionally work orientated and has a strong sense of being stigmatised because of his position. Others, he believes, wrongly consider him a 'waster'. To prove that this is not the case and to keep himself occupied he works four hours every day in the YMCA kitchens, for which he gets £4 p.w. (This is the most he can earn before his benefits are cut.) Much of the rest of the time he spends looking for unskilled manual jobs. Summing up he said 'I can cope. I'm alright but I'd much rather get a job'.

Gillian

Gillian is 18 and has been unemployed for one year. She lives at home with her parents in a small village. Her father is a policeman. She is slightly mentally disabled and although she is perfectly capable of working this may well be a disadvantage in a competitive situation. Previously she was on a YTS scheme and she is bored and frustrated in her present situation.

Isobel

Isobel is 20, living at home, and is another exception in that she does not object to her situation. In fact she is hardly unemployed except officially; she is a student and signing on because she cannot get a grant. Her parents are teachers and are very supportive, for example they do not charge her for food or accommodation. Her assessment of her future was 'straight down the road to success' and since this interview she has got her A levels and gone to Art College. A more generous system of grants would have removed her from the uneployment statistics.

Ian

Ian aged 17, lives in the YMCA having previously lived with his mother - a single parent. He had only been unemployed for one month at the time of interview but had previous spells of unemployment. He left a YTS scheme because he felt he was being exploited by being made to do unskilled work rather than training, whilst being paid the YTS rate.

He reports being bored and very dissatisfied. He would like to train as an engineer but in the meantime is looking for anything. He has had some unofficial work but this has been intermittent and very badly paid.

Joanne

Joanne 21, has been unemployed for six months and lives with her parents. Her father is a glazier and her mother works in a pub.

Joanne is another exception who is not unhappy with her situation. In her case this is because she has a driving ambition to be a dancer. She spends her time practising and socialising with the other members of her dance troupe and feels a full time job would interfere with this. She had already had several bookings with holiday centres and 'entertaining the troops' in Northern Ireland and the Falklands. She would probably have been unemployed whatever the job situation, using the time as a kind of apprenticeship before hopefully becoming a full time professional dancer.

James

James was 21 and had been unemployed this time for six months. Before that he had a temporary job working for the DHSS! He lives in a remote village with his parents. His father is a teacher and his mother a secretary.

He finds unemployment very difficult, missing the money and the social life it makes possible. He feels lonely and isolated during the day. He has some regular but low paid unofficial work gardening and decorating which he values because it keeps him occupied and because of the money ...'Filling in time - that's the hardest thing.'

Jessie

Jessie was 18, living independently in a shared house and had been unemployed for one year.

Her sub-cultural semi-punk involvement did not seem to help her much as she was one of the more depressed. She said that unemployment can be alright but 'you have to work hard at it otherwise it gets you down'. In her case it had gradually done that, paralysing her will to look for jobs or make the most of her free time. She spoke quietly with long pauses and she looked and sounded terrible and reported being depressed.

Jacky

Jacky was aged 19 and living independently in a council flat with her boyfriend. She had been unemployed for 10 months. Her mother works as a cleaner and her father as a farm labourer and they live in a remote village. Jacky had previously experienced unemployed life in a village and, unlike most, preferred it. This was because she enjoyed the company of her family and also because local contacts had enabled her to get a variety of unofficial jobs on farms, kennels, stables and cleaning for better-off neighbours. Since moving to the city this had come to an end and she and her boyfriend had fallen into joint isolation. There was a prospect of a local landowner providing accommodation in the village and she was excited about this. Of unemployment in general she says it's 'Miserable. I hate it. I don't like it at all'.

Jacqueline

Jacqueline was 24 and lived in a rented home with her unemployed boyfriend. Her father was unemployed and her mother a school cleaner. She had been unemployed for one year since being made redundant after five years working in a factory. Before that she had trained as a hair dresser.

She describes unemployment as 'Horrible. I'm not used to it. Nothing to do!' Her main preoccupation is with unfilled time in the day and lack of money to enjoy a social life.

This and the fact they had to sell their car made it difficult for them to keep in touch with friends who lived some distance and had an expensive social life. Jacqueline was in the early stages of pregnancy and she hopes that this will lead to a more fulfilled life and, very important as the rented house was in poor shape, a council house. Who looks after the baby depends on the job situation.

John

John, aged 16, lives at home with unemployed parents. He has been unemployed for six months and finds it 'boring', but he appears to be not too concerned. He gives the impression of still living a 'school holiday' existence - hanging around in the park with friends. His parents support him, charging him nothing for accommodation or food and apparently never ask him about work. He attends the Job Centre fairly regularly and is not worried about what he gets. He is optimistic about his chances of finding work eventually. He refuses to go on a YTS scheme calling them 'slave labour'.

Kate

Kate aged 20 and living in a 'cluster unit' - that is council accommodation for young people - had been unemployed for two years.

She was the only political activist to appear in the sample being involved heavily in women's groups.

She was dissatisfied with her situation and wanted to work, both to fill time and to provide money. She had attended a training course to become a carpenter and joiner and would like to do this. However she said that the course had been of such poor quality that she did not feel confident as to her ability to do the job.

Karl

Karl was 20, living at home with parents and has been unemployed for one year. His father is a motor mechanic and his mother is not employed.

Karl has several advantages that make him an exception, the most important of which is an uncle who owns a pub. Karl works there as often as he likes, and, as such, is hardly unemployed except officially. His other advantages are indulgent parents who charge him nothing for full board. He also has a supportive working girlfriend. Taken together with his dole money he is receiving more than most of his friends who are working.

Lively and cheerful he obviously considers himself as a 'bit of a lad', boasting about his illegal exploits, periods in Detention Centre and so on. This was likely to be a temporary phase of his life as his pub owning uncle has offered him a full time job in a Night Club that he plans to open.

Kevin R

Kevin was 20, had left school at 15, and since then had had three weeks temporary employment plus one year on a YTS painting and decorating scheme. He lives with his unemployed mother.

Kevin was one of the most isolated and depressed people in the sample. His mother cannot afford to subsidise him to the extent that many others do and so he pays her £30 a fortnight for board. He is also paying off fines for petty offences and has run up debts with a clothing company. Consequently he has almost no money to spend at all, has no social life and has almost entirely lost touch with his friends. Summing up he said 'It's just bad really. Don't see no friends. Depressed all the time'.

Kevin S

Kevin S was aged 18 and had been unemployed for nine months having had only temporary jobs since leaving school. He lives in a small village with his parents. His father is a farm worker and his mother is not employed.

He is dissatisfied with his situation and has a strong sense of that others are judging him unfairly, thinking that he is a 'lazy bastard', when in fact he wants to work and is looking for work. He feels that living in a village puts him at a disadvantage for the reasons given by most of those in this position - cost of transport, lack of 'things to do', and the lack of a community of people in the same position.

Mandy

Mandy was 18, living with her unemployed mother, and has been unemployed for five months. Her last job was a seasonal job in a sweet factory which takes on people for the Christmas and Easter rush and it is likely that she will get this regularly if she cannot find full time work.

She says she is bored and gets 'a bit depressed' but seems to cope. She keeps busy doing domestic work helping her mother look after her younger brothers and sisters and keeping house generally. She regularly spends time looking for work and is fairly optimistic about her chances.

One advantage she has is a working boyfriend who she sees every day during the day, as he works nights. He pays for a lot of their social life and they planned to rent a house owned by a friend of his father. This is of a higher standard than most unemployed can look forward to, made possible by his wage.

Neil

Neil had been unemployed for only three months but his last job had been only for two weeks. He lives in a small country village with his parents, his father being a self employed builder.

Neil gets regular work 'on the side' with small building firms and does both a morning and an evening paper round. However, the protective power of unofficial work has failed in his case and he is one of the most depressed individuals. There are two reasons for this. Firstly, he is a work orientated conventional individual who worries about the illegality of what he feels forced to do and wants a 'proper job'. Secondly, he is one of the few cases encountered whose parents have a hostile and blaming attitude to his unemployment. This causes tension at home and his parents take almost all his money, £25 per week, for board. He therefore gains little financially from his work and, as he is also paying off fines and debts, he can hardly afford any social life. Apart from work he spends most time searching for jobs - visiting the Job Centre - following up adverts and regularly turning up at firms to ask for work. In spite of his constantly frustrated efforts and his experience generally, he believes most people are unemployed because 'they don't want to bother'.

Nicola

Nicola, aged 18, had been unemployed for six months since a short term job nannying finished. She lives with her grandmother in a small village. This is not because she is estranged from her parents but because she considers her grandmother too frail to manage on her own. Her mother does not work and her father is a cook for a local government facility.

Nicola has managed to keep in touch with school friends, paying for a social life out of savings from her last job and two nights official work in a bar. She was worried because the savings were about to run out.

She says she has 'mixed feelings' about her situation. It was 'alright at first', but now she is starting to get 'slightly fed up with life' and describes her days as 'very empty now'. As to job search she was feeling very discouraged having had a number of interviews, mainly for shop work, which seemed to go well but then she didn't get the job. She cannot understand why and this is starting to sap her confidence.

A lively person who likes to keep active she seemed to be at a crossroads, 'trying to be optimistic about it', but finding it increasingly difficult. She had started to feel that people were 'looking down their noses' because of her unemployment. Also one time she had noticed that everyday things were starting to take longer for her to do.

Paul I

Paul lives in a small village with his parents, his father being a foreman in a factory and his mother a factory worker. He was 19 and had been unemployed for nine months but with previous periods of unemployment. His longest job had been with a building firm with which he worked for one year.

He was relatively fortunate financially having regular unofficial work and supportive parents. In fact these two factors mean that he is only a little worse off than most young workers. He is, however, far from satisfied as he wants a proper job with training and a future, not bits of illegal work here and there. He also has a strong sense of stigma describing how he sometimes hides the fact that he is unemployed, feels bad if strangers see him cashing his Giro and so on.Also time hangs heavily when he is not working as he likes to be constantly kept busy. Lively and talkative his relatively fortunate financial position has protected him from depression but not made him satisfied.

Paul D

Paul was aged 19 and living with parents in a small village. He had been unemployed for six months this time but had only temporary jobs since leaving school - with a chicken factory and a small building firm. He has had odd bits of unofficial work but very little. He hates being unemployed, feels stigmatised and finds great problems with filling time. Not yet too depressed he feels it is slowly getting to him and says that he is slowly losing confidence as his constant attempts to find work come to nothing. He is also concerned about losing touch with friends, is embarrassed at not having money and so he has adopted the common pattern of the 'big weekend' after Giro day followed by a week and half without any social life.

At first he looked only for outside labouring, hating the idea of factory work. Now he is 'gettng desperate' and will take anything.

Peter

Peter aged 16 had left school at Easter but at the time of interview in September had only just been allowed to sign on. Since leaving school he had had a one week labouring job which he enjoyed, 'because I'm quite strong and that'. He lives at home with his mother who is a hospital cleaner and his father who works for a small builder.

He earns a little money singing in pubs and tends to stay up all night and sleep until the afternoon.After a period of treating it as a holiday he has become bored and dissatisfied and is making more effort to find work. He wants money for decent clothing, a night life and Elvis memorabilia.

Phillip

Phillip aged 22 lived in a rented house with his working girlfriend. His mother was a nurse and his father a newsagent. He had been unemployed for five years and had been an exception, enjoying life on the dole for the following reasons. Firstly, he had regular unofficial work, for a friend who was a small builder and repairing and restoring motor bikes. Secondly, he shares his girlfriend's wage. Thirdly, and very importantly he is a member of the 'biker' sub culture. This means he does not worry about new clothes, consumer goods or a commercial social life so his money goes further. He has friends in the same position around during the day. His reputation in their sub-culture supplies him with customers for his unofficial motor bike business. So these factors means he had adequate money for his needs and his time filled with activities he enjoys.

At the time of interview, he hoped this period of his life was coming to an end. He and his girlfriend had decided to buy a house so, for the first time in five years, he was energetically looking for work.

Rachel

Rachel was aged 16 and had been unemployed six months. Her parents, both office workers had divorced, and she had decided to live in the YWCA.

She was fairly contradictory about unemployment saying she was bored early in the interview that she liked it later. On the whole she appeared dissatisfied and certainly she was energetically looking for work, having had five interviews in two weeks. She claims that she will inherit £118,000 when she is 18.

Richard

Richard aged 19 had been unemployed for two years and was living at home with his parents. His father worked at a double glazing factory, his mother was not fully employed but found temporary work from time to time.

Richard looked and reported feeling depressed, describing his life as 'Boring, fed-up, I mean really fed up - all I do is go round looking for a job.... ain't got no money to go out evenings.' He said that he had often considered suicide.

He had enjoyed his year spent on YTS painting and decorating scheme but had been terribly disillusioned when it had not led to anything permanent.

He used to go out socially regularly and participate actively in sport but now he could no longer afford it and resented this bitterly.

An added burden is that he is one of the very small group whose parents are not supportive, blaming him for his unemployment. In spite of the fact he constantly searches for work, going to the Job Centre everyday for example, he has arguments frequently with his parents about this.

Susan C

Susan was living with parents, who were retired due to ill health, in a small village. She was aged 20 and had been unemployed for just over a year, having terminated nurse training due to a bad back. Since then she had had a short term job as a care assistant in a private home for the elderly and as a mothers help. She now works part time in a pub.

Of unemployment she says 'its boring I'm going up the wall slowly'. Her doctor has prescribed anti-depressants because she found she was crying on her own and she says that without her part time job she would have considered suicide.

All her friends work and she felt very discouraged when the younger ones left school and found work immediately while she was rejected at interview or had her letters unanswered. Friends often ask her out but she feels too ashamed to go unless she can pay her way - buy rounds of drinks and so on.

Like most of the young people living in villages she considers it a disadvantage for the reasons described earlier.

Susan F

Susan, aged 17, had been unemployed for six months and was living in the YMCA having spent a lifetime in care. She had worked in a supermarket on the cash tills but had been sacked for being too slow.

She describes unemployment as 'horrible' and herself as 'so depressed'. Certainly she seemed it as she answered questions with a barely audible voice while staring at the floor. She wants to work she says to 'meet people' and to keep occupied, stating that she 'doesn't care about the money'.

It may not be possible for her to work as she was pregnant and no longer sees the father. She was about to move into a housing association flat and hoped that her new role would solve her problems.

Susan L

Susan, aged 18, was living in a council flat with her baby. Her father worked for a scrap merchant, her mother was not employed. They were divorced and she no longer had regular contact with them, having lived much of her life 'in care'. Before obtaining the flat she had lived in the YMCA.

One of the 'exceptions', she enjoyed life since she had the baby (so there may be room for optimism with regards to Susan F although I have my doubts). She constantly compared her boring, depressing previous life with her busy fulfilling experience of motherhood. She was full of pride as she showed me round her spotless flat and presented her happy well cared for baby.

Her flat had become something of a centre for friends she had met at the YMCA and, at the time of interview, they were helping decorate a bedroom. A main source of entertainment seemed to be watching videos (horror!), a very economical pastime as the group clubbed together to hire films and pay the recorder rental.

Susan W

Susan was aged 17, living at home with parents who were poultry farmers. She had been unemployed for six months.

She said that she was bored and depressed and off her food, complaining of lack of a social life because of money shortage and isolation during the day. She has a working boyfriend and said that their relationship had become strained because she was 'ratty' because of her feeling so 'down'. Her boyfriend was willing to pay for her social life but she did not like this.

Later she joined a YTS scheme and seemed altogether more cheerful. She enjoyed it because she was doing something positive, meeting people and because of the money. After unemployment, even the low YTS wage seemed important - 'even that little extra helps'.

Sarah

Sarah was 18 and living at home with her parents. Her mother worked serving in a cafe, while her father was unemployed. She had been unemployed for seven months and had only had temporary jobs. She worked Saturdays serving in a shoe shop for £10 each week.

She seemed very low and lacking in confidence 'It's alright when you are busy when you are not its terribly depressing, terribly boring'.

She used to look for jobs but after many rejections she had become pessimistic and had given up. Her explanation for her failure was 'I just think I am no good ....a failure'. Her vision of the future ends in suicide.

Tracey

Tracey was 18, living with her boyfriend in his mothers house. She had been unemployed for two years.

Apart from her boyfriend she had lost contact with friends because she could not afford to match their expensive social life. Now he was going to college and they were drifting apart leaving her in a difficult isolated position. Unemployment she describes as 'horrible' and she says that she is depressed and finds herself crying for no reason. She would like to work with children or do something artistic but feels pessimistic about achieving these ambitions. She also feels a strong sense of stigma especially believing the DHSS staff look down on her.

She looked very much a member of the punk sub-culture but by having drifted away from like minded friends she has lost group support.

Wendy

Wendy aged 17 had been unemployed for three months. Before that, she had a temporary office job. She lives at home in a small village with her mother who is not employed and her father who is a plant manager.

She manages to have a active social life partly subsidised by her parents.Another survival tactic she uses is to exploit her charms for young men who pay for her drinks, entrance to night clubs and buy her clothes. She refers to them as 'mugs'. Certainly not depressed she is bored and dissatisfied particularly during the day. She is looking for shop or office work partly to buy more clothes, make up and to have an even more active social life, but mostly to 'meet people'.

Bibliography

Allan, S. Walton, A. Purcell, K. and Woods S. (eds) 1986, *The Experience of Unemployment,* Explorations in Sociology 21, British Sociological Association.

Allan, R., Boti, A. and Bragard, J. C. 1981, *The shattered dream: Unemployment in the eighties,* Arrow Books, London.

Analysis 1992, 'A class of their own?', *BBC Radio 4*

Anthony, P. D. 1977, *The Ideology of Work,* Tavistock Publications, London.

Archer, J. Rhodes, V. 1987, 'Bereavement and reactions to job loss: A comparative review.' *British Journal of Social Psychology,* 26

Ashton, D. N. 1986, *Unemployment under Capitalism*, Wheatsheaf Books Ltd. (Harvester Press Publishing Group),

Bakke, E. W. 1933, *The unemployed man,* Nisbet, London.

Banks, M. H. and Jackson, P. R. 1982, 'Unemployment and risk of minor psychiatric disorder in young people: cross-sectional and longitudinal evidence.' *Psychological Medicine.* Vol. 12 pp789-98.

Banks, M. H. and Ullah, P. 1987, 'Political attitudes and voting among unemployed and employed youth.' *Journal of Adolescence No 10.*

Banks, M. H. and Warr, P. 1980, 'Work and mental health amongst lesser qualified school leavers.' *SSRC Final Report 1980.*

Bates, I. et. al. 1984, *Schooling for the dole? The new vocationalism.* Macmillan. London

Beales, A. L. and Lambert, R. S. 1934, *Memoirs of the Unemployed,* Collencz. London.

Beal, N. Nethercott, S. 1985, 'Job loss and family morbidity: and study of factory closure.' *Journal Royal College General Practitioners Vol 35 No 280*

Beynan, H. 1982, 'Jeremy Seabrook and the British Working Class.' *The Socialist Register,* Merlin Press, London.

Binns, J. and Mars, G. Nov 1984, 'Family, community, and unemployment.' *The Sociological Review, Vol. 32 No 4.*

Bleasdale, A. 1982, *Boys from the Black Stuff,* BBC TV Series.

Bradshaw, J.and Holmes, H. 1989, *Living on the Edge: a study of the living standards of families on benefits in Tyne and Wear,* CPA6, Tyneside

Brakwell, G. Collie, A. Harrison, B. and Popper, C. Feb. 1984, 'Attributes towards the unemployed: effects of threatened identity.' *British Journal of Social Psychology.*

Brenner, H. 1973, *Mental illness and the economy,* Harvard University Press, Cambridge - Mass.

Brenner, and Bartell. 1983, 'Psychological approaches to unemployment.' *Journal of occupational psychology. No. 56.*

Bryant, J. 1980, *An introductory bibliography to work on the informal economy in Third World Literature,* Mimeo, SSRC Research Initiatives on Local Labour Markets and the Informal Economy, University of Sussex

Burns, S. 1977, *The Household Economy,* Beacon Press, New York

Brown, G. Harris, T. 1978, *The social origins of depression,* Tavistock Publications, London

Caffrey, J., Mckeller S., Woodhead, .P 1986, 'Youth Unemployment: more than just a waste of a generation.' *Youth in society (Journal).*

Carr-Hill, R. A. 1985, 'Wither Unemployment? in -', Roberts B et al (eds), *New approaches to economic life,* Manchester University Press.

Carrol, .P 1979, 'The social and psychological effects of unemployment upon young people, A review of the literature.' *Department of Employment sponsored research Sept. 1979.*

Cashmore, E. E. 1984, *No Future: Youth and Society,* Heinemann, London.

Clarke, J. Critcher, C. 1985, *The Devil makes work - leisure in capitalist Britain,* MacMillan, London

Clarke, R. 1982, *Work in crisis: Dilemma of a Nation,* The Saint Andrews Press, Edinburgh.

Cockburn, J. 1983, *The use of interviewing in Social Science Research,* Unpublished PHD Thesis, University of East Anglia.

Coffield, F. Borrill, C. Marshall, S. 2nd June 1982, 'How Young people try to Survive Unemployment.' *New Society.*

Coffield, F. 26-1-1984, 'Is there work after the MSc?' *New Society.*

Coffield, F. Borrill, C. Marshall, S. 1986, *Growing up at the Margins,* Open University Press, Milton Keynes.

Crow, G. Feb. 1989, 'The use of the concept of 'strategy' in recent Sociological literature.' *Sociology. Vol 23 No 1.*

Crow, I. July 1982, 'The unemployment/crime link.' *Unemployment Unit Bulletin No 4,* London.

Daniel, W. M. 19. Aug 1974, 'The reality of Unemployment.' *New Society.*

Davies, M. 1986, *What it's like to be unemployed in Norwich; a report to the community*, Norwich: Welfare Industry Research Group, University of East Anglia.

Davies, M. 1986, *Towards a classification of the unemployed,* Norwich: Social Work Monographs for the Welfare Industry Group, University of East Anglia.

Daucey, G. 1982, *The Unemployment Handbook,* National Extension College, Cambridge.

Daucey, G. 1986, *Nice Work (if you can get it),* National Extension College in conjunction with Yorkshire TV.

Dickerson, D. 1994, 'Study links crime to jobless rise', Cambridge, Nuffield Foundation, reported in *The Gaurdian 7 -1 - 1994.*

Donovan, A. Oddy, M. 1982, 'Psychological aspects of unemployment: an investigation into the emotional and social adjustment of school leavers.' *Journal of Adolescence, No. 5.*

Dooley, M. 12 Aug. 1983, 'I'm going mad!' *New Society.*

Eisenberg, P. Lazerfield. 1938, 'The psychological effects of unemployment', *Psychological Bulletin No. 35.*

Taylor, M. Alaluf, M. 1983, *Growing up without work: a study of young unemployed people in the West Midlands,* European Centre for work and Society, Assen.

Fagin, L. Winter 1979/80, 'Unemployment and family crisis.' *New University Quarterly. Vol. 34 no 1.*

Fagin, L. Little, M. 1984, *The Forsaken families*, Hamondsworth, Penguin.

R, Fiddy. (ed) 1983, *In Place of Work: Policy and provision for the young unemployed,* Falmer Press, London.

Field, F. 1986, *Losing out,* Blackwell, London.

Fineman, S. (Ed) 1987, *Unemployment - Personal and Social Consequences,* Tavistock Publications,London.

Finlay-Jones, R., Echardt, B. 1981, 'Psychotic disorder amongst the young unemployed.' *Australia NZ Journal of Psychiatry. No 15.*

Francies, L. 1984, *Young and Unemployed,* Costello, Tunbridge Wells, Kent.

Fraser, C., Marsh, C. Jopling, R. 1985, 'Political responses to unemployment, in Roberts, et al.' *New Approaches to Economic Life,* Manchester University Press.

Freeman, R. B. Wise D. A. 1982, *The Youth Labour Market Problem,* University of Chicago Press.

Fryer, D., Payne, R. 1984, *Proactive behaviour in Unemployment: findings and implications,* Leisure Studies.

Fryer, D., McKenna, S. 1987, 'The laying off of hands: unemployment and the experience of time.' in Fineman (ed), *Unemployment - Personal and Social consequences.*

Fryer, D., Ullah, P. (eds) 1987, *Unemployed People,* Open University, Milton Keynes.

Furnham, A. 1982, 'The Protestant Work Ethic and Unemployment.' *Journal of Occupational Psychology. No 55.*

Galbraith, JK. 26-1-1994, 'Towards a new world deal', *The Guardian*

Gallie,D. Marsh, C. Vogler, C. 1994, *Social change and the experience of unemployment,* Oxford University Press, Oxford.

Gaskell, J. Lazerson, M. 1980, *Between School and Work,* Faculty of Education, University of British Columbia, Vancover, Mimeo.

Gershuny, I. Pahl, R. E. Jan 1980, 'Britain in the decade of the two economies.' *New Society.*

Gershuny, I. Patal, R.E. 1979, 'Work outside employment: some preliminary speculations.' *New Universities Quarterly,* Vol. 34.

Glaser, B. G. Strauss, A. L. 1967, *The Discovery of Grounded Theory,* Aldine Publishing Co, Chicago.

Glyptis, S. 1989, *Leisure and Unemployment,* Open University Press, Milton Keynes.

Goffman, E. 1968, *Stigma: Notes on the Management of spoiled identity,* Harmondsworth, Pelican Books, London.

Goffman, E. 1969, *The Presentation of Self in Everyday life,* Allan Lane, London.

Gore, S. June 1978, 'The effects of social support in moderating the health consequences of unemployment.' *Journal of Health and Social Behaviour. Vol 19.*

Gouldner, A. W. 1960, 'The Norm of reciprocity: a preliminary statement.' *American Sociological Review. Vol 25.*

Greyson, J. P. 1985, 'The Closure of a factory and its impact on Health.' *International Journal of Health Services.*

Griffin, C. 1985, *Typical Girls?*, Routledge, London.

Gurney, M. 1980, 'The effects of unemployment on the psycho-social development of school leavers.' *Occupational Psychology, No. 33.*

Harrison, R. April 1976, 'The demoralising effect of prolonged unemployment.' *Dept of Employment Gazette.*

Hayes, J., Nutman, P. 1981, *Understanding the unemployed: The Psychological Effects of Unemployment,* Tavistock, London.

Henry, S. Aug. 1982, 'The Working Unemployed.' *Sociological Review. Vol. 30. No. 3.*

Hepworths. S. J. May 1979, *Moderating factors and the psychological impact of unemployment MRC Social and Applied Psychology Unit,* Sheffield University. Memo 321.

Hill, J. 19 Jan. 1978, 'The Psychological impact of unemployment.' *New Society.*

Hutson, S. Jenkins, R. 1989, *Taking the strain: Families unemployment and the transition to adulthood,* Open University Press, Milton Keynes.

Hurstfield, J. 1986, 'Womens unemployment in the 1930s some comparisons with the 1980s.', in Allan, S. et. al.

Jahoda, M., Lazerfield, P. F. Zeisel, H. 1933. & 1972, *'Marienthal. The Sociography of an unemployed community.'* Tavistock, London.

Jahoda, M, 6 Sept. 1979, 'The psychological meaning of unemployment.' *New Society.*

Jahoda, M., - 1979, 'The impact of unemployment in the 1930s and 1970s.' C.S. Myers Lecture, *Bulletin of the British Psychological Society. No. 32.*

Jahoda, M. 1982, *Employment and Unemployment: A social psychological analysis,* Cambridge Universities Press.

Kasl, S. V. 1975, 'Work and Mental Health. in O'Toole, J. (ed)', *Work and the quality of life,* Cambridge, Mass.

Kasl, S. V. Cobb, S. 1970, 'Blood Pressure changes in men undergoing job loss: a preliminary report.' *Psychosomatic Medicine. Vol. 32.*

Kasl, S.V. Gore S. Cobb, S. 1975, 'The experience of losing a job: reported changes in health, symptoms and illness behaviour.', *Psychosomatic Medicine. Vol. 37. No. 2.*

Kelvin, P. 1984, 'The historical dimension of social psychology: The case of unemployment in Tajfel, H (ed)', *The social dimension. Vol. 2,* Cambridge University Press.

Kelvin, P. & Jarrett, J. 1985, *Unemployment: Its Social Psychological effects,* Cambridge University Press.

Kielselbach, T. 1988, 'Youth Unemployment and Health Effects.', *The International Journal of Social Psychiatry, Vol. 34. No. 2.*

Komarovsky, M. 1940, *The unemployed man and his family,* Octagon Books, New York.

Lawrence, 21. March. 1986, 'Unemployment: Health Hazards.' *New Society.*

Linn, M. W. Sandifer, R, Stein, S. 1985, 'Effects of unemployment as mental and physical health.' *American Journal of Public Health No. 75.*

Little, C. B. July. 1973, 'Stress responses among unemployed technical professionals.' *Dissertation Abstracts International. Vol. 34*

Mann, K. 1992,*The making of the English 'Underclass'*, Open University Press, Milton Keynes.

Marsden, D., Duff, E. 1975, *Workless,* Harmonsworth, Pelican Books, London.

Marshall, G., May. 1984, 'Womans Unemployment - its neglect.' *Sociological Review. Vol. 32. No. 2.*

Marshall, S., Barril, C. Summer. 1984, 'Understanding the invisibility of Young Women.' *Youth and Policy. No. 9.*

McLaughlin, E. 1992, *Understanding Unemployment*, Routledge, London

Miles, I. 1984, *Unemployment time use and the content of experience,* Science Policy Research Unit, University of Sussex.

Miles, I. 1983, *Adapting to Unemployment?*, SPRU Occasional Paper Series, No. 20.

Moser, K. A., Fox, A. J. 1984, 'Unemployment and Mortality in the OPCS longitudinal study.', *The Lancett.*

Murry, C. 1990,*The emerging British Underclass,* IEA Health and Welfare Unit.

Oakley, Ann. 1974, *The Sociology of Housework,* Martin Robinson, Oxford.

Oppenheim, C. 1993, *Poverty: The Facts,* CPAG, London

Osgood, M. H. Jan. 1977, 'Rural and Urban attitudes towards welfare.' *Social work, Vol. 56, No. 6.*

Pahl, R. E. 2. Nov. 1978, 'Living without a job: how school leavers see the future.' *New Society.*

Pahl, R. E. and Wallace, C.D. 1980, *17-19 and unemployed on the Isle of Sheppy,* Mimeo.

Pahl, R. E. 1984, *Divisions of Labour,* Basil Blackwell.

Pahl, R. E. Wallace, C. D. 1985, 'Forms of Work and Privatisation on the Isle of Sheppy.' in Roberts, et. al., *New approaches to economic life.*

Payne, J. May. 1989, 'Unemployment and family formation among young men.' *Sociology. Vol. 23. No. 2.*

Pilgrims Trust. 1938, *Men without work,* Cambridge University Press.

Plant, M. A. Peck, D. F. Samual, E. 1986, *Alcohol, drugs and school leavers,* Tavistock,London.

Platt, S. 1984, 'Unemployment and Suicidal behaviour: A review of the literature.' *Soc. Sc. Med. No. 19.*

Roberts, K. 1985, *Young people in society 16-19 initiative: A sociological View of the Issues,* ESRC.

Roberts, Finnegan, Gallie, (eds) 1985, *New approaches to Economic life,* Manchester.

Ridley, F. F. 1986, 'When will the army of Ghosts begin to fight?' *The Guardian.*

Seabrook, J. 1982, *Unemployment,* Quartet books, London.

Sennett. Cobb. 1972, *Hidden Injuries of Class,* Alfred A Knopf, New York.

Sinfield, A. 1981, *What Unemployment means,* Martin Robinson, Oxford.

Singer, H. 1937, *Unemployment and Health,* Pilgrims Trust, London.

Smith, D. (ed.) 1992, *Understanding the Underclass,* Policy Studies Institute.

Smith, R, weekly series of articles from 12. Oct. 1985, 'Occupationless Health.' *British Medical Journal.*

Solomos, J. May. 1985, 'Extended Review: Youth training, Unemployment and state policies.' *The sociological review. Vol. 33. No. 2.*

Starrin, B. Jarrsson, G. 1987.
'Coping with Unemployment. A contribution to the understanding of womens unemployment.' *Social Science Medical Journal. Vol. 25. No. 2.*

Stokes, G. 1983, 'Work unemployment and leisure.' *Leisure Studies. No. 2.*

Stokes, G. Cockrane, R. 1984, 'A study of the psychological effects of redundancy and unemployment.' *Journal of Occupational Psychology. No. 54.*

Tiggerman, Winfield, 1984, 'The effect of unemployment on Mood, Self Esteem and Locus of control.' *Journal of Occupational Psychology. No. 57.*

Wallace, C. 4-12 1987, 'Dole Girls', *New Society,* London.

Wallace, C. 1987, *For Richer, For Poorer: growing up in and out of work,* Tavistock.

Warr, P. 1987, 'Psychological aspects of employment and unemployment.', *Psychological Medicine. Vol. 12.*

Warr, P. 1985, '12 questions about unemployment and health.', *in New approaches to Economic Life,* Roberts, Finnegan, Gallice (eds), Manchester University Press.

Warr, P. 1984, 'Job loss, unemployment and psychological well being.', in Allen, U. L. Van de Vlert, E. eds, *Role transistions,* Plenum Publishing, New York.

Warr, P. 10 July. 1987, 'This Unhappy Breed.', *New Society.*

Warr, P. Banks, M. Ullah, P. 1985, *'The experience of unemployment among black and white urban teenagers.',* British Journal of Psychology. Vol. 76.

Warr, P. Jackson, P. 1984, 'Men without jobs: some correlates of age and length of unemployment.', *Journal of Occupational Psychology. 57.*

Warr, P. Parry, G. 1982, 'Paid Unemployment and Womens Psychological well being.', *Psychological Bulletin. 91.*

Warr, P. Payne, R. 1985, 'Social Class and Reported changes in behaviour after job loss.', *Journal applied and social Psychology. No. 13.*

Williamson, J. B. 1974, 'Beliefs about the Motivation of the poor and attitudes towards poverty policy.', *Social Problems, Vol. 21.*

Willis, P. 1979, *Learning to Labour,* Saxan House, Farnborough.

Willis, P. 1984, 'Youth Unemployment 1. A New Social State? 29 March.', 'Youth Unemployment 2. Ways of Living. 5 April.', 'Youth Unemployment 3. The land of Juventus. 12 April.', *New Society.*

Willis, P. 198, *The Social Condition of Young people in Wolverhampton,* Wolverhampton Information Centre.

Willis, P. 1986, 'Unemployment: the final unequality?', *British Journal of Sociology of Education. Vol. 7. No. 2.*

Zawadski, B. Lazerfield, P. 1935, 'The Psychological consequences of unemployment.', *Journal of Social Psychology. Vol. 6.*